DAY SKIPPER FOR SAIL AND POWER

OTHER TITLES OF INTEREST

Day Skipper Exercises for Sail and Power
Alison Noice
978-0-7136-8271-7

Complimenting *Day Skipper for Sail and Power*, this practical book includes a free practice chart and contains additional question papers on chartwork, tides, pilotage and passage planning, all with fully explained answers and new general knowledge questions on seamanship, anchorwork, ropework and rules of the road. An ideal exam revision guide and a practice book for anyone wanting to brush up on their practical navigation skills.

Reeds VHF/DSC Handbook
Sue Fletcher
978-0-7136-7573-3

A user-friendly guide covering both the analogue and digital functions on the radio. Sue Fletcher's straight-forward explanations and tips describe the leisure craft VHF DSC radio system in detail and its place within GMDSS.

'If you are looking for just one book to explain all marine VHF operating code and procedure, you need look no further...Packed with hints, tips and sound advice.' *Yachting Monthly*

Pass Your Day Skipper
David Fairhall
978-0-7136-7400-2

This concise and comprehensive 'crammer' covers all the essentials, and has helped thousands of students through their shorebased Day Skipper course. Arranged and highlighted to make revising easier, and updated for its second edition, each section is enlivened with Mike Peyton's best loved cartoons.

The Weather Handbook
Alan Watts
978-0-7136-6938-1

This is the perfect book for anyone who finds general weather forecasts frustrating because they don't give sufficient local detail. It answers such questions as: Is it likely to rain, be sunny or windy? Should I take an umbrella to work? Will there be plenty of wind for sailing? Alan Watts explains in straightforward terms how to interpret what the clouds indicate about the coming weather, and how to combine this with the information given in weather forecasts to arrive at a correct assessment of what the weather will really do.

Reeds Skipper's Handbook
Malcolm Pearson
978-0-7136-8338-7

The Reeds Skipper's Handbook has been a bestseller since first publication. A handy pocket size, it is an aide-memoire of everything a boater would need to know at sea. This treasure trove of essential information is frequently recommended by Yachtmaster™ Instructors as a quick reference guide, and as a revision aid for anyone taking their Day Skipper and Yachtmaster™ certificates.

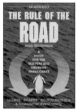

Learning the Rule of the Road
Basil Mosenthal
978-0-7136-7100-1

This guide takes those sections of the International Regulations for Preventing Collisions at Sea that particularly affect small craft, and explains them briefly and simply. Ideal for beginners and as a useful reminder.

'Don't put to sea without a copy! A first class guide.' *Cruising*

'As clear and unambiguous as you could possibly ask for...Thoroughly recommended.' *Practical Boat Owner*

Available from all good bookshops or online. For more details on these and other Adlard Coles Nautical titles, please go to www.adlardcoles.com

DAY SKIPPER

FOR SAIL AND POWER

ALISON NOICE

ADLARD COLES NAUTICAL
LONDON

Published by Adlard Coles Nautical
an imprint of A & C Black (Publishers) Ltd
38 Soho Square, London WC1D 3HB
www.adlardcoles.com

First edition 2007

ISBN 978-07136-8272-4

A CIP catalogue record for this book is available
from the British Library.

Designed by Susan McIntyre
Typeset in 9 on 11.5pt Dax Wide light

Printed and bound in Malta by Gutenberg Press Ltd

This book is produced using paper that is made
from wood grown in managed, sustainable forests.
It is natural, renewable and recyclable. The logging
and manufacturing processes conform to the
environmental regulations of the country of origin.

CONTENTS

INTRODUCTION

You are about to embark on a great adventure, following in the steps of great and famous sea-farers – Horatio Nelson, Robin Knox-Johnson and Ellen MacArthur, to name but a few. I suspect they all started where you are about to begin – learning seamanship, pilotage and navigation from a book before putting it all into practice on the water and taking charge of a boat for the first time.

Their first 'voyage' in a small boat would have been a short passage in sheltered water in daylight – exactly what is expected of a student participating in a Royal Yachting Association Day Skipper course at a practical teaching centre.

RYA theory courses are for both powerboaters and yachtsmen and form part of the Yachtmaster™ training scheme, which is internationally respected and the envy of the world.

This book covers all the subjects in the Day Skipper theory course syllabus and a lot more besides. Questions have been included at the end of each chapter so that you can practise your new skills, and I hope that I have achieved a balance between traditional methods and the use of the wonderful electronic equipment that was not available to many of us when we skippered for the first time. Good luck and happy learning.

Alison Noice
September 2007

ACKNOWLEDGEMENTS

My grateful thanks go to the following people who gave permission for me to use their photographs and material:

Adlard Coles Nautical
Avon Inflatables
Beneteau – France
C Map software
Cranchi – Italy
Crewsaver
Firdell Radar Reflectors
Firemaster Fire Extinguishers
Hallberg Rassy Yachts
Hamble School of Yachting
Ken Waylen (Hi-line transfer)
Lewmar
Lucas Injectors
McMurdo

Met Office
Natasha Wetherall
Neptune Software
Pains Wessex
Raymarine
Reeds Nautical Almanac
Sealine
Simrad Yachting
Stanford Maritime
Trinity House
UK Hydrographic Office
Volvo-Penta UK
Wetterzentrale

A special mention for:

Steve at www.stephenrichard.com who freely gave me his excellent photographs.

Roger Seymour for words of wisdom and for checking through the text.

Peter Noice for his encouragement, the majority of the photographs, sound advice and giving me the courage to live through the nine months it took to write this book!

RYA NATIONAL CRUISING SCHEME – SAIL CRUISING COURSES

Course (and duration)	Suggested minimum pre-course experience	Assumed knowledge	Course content	Ability after course
Basic Navigation shorebased* (2 days)	None	None	Basic navigation and safety	Introductory knowledge of navigation and safety
Start sailing Practical (2 days)	None	None	Introduction to sailing and seamanship	Basic sailing experience
Competent Crew Practical (5 days)	None	None	Basic seamanship and helmsmanship	Useful crew member
Day Skipper shorebased*	Some practical experience desirable	None	Basic seamanship and introduction to seamanship and meteorology	Knowledge to skipper a small yacht in familiar waters by day
Day Skipper practical (Yacht) ** (5 days)	5 days 100 miles 4 night hours	Basic navigation and sailing ability	Basic pilotage, boat handling, seamanship and navigation	Skipper a small yacht in familiar waters by day
Watch Leader Practical (Sail training ships) (5 days)	5 days 100 miles 4 night hours	Basic navigation and sailing ability	Navigation, seamanship and watch organisation	Take charge of a watch on a sail training vessel
Coastal Skipper/ Yachtmaster™ Offshore shorebased*	Some practical experience	Navigation to Day Skipper shorebased standard	Offshore and coastal navigation, pilotage and meteorology	Knowledge to skipper a small yacht in familiar waters by day and night
Coastal Skipper practical ** (5 days)	15 days (2 days as skipper) 300 miles at sea 8 night hours	Navigation to Coastal Skipper shorebased standard. Sailing to Day Skipper practical standard	Skippering techniques for coastal and offshore passages	Skipper a yacht on coastal passages by day and night
Yachtmaster™ Ocean shorebased course	Coastal and offshore sailing	Navigation to Coastal Skipper/ YM shorebased level	Astro-navigation, ocean meteorology and passage planning	Background knowledge to skipper a yacht on ocean passages

* Syllabus is the same for sailing and motor cruising.
** Different courses for tidal and non-tidal waters.

RYA NATIONAL CRUISING SCHEME – MOTOR CRUISING COURSES

Course (and duration)	Suggested minimum pre-course experience	Assumed knowledge	Course content	Ability after course
Basic Navigation shorebased* (2 days)	None	None	Basic navigation and safety	Introductory knowledge of navigation and safety
Helmsman's Practical course (2 days)	None	None	Boating safety helmsmanship and boat handling. Introduction to engine maintenance	Competent to handle motor cruiser of specific types in sheltered waters
Day Skipper shorebased course *	None	None	Basic seamanship and introduction to seamanship and meteorology	Knowledge to skipper a motor cruiser in familiar waters by day
Day Skipper practical course ** (4 days)	2 days	Basic navigation and helmsmanship	Pilotage, boat handling, seamanship and navigation. Engine maintenance	Skipper a motor cruiser in familiar waters by day
Coastal Skipper/ Yachtmaster™ Offshore shorebased course*	Some practical experience	Navigation to Day Skipper shorebased standard	Offshore and coastal navigation, and pilotage, meteorology	Knowledge to skipper a motor cruiser on coastal passages by day and night
Coastal Skipper practical course ** (5 days)	15 days (2 days as skipper) 300 miles at sea 8 night hours	Navigation to Coastal Skipper shorebased course. Standard boat handling to Day Skipper standard	Skippering techniques for coastal and offshore passage	Skipper a motor cruiser on coastal passages by day and night
Yachtmaster™ Ocean shorebased course	Coastal and offshore passages	Navigation to Coastal Skipper/ Yachtmaster™ Offshore Shorebased standard	Astro-navigation, ocean meteorology and passage planning	Background knowledge to skipper a yacht on ocean passages

* Syllabus is the same for sailing and motor cruising.

** Different courses for tidal and non-tidal waters.

RYA DAY SKIPPER SHOREBASED COURSE SYLLABUS

This theory course provides a comprehensive introduction to Navigation, Pilotage, Chartwork, Meteorology and the International Regulations for Preventing Collisions at Sea. It provides the necessary background knowledge for students prior to commencing the Day Skipper Practical course and enables them to get full benefit from that course. The RYA Shorebased Day Skipper course is also an ideal refresher for those about to start a Coastal Skipper and Yachtmaster™ Shorebased course, which contains many of the subjects, taught on the Day Skipper Shorebased course, but to a greater depth of knowledge.

1 **Nautical terms** · Parts of a boat and hull · General nautical terminology.
2 **Ropework** · Knowledge of the properties of synthetic ropes in common use.
3 **Anchorwork** · Characteristics of different types of anchor · Considerations to be taken into account when anchoring.
4 **Safety** · Knowledge of the safety equipment to be carried, its stowage and use · Fire precautions and fire fighting · Use of personal safety equipment, harnesses and lifejackets · Ability to send a distress signal by VHF radiotelephone · Basic knowledge of rescue procedures including helicopter rescue.
5 **International Regulations for Preventing Collisions at Sea** · Steering and Sailing Rules 5, 7, 8, 9, 10 and 12–19 (Full knowledge) · All other rules (outline knowledge).
6 **Definition of position, course and speed** · Latitude and longitude · Knowledge of standard navigational terms · True bearings and courses · The knot.
7 **Navigational charts and publications** · Information shown on charts, chart symbols, representation of direction and distance · Navigational publications in common use · Chart correction.
8 **Navigational drawing instruments** · Use of parallel rulers, dividers and proprietary plotting instruments.
9 **Compass** · Application of variation · Awareness of deviation and its causes · Use of hand-bearing compass.
10 **Chartwork** · Dead reckoning and estimated position including an awareness of leeway · Techniques of visual fixing · Satellite-derived positions · Use of waypoints to fix position (full knowledge) · Course to steer.
11 **Tides and tidal streams** · Tide definitions, levels and datum · Tide tables · Use of Admiralty method of determining tidal height at standard port and awareness of corrections for secondary ports · Use of tidal diamonds and tidal stream atlases for chartwork.
12 **Visual aids to navigation** · Lighthouses and beacons, light characteristics.
13 **Meteorology** · Sources of broadcast meteorological information · Knowledge of the terms used in shipping forecasts, including the Beaufort scale and their significance to small craft · Basic knowledge of highs, lows and fronts.
14 **Passage planning** · Preparation of navigational plan for short coastal passages · Meteorological considerations in planning short coastal passages · Use of waypoints on passage · Importance of confirmation of position by an independent source (full knowledge) · Keeping a navigational record (full knowledge).
15 **Navigation in restricted visibility** · Precautions to be taken in, and limitations imposed by, fog.
16 **Pilotage** · Use of transits, leading lines and clearing lines · IALA system of buoyage for Region A · Use of sailing directions · Pilotage plans and harbour entry.
17 **Marine environment** · Responsibility for avoiding pollution and protecting the marine environment.

CHAPTER ONE

ABOUT BOATS – SAIL AND POWER

Enthusiasts who decide to take to the water will probably have first visited a boat show and enjoyed its gloss and hype or wandered down to the harbour when on holiday and chatted to the owners of boats secured to the quay. Either way they quickly realise that boats come in all shapes and sizes, are powered by different means, and that the sea has a language of its own!

This chapter doesn't aim to replace the nautical dictionary – this quick introduction will give the basics while the rest of the book, and some time on the water, will fill in the gaps. To begin with, you need enough knowledge to know what to look for at the yacht broker, or when you embark on your first cruising course.

Nautical Terms

Directions

All boats, whether powered by engine or sail, are affected by the wind. Motor cruisers often have high superstructure supporting the upper steering position and are liable to be affected by the wind, particularly when manoeuvring at slow speed. Sailing yachts use the wind to drive them forward but are also pushed sideways – making leeway – when heeled over by the wind.

The upwind side of the boat is called the *windward* side and the sheltered side is the *leeward* side (pronounced 'loo-erd').

The widest part of the boat is called the *beam*, so an object sighted at right-angles to the boat on the right-hand side would be described as being *on the starboard beam*.

When looking ahead, the left-hand side of the boat is the port side and Figure 1.1 shows that side shaded red – the colour of the port navigation light. A quick memory jogger is to remember that port wine is red.

Fig 1.1 *An object seen behind the boat is described as being* astern *or* aft.

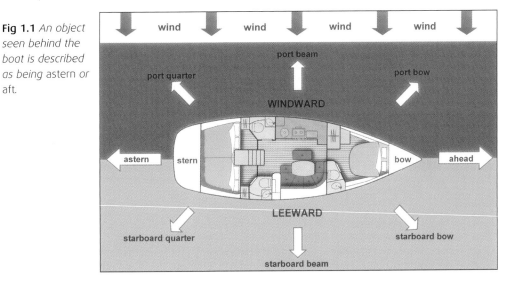

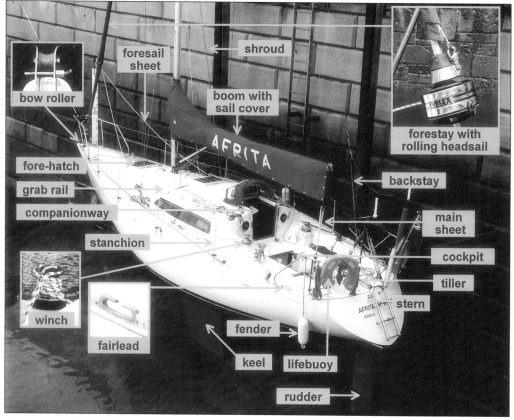

Fig 1.2 *Just a few of the more important boat parts.*

Parts of a Sailing Yacht

Foresail furling system In Figure 1.2 the inset photograph (right) shows that the foresail is furled around the wire that supports the mast at the bow (the forestay). The line used for furling and unfurling the sail is rolled around the black metal drum on the bow and is controlled from the safety of the cockpit, making it convenient for cruising and shorthanded sailing.

Fairlead Ropes, which secure the yacht to the shore, are led through the fairlead (inset in Figure 1.2) so that the ropes are not chafed by sharp metal edges.

Bow roller The bow roller is used to lead the anchor chain or anchor rope (called a warp) safely into the boat over the bow. The metal bar on the roller slides sideways to allow the chain to be laid on the roller and is then slid back above the chain to prevent the chain jumping off the bracket.

Winches See Chapter 2.

Parts of a sail

These are shown in Figure 1.3.

Both the mainsail and the foresail are hoisted by *halyards*. The mainsail is hoisted by the *main halyard* and the foresail by the *genoa* or *jib halyard*.

The *reefing pennants*, which are used to decrease the size of the sail when the wind is strong, pass through small metal rings set into the sail. These rings are called *cringles*.

The sails are hoisted when the boat is heading into – or almost into – wind, so that they are empty of wind and therefore easy to manage.

Types of Hull and Keel for Sailboats

Short keel and balanced rudder

The 10-metre cruiser-racer in Figure 1.2 has a short-fin keel with a relatively deep draught (measurement from the waterline to the bottom of the keel) and a large rudder which is unsupported at the bottom. This keel and rudder configuration produces a boat that is lively, responsive and fast, but makes hard work for the crew who will need to trim the sails frequently to keep her in check. The short keel will give a tight turning circle and allow her to go astern under power easily, but she will be difficult to berth in a marina in any sort of blow as she will get blown off line easily. A fun boat, but probably not the one to choose if going into Southern Ocean weather with anyone other than Ellen MacArthur!

Traditional long keel

Yachts with long keels (Figure 1.4) are generally heavier and narrower than the modern short-keeled boat and are favoured by blue water sailors for their stability and seakindliness in a blow. The narrow beam reduces living space down below and the long keel

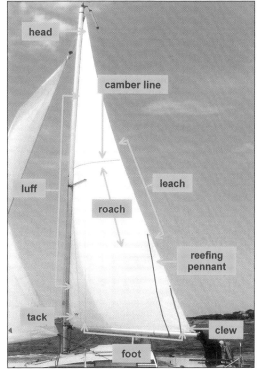

Fig 1.3 *Parts of a sail.*

Fig 1.4 *A long keeled yacht. The rudder is attached to the keel along its full length.*

means that the turning circle is greater than shorter-keeled boats. It will be difficult to take her astern in a straight line under power so berthing stern first is not a good option. However, many famous circumnavigators such as *Lively Lady* and *Gypsy Moth* are this type of boat.

Mid-length keel and rudder with skeg

'Moderation in all things' is often a good philosophy; those who want a good working compromise will choose a hull with a medium-length keel and a rudder that is supported over its full length with a skeg (Figure 1.5 overleaf). This type of yacht will handle tolerably well under power and has a large enough keel area to limit the amount of leeway she makes. Many production cruising boats are of this design and have sufficient beam to satisfy the demand for separate cabins and spacious saloons.

None of the fin keel boats are really suitable for mooring in a shallow creek that dries out at low water. It is very unkind to lay a boat down on its side at every low water and there is a risk of swamping if she lies with her cockpit downhill on a sloping seabed.

Twin bilge keels

A boat with bilge keels (Figure 1.6) would be the better bet as this type will sit down on both keels if the seabed is even and not tip its owners out of bed in the middle of the night as it takes to the ground! Many cruising folk like to keep berthing costs down and to enjoy quiet corners away from marinas and bustle, and this is made possible by the shallow draught of a bilge keeler when upright. The downside is that performance upwind can be affected by the water flow around the uppermost keel.

Lifting or swing keel

A lifting keel may be the perfect answer for a berth with restricted water, and the one in Figure 1.7 has a very shallow draught. There usually has to be some compromise for convenience: space will be taken up in the cabin by the keel housing which is often heavily disguised as part of the saloon table. Early models of swing and lifting keels made a lot of noise down below when the boat was sailing downwind.

Fig 1.5 *A yacht with a rudder supported by a skeg and a medium-length keel.*

Fig 1.6 *A yacht with bilge keels.*

Fig 1.7 *A French production yacht with a lifting keel.*

Fig 1.8 *This cruising catamaran is used for charter in the Caribbean.*

Catamaran

Twin-hulled yachts (Figure 1.8) are favoured by those chartering in exotic places because their boat remains flat while sailing and accommodation is spacious. Sailing performance when running downwind is good, but their windward performance is generally poor and the bow turns through the wind slowly. Berthing in a marina can be difficult as many visitors' berths are not wide enough for the two hulls, but lying-to a mooring is no problem if there is plenty of swinging room. Marinas often charge double to berth a 'cat'.

Wing keels

Short fin keels are sometimes given 'wings' to reduce the draught without decreasing the weight of the ballast (Figure 1.9). Sailing performance is not affected, but if the boat accidentally runs aground, any attempt to re-float her by heeling just digs one of the wings even deeper into the mud!

Fig 1.9 *A wing keel.*

Types of Rig

Sloop

A sloop is designed to have one mast and one foresail and will be described as a 'masthead sloop' or as having a 'fractional rig'.

A masthead sloop has the forestay attached to the top of the mast, which in turn means that the largest foresail is also hoisted to the top (Figure 1.10).

The fractional rig has a taller mast in comparison, but the forestay is attached to a lower point on the mast, which can be between three-quarters and seven-eighths of the total mast length from the deck (Figure 1.11).

Fig 1.10 *A masthead-rigged sloop.*

Fig 1.11 *A fractional-rigged boat has a tall rig with a bendy mast for higher speeds.*

Fig 1.12 *A cutter-rigged yacht.*

Cutter rig

A cutter is very similar to the masthead sloop but has a second foresail and the mast is stepped slightly further aft. Blue water cruising yachtsmen often buy cutter-rigged yachts as it gives them greater flexibility to vary the sail pattern either downwind or in a blow. The yacht shown in Figure 1.12 is an Island Packet, a popular American cruiser.

▶**Fig 1.13** *A ketch-rigged cruising yacht.*

▼ **Fig 1.14** *A schooner moving fast under power.*

Two-masted craft

Yachts with two masts can be rigged as any of the following:

Ketch The ketch (Figure 1.13) has the main mast taller than the smaller mizzen mast. To be classified as a ketch the rudder post has to be positioned aft of the mizzen. This rig is considered versatile for the cruising sailor and in strong winds the mizzen and foresail can be used alone without the mainsail to give a balanced boat with reduced sail.

Yawl This is similar to the ketch rig except that the after mast is shorter and the rudder post is forward of the mizzen mast. Very few yawls are built nowadays – the ketch rig is more popular.

Schooner The schooner rig (Figure 1.14) has the after mast taller than the foremast and is mostly used on larger craft and sail training vessels. The aftermost sail is the largest sail and this is often used with one of the foresails in stronger winds.

Points of Sail

When the boat is head-to-wind the sails act as a flag and have no drive. The boat has to alter course by about 45° in order for the sails to fill; this point of sailing is *close-hauled*.

When the wind is blowing broadside-on the boat will move well – the *beam reach* is the fastest point of sailing. The boat in Figure 1.15 that is on a beam reach has the wind blowing onto the starboard side of the boat; this is on the *starboard tack*. The vessel on a close reach in Figure 1.15 is on the *port tack*.

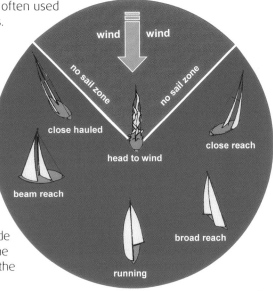

Fig 1.15 *Points of sail.*

The wind will appear to get lighter as the boat runs downwind – 'running' is the term used here.

When the bow turns through the eye of the wind to put the wind on the other side, the manoeuvre is called *tacking* or *going about*.

Parts of a Motor Yacht

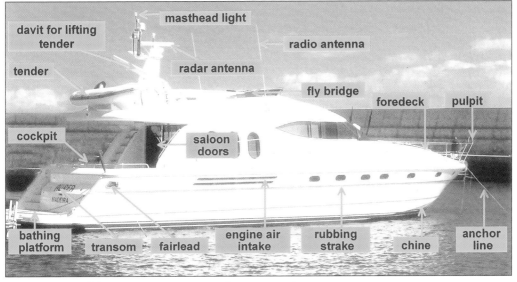

Fig 1.16 *Some of the more important parts of a motor yacht.*

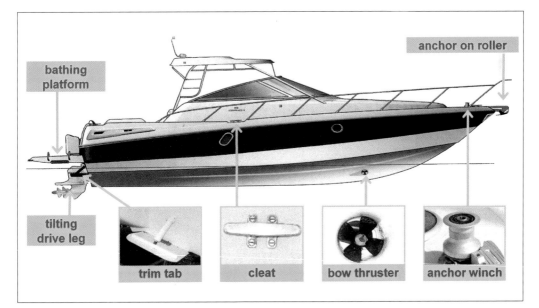

Fig 1.17 *More features of power boats.*

There are also different types of powered craft. We will run through the three main types and then describe some of the controls that improve handling at speed and manoeuvrability. (*Note*: Trim tabs and bow thrusters are explained later in the chapter.)

Motor Vessels

Fly-bridge cruiser

These high-performance craft skim across the surface of the water once they have achieved enough speed to 'plane'. They are most commonly powered by twin inboard diesel engines or twin outdrives, but now some use water jets. Speeds of over 30 knots are possible with some craft in calm or moderate conditions. In rough seas the boat may have to reduce to a speed where the whole hull is in the water – this is being in 'displacement mode' rather than slamming onto the waves, which puts both the interior fittings and the crew under stress. The boat in Figure 1.18 has two steering positions, one in the warmth and protection of the saloon, and the other on the fly-bridge; in contrast the craft in Figure 1.17 has one control position and is known as 'a sports bridge cruiser'. Many boats are fitted with bow thrusters (inset in Figure 1.17) which give added control when berthing alongside, and trim tabs (also shown in 1.17) to keep the vessel on an even keel.

Semi-displacement

The semi-displacement (Figure 1.19) hull is used for many working boats such as pilot and police launches which have to keep working in all weathers. At speed the forward part of this tough boat rises onto the plane, making it far more comfortable for the crew heading into a rough sea. It will usually have twin diesels with propeller shafts, rudders, trim tabs, and a bow thruster – not outdrives.

Displacement craft

The displacement boat cuts through the water rather than skimming over it. This makes it much slower than the planing hull, but craft such as the one in Figure 1.20 will show their good sea-keeping performance while trawling in foul weather. It may have a single screw (propeller) instead of twin engines, and older boats rarely have bow thrusters.

Rigid inflatable

Boats such as the one in Figure 1.21 are currently very popular because they are fast, fun and unsinkable due to the separate inflatable compartments. Most are fitted with twin petrol out-boards, but inboard diesels and outdrives are now quite common in the larger boats. They may be stored at home and trailed to a launching slipway so berthing costs are minimal and distant harbours can be explored.

Sports boat

The small sports boat in Figure 1.22 has a single engine and is very definitely a fair weather dayboat. It can be trailed from area to area and is often used as a water-ski boat.

Most harbour authorities have very strict rules about water-skiing close to a beach frequented by swimmers, so you need to consult the local guide book and harbourmaster's notice board to find out whether there is a specific water skiing area before opening up the throttles. These boats are very liable to swamp if the sea kicks up rough, so always wear a life-jacket even if the weather is calm when you first launch.

▶ **Fig 1.18** *A large planing craft in calm seas.*

◀ **Fig 1.19** *A Ministry of Defence launch in Portsmouth harbour.*

▲ **Fig 1.20** *This fishing boat is a displacement craft.*

◀ **Fig 1.21** *A rigid inflatable boat alongside a pontoon.*

▶ **Fig 1.22** *A sports boat in a calm sea. The helmsman should be wearing a lifejacket, and the boat equipped with flares and a hand-held VHF radio.*

A major safety feature with sports boats and RIBs is the ability to cut the engines quickly in the event of an emergency. A stretchy plastic cord that joins to the cut-off switch is worn round the helmsman's wrist so that if he goes overboard the engines will cut out immediately. You would never forget the sight of a sports boat with a 100hp outboard engine going flat out with no one to control it – I certainly haven't.

Motor Vessel Controls

Stern drive

The stern drive engine could be described as an inboard outboard! The main body of the engines are mounted inside the boat but legs protrude out through the stern as shown in Figure 1.23. The boat is steered by turning these legs and the use of propellers on one or both legs.

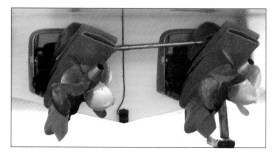

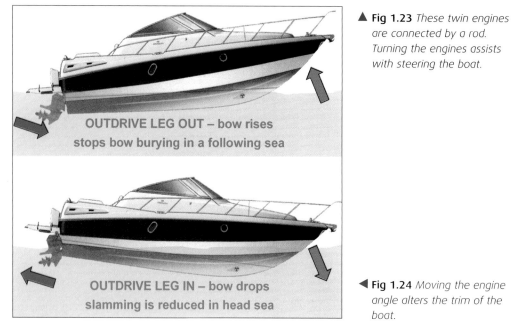

OUTDRIVE LEG OUT – bow rises
stops bow burying in a following sea

OUTDRIVE LEG IN – bow drops
slamming is reduced in head sea

▲ **Fig 1.23** *These twin engines are connected by a rod. Turning the engines assists with steering the boat.*

◀ **Fig 1.24** *Moving the engine angle alters the trim of the boat.*

Power trim

The legs that hold the props and the water cooling system can be lifted or lowered using a hydraulic ram. This alters the fore-and-aft trim of the boat. Figure 1.24 shows that moving the leg away from the boat allows the bow to rise, the attitude required when coping with a following sea. If this is not done the bow is likely to bury when the stern is lifted by a wave. The leg is brought forward to keep the bow down to stop it slamming into a head-sea.

Trim tabs

The trim tabs, which are also operated by hydraulic rams, are situated on each side of the boat on the lower edge of the transom. They can alter the fore-and-aft trim of the boat (Figure 1.25) to make the boat ride more comfortably when a head wind is kicking up the sea or when a swell from astern is tending to bury the bow. Both trim tabs up will bring the bow up to stop it burying; both tabs down will prevent slamming (see Figure 1.26).

▶ **Fig 1.25** *The trim tabs alter the fore-and-aft and port/starboard trim.*

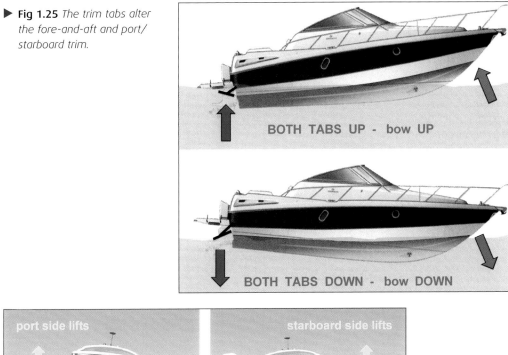

BOTH TABS UP - bow UP

BOTH TABS DOWN - bow DOWN

port side lifts

starboard side lifts

port tab down

starboard tab down

▲ **Fig 1.26** *The trim tabs can correct the angle of heel.*

Windage on the boat can sometimes heel it so that it rides on one of the chines instead of sitting upright. The trim tabs can again be activated on both sides, but with one raised and the other lowered (Figure 1.26).

Bow thruster

The bow thruster (Figure 1.27) is a small electrically driven propeller installed near the bow to assist with berthing in close quarters. If it is used carelessly or accidentally applied in the wrong direction, it can prove disastrous.

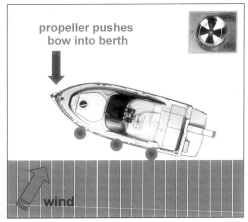

propeller pushes bow into berth

wind

▲ **Fig 1.27** *A bow thruster is extremely useful to assist with berthing when the boat is affected by windage.*

Ensigns and Burgees

Ensigns You will have noticed that most of the boats illustrated in this chapter are flying their national flag either on the stern or close to the mast. It is a legal requirement to fly such a flag when under way in territorial waters, but it is lowered between sunset and sunrise when in harbour. The yacht in Figure 1.28 is flying the red ensign, which is the national maritime ensign of the UK. Members of certain royal yacht clubs have obtained special permission to fly a blue or a white ensign but others hoist the red.

Burgees A burgee is a small triangular flag flown to indicate membership of a yacht club or organisation. They were traditionally flown at the mast head but modern yachts often fly them from the starboard spreaders as so many instruments are mounted at the mast head.

Courtesy ensigns When abroad, the ensign of the host country is flown by the visitor on the starboard spreaders – never on the port side as this is considered to be discourteous. This may seem an old-fashioned tradition, but some countries get very tetchy about it. The yacht in Figure 1.29 is flying the French tricolour and two yacht club burgees.

Fig 1.28 *The red ensign is flown by the majority of UK vessels.*

Fig 1.29 *Here the tricolour is flown as a courtesy when visiting a French port. The burgees have been temporarily moved to the port side.*

ABOUT BOATS – SAIL AND POWER: KNOWLEDGE CHECK

1 What is the downwind side of a boat called?
2 Is the leading or forward edge of the sail
  a) the leech? b) the foot? c) the luff?
3 Does a long-keeled yacht handle well or badly when going astern under power?
4 Who is likely to use a semi-displacement powered craft?
5 How would you position the trim tabs to return the boat in Figure 1.30 to an even keel?

Fig 1.30 *Knowledge Check: Question 5.*

CHAPTER TWO

KNOWING THE ROPES

Old sea dogs will tell you that they can tell a seasoned hand by the way that lines and warps are handled, so the aim of this chapter is to help you look cool and competent on the foredeck!

The average sailing yacht uses many hundreds of metres of rope for mooring the boat, hoisting and sheeting the sails and for anchoring and the type of rope used is different for each of these tasks. Synthetic materials are generally used for all types of cordage as they are stronger and lighter than natural fibres such as sisal and manilla.

Types of Rope

Rope can be constructed in three main ways and made of several different materials.

Construction

Laid Usually three strands of rope are twisted together in a clockwise direction – called *hawser laid*. More expensive rope has four strands, is also twisted clockwise, and is called *shroud laid* – the argument being that, in days gone by, the best rope was required to support the mast! Figure 2.1 shows three-stranded polyester rope that is twisted to the right and therefore needs to be coiled in a clockwise direction to reduce kinking.

Braided A woven cover is used to protect low-stretch cores from abrasion and UV radiation. This gives a rope that is flexible and easy to handle. Polyester is used for economy, but racing boats that need strength, lightness and little stretch will use the more expensive Kevlar-type yarns – Spectra, Technora or Vectran. Figure 2.2 shows braided sheets on a charter yacht.

Plaited The rope in Figure 2.3 has eight strands of which four are plaited clockwise and four anticlockwise. The result is a rope that is strong, flexible and resists kinking.

Fig 2.1 *Polyester laid rope.*

Fig 2.2 *Braided polyester sheet.*

Fig 2.3 *Plaited nylon anchor line.*

Materials

Polyester This is very popular for laid mooring lines as it is relatively strong with moderate stretch and good abrasion resistance. To make it even more attractive it is also moderately priced. When braided, it is the most suitable material for sheets (Figure 2.2), and when pre-stretched can be used for rope halyards – although intermittent tightening may be needed.

Nylon This is ideal for anchor warps as it is strong, stretches up to 15% and absorbs shock. It is fairly resistant to abrasion, but has poor resistance to UV light. It is frequently used for dock lines, but if the boat is to be left unattended for any length of time, stretching may allow the boat to surge backwards and forwards too much.

Polypropylene Buoyant and light, this fibre does not absorb water. It has stretch properties very similar to polyester, but has poor resistance to UV light. It is used extensively for rescue equipment such as danbuoys, lifebelts and heaving lines because it floats (Figure 2.4).

Fig 2.4 *A polypropylene throwing line.*

Knots

Although there are hundreds of different knots, you should manage to impress others with just a handful of those used frequently on both power and sailing yachts.

Bowline

Probably the most important knot of all, the *bowline* is used to put a temporary non-slip loop in the end of a rope. It may be used to secure the boat to a cleat or post ashore; to fasten sheets to a foresail; and to go around a casualty's waist in a rescue. It is a secure knot, but difficult to undo when under load.

When tying a bowline the secret is to start off with the short end in the right hand and make a figure 6 with the rope in your left. Once that is done, the rabbit comes up out of the hole, round the tree, and back down the hole again! Study Figure 2.5 and then get practising!

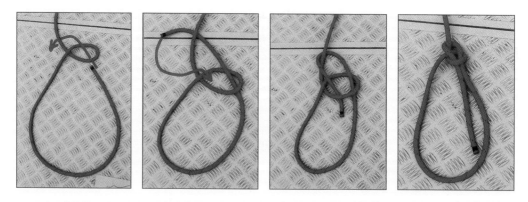

Fig 2.5 *The bowline is tied to make a temporary non-slip loop in the end of a rope.*

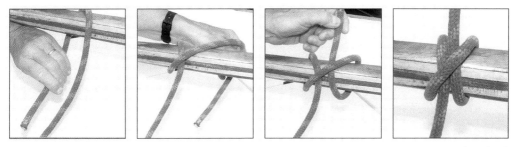

Fig 2.6 A clove hitch.

Clove hitch

The *clove hitch* is useful for attaching fenders to the guardrail because it is easy to slide the fender sideways to reposition it and the height above the water can be adjusted quickly. It requires an extra half-hitch for security if the boat is to be left for any length of time as it can shake loose.

It may also be used on tiller-steered boats for securing the helm mid-ships to avoid rudder damage. Figure 2.6 shows how it is tied.

Round turn and two half-hitches

This secure knot, which is easy to tie and undo under load, is for securing a line to the base of a cleat or to a ring. It is also preferred by some skippers for securing fenders to the rail as it does not shake loose as easily as a clove-hitch. See Figure 2.7.

Figure of eight

A quick and easy knot to tie, the *figure of eight* stops the end of a rope running out through a block (Figure 2.8). It is known as a 'stopper' knot for that reason. See Figure 2.9.

▲ **Fig 2.7** A round turn and two half-hitches.

◀ **Fig 2.8** The sheet is led through this turning block.

▼ **Fig 2.9** A figure of eight knot – a stopper knot.

figure of eight - forming

figure of eight - finished

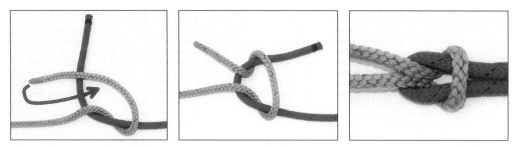

Fig 2.10 *A reef knot. It is used to join lines of equal thickness.*

Reef knot

The *reef knot*, as its name suggests, is used for *reefing*. Reefing reduces the size of the mainsail in windy weather and the unwanted sail is rolled and tied to the boom with a short length of line. This knot is shown in Figure 2.10.

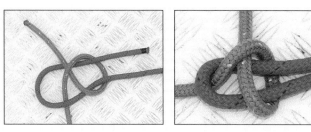

Fig 2.11 *A single sheet bend.*

Sheet bend

The *sheet bend* is used for joining two ropes of different diameters. It is often used to lengthen lines to the shore when a number of yachts are alongside one another on a harbour wall. It is said that the two ends of the rope should finish up on the same side of the bend to prevent the knot from collapsing. In Figure 2.11 they both exit at the top.

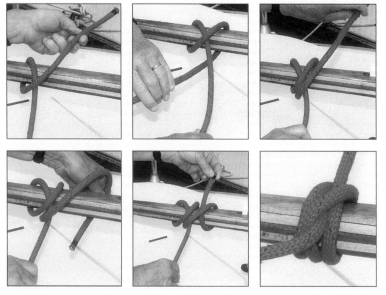

Rolling hitch

The *rolling hitch* is similar to a clove hitch but has an extra turn before it is finished off. This extra turn locks the rope in place on a spar, which in the case of Figure 2.12 allows the finished knot to slide down to the right, but locks if an attempt is made to pull the rope to the left.

Fig 2.12 *The rolling hitch.*

Fig 2.13 *Coiling a rope.*

Coiling a rope

Lines stowed away in the cockpit locker should be coiled so they are ready for immediate use. If the rope is laid then it will almost certainly need to be coiled in a clockwise direction but the rope in Figure 2.13 is braided rope and can be coiled in either direction.

Once the initial coils are complete, leave enough end to wind several turns around the coil – working upwards towards your hand. To finish, push a loop of rope through the coil and pull it down over the top as illustrated.

Winching

As sheets are under enormous strain in even a moderate wind we use winches to assist us with sail trim. The average sailing yacht has four or more winches for halyards, sheets and reefing pennants. These winches usually have two gears, single or double speed, which makes it much easier to adjust the sheets. They rely on friction to hold the rope securely on the drum; notice that the winch in Figure 2.14 is large enough to take four full turns of rope, and in a blow all four will be needed to stop the rope from slipping. Because of the strains involved, great care is needed to keep vulnerable fingers out of danger when loading or unloading the winch.

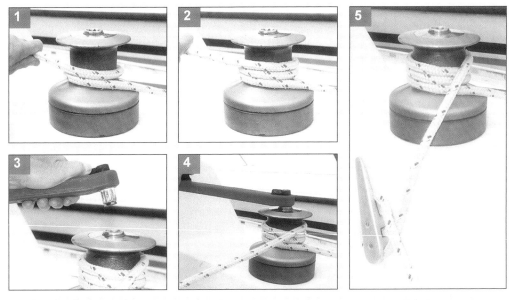

Fig 2.14 *Loading a winch.*

Initially, put two or three turns around the drum in a clockwise direction and pull in as much rope as you can without straining (as shown in pictures 1 and 2 in Figure 2.14). Now insert the handle and wind in the remainder of the rope. The handle may be turned in either direction, the hard way or the easy way – you'll soon find out which is which! Finally cleat the rope – the one in picture 5 in Figure 2.14 is a 'jam cleat', where the rope is forced into an ever-narrowing gap.

Before removing the rope from the cleat take the strain by pressing the flat of the hand on the drum, as in Figure 2.15. This will prevent the rope from slipping before the left hand is slid out of harm's way.

Most cruising and charter yachts replace the cleat with a device for gripping the rope which is added to the top of the winch – known as a *self-tailing winch*. Figure 2.16 shows that the rope is wound in a clockwise direction as normal, but the last turn is jammed between the black 'jaws'.

Halyards and reefing pennants often pass through 'rope clutches' before being wound onto the winch. These devices, which are mounted on the cabin (coach) roof close to the companionway, replace cleats to grip the rope while the lever is down, but leave it free to run when the handle is up (Figure 2.17). The rope may be tightened with the handle in the down position, but cannot be loosened without lifting the handle.

A couple of DO NOT warnings next as safety issues come into play here:

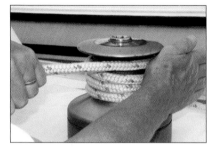

Fig 2.15 *Safely taking the strain.*

Fig 2.16 *A self-tailing winch.*

Fig 2.17 *Rope clutches for halyards and reefing pennants.*

1 Ropes are often wound extremely tightly before the clutch handle is engaged, so DO NOT attempt to lift the clutch handle unless the rope is loaded onto a winch first. Two things could happen if you do – the handle may break before it releases the rope or the rope could rush back through the clutch, taking your fingers into the clutch as well – not a good result either way!
2 If the mainsheet leads through a rope clutch, DO NOT close the clutch; take the strain with the self-tailing device instead – it can be released more quickly if required.

Cleating

A boat is secured alongside with lines or warps that are 'made up' on cleats – one on each corner of the boat and often one on each side amidships. The rope must not slip off the cleat, but neither must it be inextricably jammed. The way to get a satisfactory end result is to wind the word OXO onto the cleat. Begin with one round turn, then a figure of eight, and finally another round turn around the base of the cleat and pull tight. If the rope is very thin or slippery, perhaps OXXO will be needed to stop it slipping. See Figure 2.18.

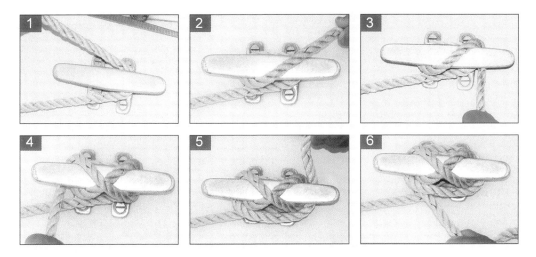

Fig 2.18 *Making up a rope on a cleat.*

Mooring Alongside

The yacht in Figure 2.19 is safely moored to a floating pontoon in a sheltered marina. It has five chunky fenders to protect the hull and is secured by four lines. These lines are fastened to the base of cleats with a round turn and two half-hitches, but a bowline would also be a suitable knot.

The lines that cross over at the centre of the boat stop the hull moving ahead and astern, while the two at each end keep the bow and the stern parallel to the pontoon. Figure 2.20 gives the names of these lines. Had this craft been secured to a harbour wall with a tidal rise and fall, the bow and stern lines would have to be longer or continuously tended to prevent the boat from hanging itself – a situation that is both embarrassing and dangerous!

Fig 2.19 *A snug marina berth.*

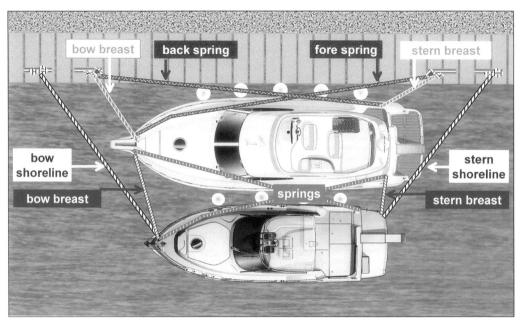

Fig 2.20 *The owner of the outside boat has put lines to the shore so that there is not too much strain on the inner boat's lines. If the outside vessel had no lines to the shore, it would also make it very difficult for the inner boat to depart without casting the other boat loose.*

Rafting up

It is quite common to see four or five boats rafted alongside one another in busy ports. Harbourmasters usually take care to berth motor cruisers in one raft and yachts in another so that there is no incompatibility with hull shapes. In a mixed raft, yacht skippers will have to check that their stanchions are not damaging the motorboat's hull or, if alongside another yacht, that the rigging could not become entangled.

Fig 2.21 *Three yachts rafted together in St Peter Port. The outside yacht has just arrived and is rigging lines to the pontoon.*

With so many boats secured alongside, the few cleats on the pontoon become full of rope so be careful not to add to the problem by leaving piles of spare line lying on the pontoon where others could trip over it. It is a pity that the skipper in Figure 2.22 was not so thoughtful.

Etiquette

When walking across other boats to reach the shore it is customary to walk around the bow – not across the cockpit unless you are invited to do so. Be as light footed as possible and do not kick the spinnaker pole or twang the rigging as you walk across. Try not to peer into open hatches or saloons and keep the noise down when returning from a good evening ashore.

Chafe

Whether attached to a mooring or rafted alongside, a line that chafes through on something sharp or by rubbing on a bow roller puts the boat at risk. Wise skippers always keep a short length of split plastic hose to place over ropes that are subject to chafe. If no hose is available, wrap a dish cloth or tea towel around the rope and keep it in place with tightly wound whipping twine. Figure 2.23 illustrates what happened to a line in just a few hours in a bumpy marina in Madeira.

Fig 2.22 *An accident waiting to happen!*

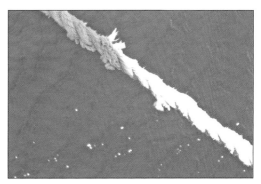

Fig 2.23 *Serious chafe on a breast rope.*

Mediterranean Moor

In the Mediterranean and the Caribbean where there is little rise and fall of the tide, boats frequently moor stern to a quay instead of alongside so that everyone has easy access to the shore and more boats can be fitted in. Figure 2.24 (overleaf) shows where the anchor should be dropped and how the stern lines are secured. Try to get the boat moving astern in a straight line before dropping – you are less likely to be blown off course by the wind if you can manage this.

anchor dropped here

stern lines should be crossed over to restrict sideways movement

Fig 2.24 *As the boat is driven astern, the anchor chain has to run freely without being checked until the stern reaches the dock.*

KNOWING THE ROPES: KNOWLEDGE CHECK

1 Is laid rope used for:
   a) sheets? **b)** anchor lines? **c)** mooring lines?
2 What type of rope is likely to be used for a heaving line?
3 What is a 'back spring'? What does it do?
4 Would you place a rope on a winch in a clockwise or anticlockwise direction?
5 How could you limit chafe on a rope?
6 Why are the stern lines crossed over when mooring stern-to a harbour wall?

CHAPTER THREE

ANCHORS AND ANCHORING

Our coastline provides an abundance of sheltered bays, rivers and creeks in which to 'drop the hook' for lunch or for an overnight stay. A peaceful anchorage away from the hurly-burly of a marina can give immense joy – *and* will be a lot cheaper!

However, if we are to sleep soundly in the knowledge that the pick is snugly dug in we have to give the problem some thought beforehand.

The Anchors

One of the first considerations is the type and size of the ground tackle. The anchor itself has to be heavy enough to dig into the seabed when it is given a hefty pull and the attached anchor cable has to be man enough to take the strain of the boat. This cable may consist of all chain or a mixture of chain and warp, depending on whether the boat is used mainly for racing or cruising. The chain should be galvanised steel and as heavy as possible if it is to do a good job. Boats fitted with a windlass are restricted to the size of chain that fits the windlass, but if you have a choice of chain size and the stemhead fitting can cope, try to fit something beefy – a 15-kilogram anchor is recommended for an 11-metre boat which, together with 10 millimetre chain, should give peace of mind. If a rope and chain mix is used, then at least a boat length of chain is needed to prevent rocks and obstructions chafing the rope. The rope should be nylon as it is strong and stretches – plaited rope is ideal.

Fig 3.1 *A peaceful dawn at anchor in the Caribbean.*

Figure 3.2 shows how the rope is spliced to the chain when the equipment is bought as a package. New types of anchors have been marketed over the past few years, but most are variations of the unhinged plough or claw anchors.

The CQR

The *CQR* anchor is of the plough variety, with a hinge joining its two parts. This means that it can be folded to stow in a bow locker, but watch your fingers as the anchor sometimes bites!

It holds well in mud and soft sand, but does not dig into kelp or hard sand too easily.

Notice in Figure 3.3 that it has an eyelet near the plough blades – the flukes. This is for attaching a tripping line (see later in this chapter).

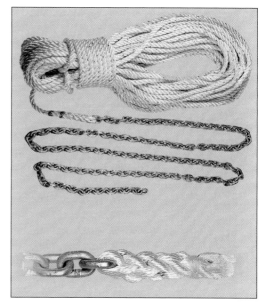

Fig 3.2 *The line is spliced to the chain.*

Fig 3.3 *A CQR anchor on the stemhead roller.*

Fig 3.4 *A Delta one-part anchor.*

Delta

Made of manganese steel, the Delta one-part anchor, is immensely strong and has very high holding power. It is balanced to set easily after an unattended drop from the bow roller using a windlass, so it is ideal when you are short handed. See Figure 3.4.

Bruce

Originally designed for mooring oil rigs, the Bruce is a one part claw anchor of high tensile strength and digs well into most surfaces with the exception of kelp. It remains stable in most sea and wind conditions and stows well on the bow without becoming a battering ram to other boats!

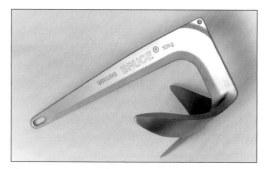

Fig 3.5 *A Bruce anchor.*

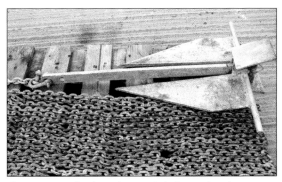

Fig 3.6 *A Danforth anchor and chain. Notice the coloured length marks painted on the chain.*

Fig 3.7 *Marking the cable.*

Danforth

This anchor is in two parts with a 32° shank angle, which allows the anchor to dig in well and bury itself. It is most commonly used as a second or smaller anchor because it folds flat in a cockpit locker. It can be difficult to break out, and can trap fingers very painfully.

Marking the anchor cable

When using an electric windlass for anchor work it is difficult to judge just how much cable you have veered if it is not marked. The chain in Figure 3.6 has been painted with the owner's secret code, and the anchor rode in Figure 3.7 was marked by threading a small length of spinnaker cloth through a strand and marking it with a permanent marker. This marking has lasted over ten years with just one quick re-mark with the pen.

DO NOT mark the chain with electrical cable ties, shown in Figure 3.8, as they can rip your hands to shreds if the chain accidentally runs out through them.

Fig 3.8 *Cable ties can seriously damage your hands if the chain runs through them.*

Windlasses

Windlasses in small boats are generally electrically or mechanically operated. If electrically operated, the engine must be running with some throttle if the battery is to cope with the strain of weighing anchor. Many have a remote control on the fly-bridge and some have foot-operated buttons on the foredeck.

The windlass in Figure 3.9 has a hand control, a winch drum for rope and a toothed holder for the

Fig 3.9 *An electrically operated small boat windlass.*
Photograph: www.stephenrichard.co.uk

chain (known as a *wildcat*). The windlass can also be operated manually using a long handle that fits onto the windlass.

Anchoring

Factors to consider when anchoring

There are many things to think about when getting ready to anchor and it is a great idea to have a checklist so that we don't forget something vital at this busy time. After all, no self-respecting pilot would land a plane without his checklist, would he?

Checklist
1 Is the location sheltered enough for the present and forecast wind?
2 Does the chart show that anchoring is allowed?
3 Is the holding good?
4 Is there enough room for the boat to swing on the tide without getting too close to other boats or shallow water?
5 Is the anchorage out of the shipping channel and strong tidal stream?
6 Is there a valley to funnel a strong wind?
7 Could I safely leave the anchorage in the dark?
8 Is it close to a landing place?

Line of approach and lowering the anchor

Both wind and tide deserve some consideration when deciding upon the angle of approach to an anchorage. Look at other moored boats of similar design to see in which direction they are pointing. If there is any tidal stream, they will most likely be heading into it, so copy their heading. If there is no tide, then approach upwind, then stop where you want the anchor to be. The foredeck crew should be told the actual depth so that they can quickly lower the anchor and enough chain to reach the seabed. They should let the helmsman know when this has happened so that the boat can be driven astern to lay the chain along the bottom. It will not always go astern in a straight line, but this does not matter. Once the desired amount of chain has been laid, cleat it off or stop the windlass and drive the boat astern to dig the anchor in.

How much cable should I use?

Anchor chain left in the locker is little use to anybody, so if you are not sure whether you need more cable, then the advice is to let more out. If stopping for a quick lunch when everyone is awake and aware whether the boat is secure, then less cable will do.

All chain	= 4 times the maximum expected depth
Chain and rope mix	= 6 to 7 times the maximum expected depth

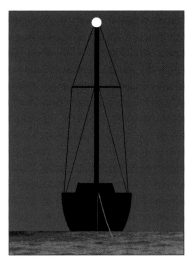

Fig 3.10 *An all-round white light is displayed at night when at anchor.*

Checking the position

Once the hook has dug itself in and the boat has settled to her anchor, we should have a good look around to check that we are far enough from other boats and the depth is as expected.

An anchor fix of some description is now a good idea – we can use the GPS to set a drift alarm or could line up two features on the shore so that we can see clearly if the boat drifts off the line. An anchor fix could also be formally plotted on the chart, and we will be learning how to do that in Chapter 14. Lastly, we need to show other boats that we are at anchor by hoisting a black circular shape near the bow during daylight hours or switching on an all-round white light at night (Figure 3.10).

Tripping line

When there is a possibility of old mooring tackle or rocks on the seabed, then a *tripping line* should be used to extricate the anchor if it becomes fouled. It is attached to the eye near the crown and needs to be long enough to reach the surface, where it will either be supported by a very small mooring buoy or brought back on board.

Figure 3.11 shows the tripping line being used to pull the anchor clear of a mooring line.

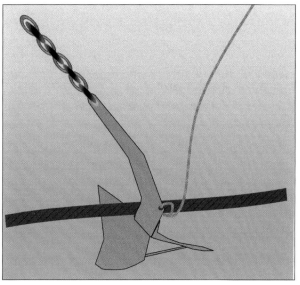

Fig 3.11 *The tripping line is attached to the crown of the anchor.*

ANCHORS AND ANCHORING: KNOWLEDGE CHECK

1 Why should the engine be run when using an electrically operated windlass?
2 Name four factors that should be considered when selecting an anchorage.
3 Should the anchorage be approached downtide or into tide?
4 If a mix of chain and rope is used, how much cable should be used for a maximum depth of 5 metres?
5 What light should be displayed at night to indicate that a boat is at anchor?

CHAPTER FOUR

KEEPING SAFE

I used to sail on a boat that had a brass plaque fastened to the cabin bulkhead upon which there was a quote from the author G.K. Chesterton. It said, 'An adventure is an inconvenience rightly considered'. Life on the sea is certainly an adventure, but if 'rightly considered' – particularly from the safety aspect – it should be possible to prepare for the very worst that can happen and then relax in the knowledge that everything has been done to avoid trouble. Good skippers seldom tell tales of disasters that have befallen them because they make every effort to see that they do not happen – they have 'what if' plans and try to make sure that, as far as possible, they are not in the wrong place at the wrong time.

Before taking part in any sport we need suitable clothing and equipment, and boating is certainly no exception. Chandleries are full of brightly coloured garments and many other safety goodies but, except for a few items, safety equipment is not compulsory for leisure craft less than 13.7 metres in length. Over that length, or if used for commercial purposes, boats must have equipment as laid down in the Merchant Shipping Rules. With smaller craft, it comes down to personal choice and this will depend on the size of the boat and how far offshore you intend to go.

In this section, we will look in detail at some of the vital safety equipment and drills for some emergency procedures that, by the law of averages, you are unlikely to experience but nevertheless need to know.

Personal Clothing

Keeping the crew warm and dry is of the first importance – getting wet and cold can ruin a good day out and wet clothes can sap the strength very quickly, often leading to misery and seasickness.

Both powerboaters and sailors need good windproof and waterproof clothing – the fly-bridge of a motor cruiser travelling at 25 knots can be a bitter place when it is chilly, and it is not always possible to steer from the wheelhouse.

Much of the modern sailing clothing, although pricey, has well-fitting hoods, reflective tape and high collars; it is also breathable so that undergarments don't feel cold and clammy. The cuffs have rubber seals and may be tightened at the ankles and wrists to prevent the ingress of water, and some pockets are lined with quick-drying fleece to warm the hands. The trousers are high fitting so there is no gap at the waist, and most have hefty plastic zips down the front. The crew members in Figures 4.1 and 4.2 are looking happy wearing hats, gloves and boots for added warmth.

Sunglasses are a must at sea as the glare from the sun reflecting off the water can cause eye damage in the long term. If you intend to spend much time on the water, buy the best pair you can afford.

Fig 4.1 *Wrapped up well!*

Fig 4.2 *A happy dry crew dressed for a cold day complete with lifejackets, harnesses, hats and gloves.*

Lifejackets and Harnesses

The crew in Figure 4.2 are wearing combined lifejackets and harnesses in the waistcoat style and are clipped onto the boat for safety while working on the exposed cabin top.

This type of lifejacket is probably the most comfortable to wear as they are unobtrusive when worn uninflated. Most are labelled as being '150N (Newton)', which gives 33 pounds of buoyancy when inflated. All but the largest adult will be supported adequately with this buoyancy (Figures 4.3 and 4.4).

The most expensive jackets have crutch straps to prevent them riding up when inflated, and a built-in spray hood to protect the face. They are also fitted with a light, and inflate automatically on contact with water. All jackets have a whistle to attract attention and a top-up tube for further inflation. Non-swimmers should be encouraged to wear their jackets at all times when out of the cabin, and many skippers nowadays require the whole crew to wear them as well. Most guidelines advise donning them when balance is likely to be disturbed by the sea state, when in a dinghy or RIB, and on deck at night. When you are the skipper, it will be up to you to decide whether the conditions are such that it would be advisable to wear a jacket or whether to relax the rules on a balmy summer afternoon with a flat calm sea.

Fig 4.3 *The Crewsaver 150N automatic lifejacket.*

Fig 4.4 *An inflated 150N automatic lifejacket showing whistle and top-up tube.*

The harness line, which has clips at each end (Figure 4.5), is attached to the metal ring on the centre of the chest and, at the other end, to a webbing strap running along the full length of the deck. Yachts should carry a harness for each member of the crew and motor cruisers are advised to have at least two harnesses and lines for crew working on the exposed foredeck.

Boating is generally a very safe sport, but every care should still be taken to ensure that people remain on the boat – falling into cold rough water is definitely not advisable and at night could be catastrophic. Without being too dramatic, cold, shock, inhaling salt water and choking are just some of the potential problems, so make a positive effort to remain on the boat.

Lifebelts, Marker Buoys and Throwing Lines

Fig 4.5 *This Crewsaver harness line has an elasticised cover to prevent it becoming a trip-line by mistake.*

Should someone fall in the water, then some additional flotation device will be needed quickly. The soft U–shaped *life ring* in Figure 4.6 rests in a wire frame on the stern of the boat so that it can be deployed quickly. Powerboats often mount one on the side of the fly-bridge (Figure 4.7) where it can also be reached from the cockpit aft. The ring must be available for quick release so it should not be tied to the boat.

The one in Figure 4.6 is attached to a marker buoy with a floating line. This buoy, known as a *danbuoy*, is about 2 metres high and has the international 'man overboard' flag mounted above the orange floats to aid visibility. The danbuoy and the ring are dropped together as one unit. For offshore boats and those intending to go out at night, it is wise to have two of these rings with a light and drogue attached. The drogue creates drag that will hinder any downwind drift.

A buoyant polypropylene line is ideal for throwing to a casualty in the water. The one in Figure 4.8 is secured to the stern rail and held in place with a quick-release toggle. At the other

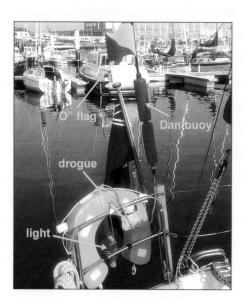

◀ **Fig 4.6** *The life ring, complete with light and drogue, are attached to the danbuoy and rest in a wire frame.*

▼ **Fig 4.7** *This life ring can be reached from the fly-bridge or from the after end of the cruiser.*

end, the rope has been worked into a 'monkey's fist' so that the casualty has something of substance to grab and hold onto. Some lines come ready packed in a throw bag.

First Aid Kit

Strictly speaking, First Aid is not part of the Day Skipper syllabus, but it is recommended that at least one member of the regular crew attend an RYA First Aid course.

Fig 4.8 *Buoyant throwing line attached to the stern rail.*

However, a First Aid kit, as shown in Figure 4.9, is part of the boat's vital equipment and it should be stowed in an accessible locker, preferably in a watertight container. Keep an up-to-date First Aid book in the box or close to it – *The First Aid Manual*, issued by St John Ambulance. Plasters should be individually wrapped, not hacked off a long strip with rusty scissors, and if antiseptic cream is carried, remember that it has a shelf life – once it is seeping out of the cracks in a rolled-up tube, it is time to throw it in the bin! Notice that the First Aid box in Figure 4.9 contains protective gloves – these are protection for the 'First-Aider' *not* to keep the engineer clean while doing an oil change on the engine!

A suggested list of contents for a First Aid kit for a craft venturing up to 60 miles from a safe haven is shown in Figure 4.10.

SUGGESTED FIRST AID KIT

Equipment
Stainless steel scissors
Pocket face mask
Safety pins
Disposable polythene gloves
Plastic burn bag or roll of Cling film

Tablets, creams etc
Seasickness tablets
Paracetamol and Ibuprofen tablets
Imodium tablets
Antiseptic cream
Antiseptic wipes

Bandages and dressings
Sterile bandages with dressing (medium)
Sterile bandages with dressing (large)
Sterile bandages with dressing (extra large)
Adhesive suture strips

Triangular bandages
Adhesive elastic bandage
Individual adhesive plasters
Sterile gauze swabs

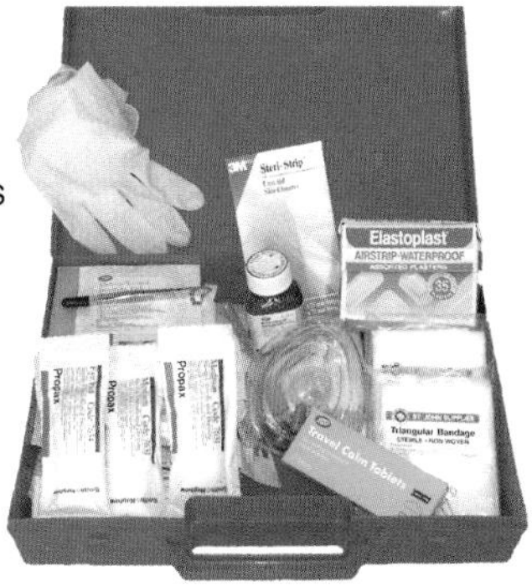

Fig 4.9 *A First Aid kit for a boat remaining within 60 miles of the coast.*

Fig 4.10 *First Aid kits can be personalised, but this type of kit will be adequate for most coastal passages.*

Fire Prevention

Fire in a GRP boat is a fearsome prospect so 'Prevention' is the key word here. There are several sites on board where care will be especially needed – the living areas, the galley, and the engine compartment.

Fig 4.11 *The saloon and galley of an Oceanis 343 – this is a typical charter boat used for flotillas.*

Living areas

Smoking down below and near sails is banned in most boats, so your crew won't think it unreasonable if you impose this rule. A cigarette not properly extinguished could cause havoc in a saloon such as the one shown in Figure 4.11.

Considerate smokers will smoke on the pontoon or sit downwind of everybody else when under way, so that ash does not blow into people's eyes and over the cockpit sole.

When lighting paraffin lamps or cookers, make sure that all matches are extinguished before putting them in with the rubbish – a small open-topped jar wedged close to the stove is a good place for putting dead matches. Better still, have a dedicated gas lighter (available from all good stores), then fingers will not get burnt either.

Engine

Boats over 10 metres long have diesel engines installed, but smaller ones and sports boats are often petrol driven. Particular care needs to be taken when storing petrol, which should be kept in cans on deck – definitely not in a cockpit locker or in the cabin. Normal land-based petrol service station rules apply when refuelling with either diesel or petrol: the engine, cooker and mobile phones should be turned off and there should be no naked lights.

Keep the engine clean and check any water pipes or wiring for chafe on the insulation. Mop up all oil and fuel spills to stop them reaching the bilges because diesel fuel slopping around can turn even the strongest stomach if it is choppy (See Figure 4.12). A disposable nappy is great for mopping up any mess, and can even be wrung out like a sponge when soaked with salt water.

Fig 4.12 *Avoid pools of oil and diesel fuel under the engine.*

Fortunately, engine fires are rare as diesel fuel is not instantly flammable, but occasionally an electrical fire can break out in the engine space. If you see smoke emerging from the engine area, stop the engine immediately and DO NOT lift the lid to peek, as this will allow more oxygen to feed the fire.

Modern sailboats now have double cabins on each quarter where you can get a bit of privacy and sleep soundly with the door shut. UK charter boats are required to fit a simple smoke alarm in these cabins due to the proximity of both engine and galley. These alarms are very sensitive to burnt toast as well, so shut the cabin doors while cooking and *do not remove the battery* to keep them quiet!

The galley

All except the very largest boats use bottled butane or propane gas for cooking (Figure 4.13). The gas cylinder and the spares should be stowed in a dedicated locker outside the living area because these gases are heavier than air and will sink into (and remain in) the bilges in the event of a gas leak – just waiting to be violently ignited by a striking match or electrical spark.

Fortunately, many craft are fitted with gas detectors and most with lockers that drain any leaking gas straight out of the boat. Gas bottles are fitted with a shut-off valve and usually there is a second valve or a solenoid close to the cooker. You should close the one down below when the stove is not being used and shut the one in the cockpit in the following conditions:

- At night.
- When leaving the boat to go ashore.
- Any time the stove is not being used, *if* there is no secondary shut-off valve.

Try to set a good example to new crew – if you are lazy turning off the gas tap, they will be too.

If, after all these precautions, gas *does* get into the bilges, then ventilate the boat well. Bailing the gas out of the bilge with a jug is effective, although one can feel a little foolish tipping (apparently) nothing overboard!

As a second line of defence, the burners themselves are fitted with a thermocouple – a flame failure device very similar to the one used on domestic gas boilers that looks like an upright metal bar near the burner (shown in Figure 4.14). When the gas is first lit the tap should be held in for about 30 seconds to override the shut-off valve while the thermocouple heats. When it is hot, the tap can be released and the gas flow will continue; if the flame blows out, the safety device takes over to turn the gas off.

Care should be taken when using the hob, and curtains should be at least 0.6 metre away from the top of the stove. If cooking under way when it is choppy, it is wise to wear waterproof trousers and boots as protection. The flaming of *crêpe suzettes* is definitely not encouraged on board a boat!

Fig 4.13 *A typical boat's gas cooker with two burners and a grill.*

Fig 4.14 *A thermocouple on a gas burner.*

'in the Unlikely Event' – Dealing with Emergencies

Fire

Fire blanket A fire blanket (Figure 4.15) should be mounted within reach of the cooker, but not so close that you have to stretch over any flames to grab it. If the worst happens, the drill is:

1 Shout 'Fire' to alert the crew.
2 Ask the cockpit crew to turn the gas off at the bottle.
3 Pull the tabs on the blanket and pull it out of its holder.
4 Wrap the blanket over your hands to protect your knuckles.
5 Holding the blanket in front of you to protect your chest, place it right over the pan and leave it in place until the burning material has cooled.

Fig 4.15 *A Firemaster fire blanket.*

Fire extinguishers Fire extinguishers can be filled with a variety of substances, but the chosen medium is generally dry powder as it is effective against burning paper and wood, fuel, flammable gas and electrical fires (Classes A, B and C).

A small-sized extinguisher, as shown in Figure 4.16, should be fitted in every cabin and in the saloon. The one in the forecabin should be mounted near the hatch so that it can be reached from the upper deck.

Inert gas extinguishers are better for use on engines as dry powder damages them. Stow a large extinguisher in a cockpit locker so that it could be used to fight a fire below from a place of safety.

Emergency fire procedure Any fire in a boat is serious and, if it takes hold, crew safety is of paramount importance. The fumes given off when GRP burns are very toxic so crew should leave the cabin as soon as possible, taking a lifejacket and a fire extinguisher with them.

The smoke given off from a fire is very combustible and firefighters fear the 'flashover' that happens when smoke ignites suddenly. The hatches should therefore be LEFT OPEN to allow this smoke and the crew to escape from below.

If you have time, turn the gas off at the cylinder and consider whether to throw the cylinders overboard. Prepare the liferaft for launching on the windward side and have the crew congregate there.

Fig 4.16 *Large and small dry powder fire extinguishers by Firemaster.*

Flares

Flares, which are considered the second line of defence after the VHF radio, are used to signal that you are in distress and to pinpoint your position to the rescue services. To protect them against damp and damage they should be kept in a rigid waterproof container similar to the one shown in Figure 4.17. This box needs to be accessible at all times and a cockpit locker is an ideal storage place.

The number required varies depending on how far offshore you intend to cruise – the table in Figure 4.18 gives an indication as to what is needed. From new, they should last three or four seasons depending on which part of the year they were purchased. Keep a note of the date by which they will have to be renewed.

Fig 4.17 *A Pains Wessex coastal flare pack.*

RECOMMENDED FLARE PACKS

Inshore - less than 3 miles from land

2 red hand flares   2 orange hand smoke

Coastal - up to 7 miles from land

2 red hand flares   2 orange hand smoke   2 red parachute flares

Offshore - over 7 miles from land

4 red hand flares   2 buoyant orange smoke   4 red parachute flares

Fig 4.18 *These recommendations are a minimum – you can always have more.*

Follow the guidelines that follow, and NEVER POINT FLARES AT PEOPLE.

Red hand flares The burning time for these is 1 minute. Use within sight of land or rescue services.
1   Use gloves if possible
2   Point downwind.
3   Extend your arm away from your body.
4   Hold up and outboard.
5   Do not look directly at the burning flare.

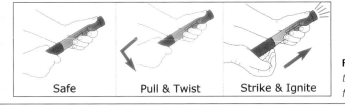

| Safe | Pull & Twist | Strike & Ignite |

Fig 4.19 *Instructions for firing the Pains Wessex red hand flare.*

Orange hand smoke This burns for 1 minute. Use in daylight in light winds. Firing instructions are the same as for the red hand flare in Figure 4.19.

Red parachute flare The burn time is 40 seconds. Height: 300 metres fired vertically, 200 metres fired at 45°.
1   Stand with your back to the wind and fire slightly downwind if the cloud is more than 500 metres, but at an angle of 45° if the cloud base is very low.
2   Do not point the bottom end of the flare at your body.

Figure 4.20 gives firing instructions for one make of parachute flare. Each manufacturer uses a different firing procedure, so read the instructions carefully.

Remove end caps & safety tab   Lever drops down   Push lever upwards to fire

Fig 4.20 *When firing the red parachute flare there is a slight recoil, so be prepared.*

The disposal of old flares

It is currently (2007) a lot easier to purchase flares than it is to dispose of them, but every effort must be taken to ensure that they are not dumped overboard or let off on bonfire night. HM Coastguard is still willing to accept small quantities as long as you take them to the Coastguard station and speak to them nicely beforehand.

The liferaft

A liferaft (Figure 4.21) must be considered a last resort and it is highly likely that your craft, although damaged or with some water inside it, will support and sustain you while it is still afloat. Unless it has an uncontrollable fire or is sinking rapidly, STAY WITH THE BOAT.

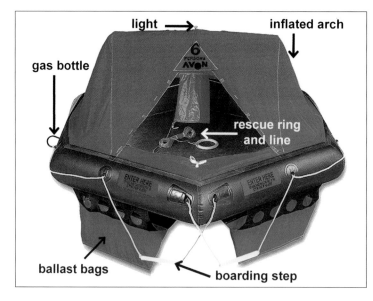

light →   inflated arch ↓

gas bottle

rescue ring and line

ballast bags   boarding step

Fig 4.21 *Avon 'Coastline' six-man liferaft. The rescue quoit and line are visible inside the raft.*

Before abandoning ship
1 Send out a *DSC* distress alert and a *Mayday* voice message (see Chapter 5).
2 Wear warm clothes and a lifejacket. Keep your boots on – they give added insulation and are useful for bailing water out of the raft.
3 Take the grab bag and anything else that is quickly to hand and useful.

Launching the raft
1 Make sure the painter is fastened to the boat.
2 Throw the raft into the water once the fastenings have been released.
3 Give a sharp tug (or two) on the painter – this will inflate the raft.

Boarding the raft
1 If possible try to keep dry when entering the raft.
2 Do not jump in – it is only made of rubber!
3 The heaviest person should go in first to give the raft stability.
4 Stream the drogue as soon as possible as this is essential for the stability of the raft if the sea is rough.
5 Bail out the water if possible.
6 Close the canopy, check for leaks and inflate the floor if it is not self-inflating.
7 Open the survival pack and give everyone (yes, *everyone*) a seasickness pill.
8 Read the survival handbook.
9 Do not drink water for the first 24 hours unless bleeding. NEVER drink sea water or urine.
10 Post a lookout and give a job to each person.
11 STAY STRONG. STAY CONFIDENT.

Lifeboat rescue

The lifeboat (Figure 4.22) may be launched to take a casualty to the shore or to take the whole crew off the boat if the situation warrants it. The lifeboat is primarily there to save life – not to tow you home because you think it less expensive than a commercial towing company.

Although the lifeboat crew are all volunteers, they are highly trained men who seek no reward for their task and know what they are doing.

The radio operator will contact you as their boat approaches, but it will help the coxswain if you have your crew ready in lifejackets. Should it be decided to take the boat in tow, one of the lifeboat crew will almost certainly come aboard to assist. The anchor winch is usually the main strong point on motor cruisers and larger yachts, but it may be necessary to spread the load of the tow by rigging a bridle around the boat. Never attach the tow around a deck-stepped mast – unless, of course, you wish to bring it down around your ears!

Fig 4.22 *The Guernsey lifeboat heading off to a 'shout'.*

Helicopter rescue

Should someone on your boat become ill or there is an urgent need to abandon ship, HM Coastguard may decide to send a search and rescue helicopter to assist you.

In the UK these helicopter crews are highly trained specialists who have developed procedures for all types of craft be they yachts with swaying masts, swiftly moving powerboats or merchant ships which make a good landing platform.

Fig 4.23 *A helicopter overhead and ready to lower a line to the deck of a yacht. Photograph: Ken Waylen*

However, before the helicopter arrives there are a number of things you can do in advance to assist the helicopter crew (Figure 4.23).

General preparation

1 Dig out the flare box as you may be asked to identify your boat using a red hand flare or orange hand smoke if you are among a crowd of other boats.
2 Put your most competent helmsperson at the wheel or tiller as steering a steady course is paramount.
3 Stow any loose items that might be caught in the down-draught from the helicopter rotors.
4 Lifejackets and waterproofs should be worn by all crew if abandonment is contemplated. This is wise anyway because sea water blown aboard by the down-draught can make you very wet.
5 If your GPS antenna could be touched by the helicopter crewman or by the line first dropped to yachts, then turn your GPS/chart plotter off, because the equipment, just like a human, does not function so well after receiving an electric shock!
6 Have one of the crew wear gloves and place a bucket in the cockpit (for keeping the hi-line tidy). Clear away the ensign staff and danbuoy if they are stowed on the port quarter as this is where the crewman will come aboard.

Before the helicopter arrives overhead and the noise is too great to hear anything you will be called on the VHF radio and given a briefing by the pilot. In this briefing you will be told what they intend to do and asked to steer a course of their choice at a speed that is agreeable to both parties.

Follow the pilot's instructions – he has done this before and knows what is required for success!

You will also be told very firmly that any lines that are lowered MUST NOT BE TIED TO THE BOAT.

Finally, you will be asked if you have any questions. If you have any doubts, now is the time to voice them – the helicopter crew are there to help in every way they can.

The methods of approach differ depending on whether you are capable of higher speeds or have a mast that may impede a safe approach.

Powerboats and motor cruisers
Procedure
1 After the initial briefing, you will be told to steer a steady compass course at an agreed speed. This course will probably be into or slightly off the wind.
2 The helicopter is likely to approach from behind on the port quarter so that the pilot, who sits on the right-hand side of most helicopters, has a good view.
3 The crewman will be lowered on the winch wire directly onto an uncluttered area of the deck – maybe the fly-bridge or cockpit.
4 Don't make a grab for him until his earth wire has touched either the sea or the boat. Once it has earthed, pull the crewman aboard.
5 Follow any instructions given to you by the crewman.

Yachts with a mast
Nowadays yachts are often asked to keep their sails hoisted while a lift-off is made as a yacht that is sailing close-hauled is more directionally stable under sail than power, and when on the port tack, the mast is tilted safely away from a helicopter approaching from the port quarter.

If the helicopter is of the type that gives a hefty downdraught, the yacht will be asked to deep reef the mainsail, furl the headsail away and to start the engine so that a steady speed is maintained.

If the downdraught is minimal then the normal sail for the prevailing conditions and engine will be asked for.

Procedure
1 The helicopter approaches from the port quarter.
2 A rope line with a weight attached is lowered onto the port side aft (Figure 4.24).
3 Crew No 1 (wearing gloves) should wait for the weight to touch the deck or the water before grabbing it. Once down, he should haul the line in with a steady pull until the winch-man indicates him to stop.
4 Meanwhile, the line is flaked into the bucket by Crew No 2 so that it will run out easily later on. DO NOT TIE IT TO THE BOAT. (If you do, the pilot will break off the transfer, and time will be lost while another line is rigged.)
5 The crewman is lowered on the wire and is hauled in by Crew No 1. Once close to the boat, the crewman should be grabbed and pulled on board.
6 The crewman will take charge and tell you what to do.

▲ **Fig 4.24** *The weighted hi-line is lowered to the deck. Photograph: Ken Waylen*

▶ **Fig 4.25** *Helicopter rescue. The crewman arrives on the deck and is pulled aboard using a 'hi-line'. Photograph: Ken Waylen*

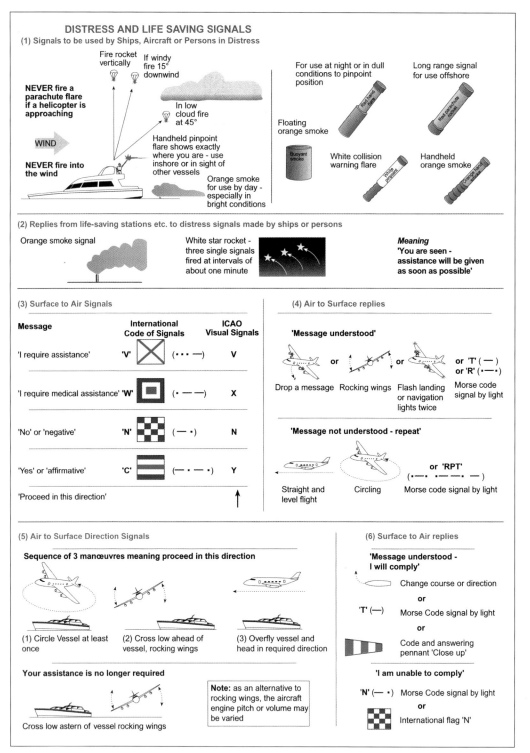

Fig 4.26 *SOLAS search and rescue signals. The law requires that a copy of these signals be kept on the boat.*

DISTRESS AND LIFE SAVING SIGNALS (continued)

(7) Landing signals for the guidance of small boats with crews or persons in distress. By night white lights or flares are used instead of white flags.

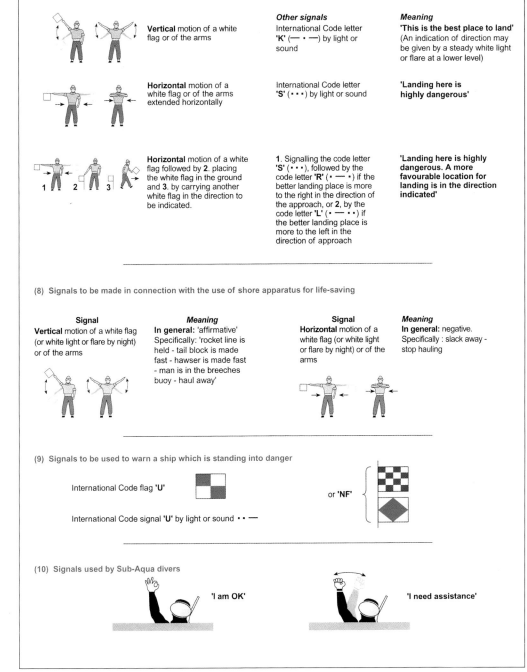

	Other signals	Meaning
Vertical motion of a white flag or of the arms	International Code letter **'K'** (— · —) by light or sound	**'This is the best place to land'** (An indication of direction may be given by a steady white light or flare at a lower level)
Horizontal motion of a white flag or of the arms extended horizontally	International Code letter **'S'** (· · ·) by light or sound	**'Landing here is highly dangerous'**
Horizontal motion of a white flag followed by **2**. placing the white flag in the ground and **3**. by carrying another white flag in the direction to be indicated.	1. Signalling the code letter **'S'** (· · ·), followed by the code letter **'R'** (· — ·) if the better landing place is more to the right in the direction of the approach, or **2**, by the code letter **'L'** (· — · ·) if the better landing place is more to the left in the direction of approach	**'Landing here is highly dangerous. A more favourable location for landing is in the direction indicated'**

(8) Signals to be made in connection with the use of shore apparatus for life-saving

Signal	Meaning	Signal	Meaning
Vertical motion of a white flag (or white light or flare by night) or of the arms	**In general:** 'affirmative' Specifically: 'rocket line is held - tail block is made fast - hawser is made fast - man is in the breeches buoy - haul away'	**Horizontal** motion of a white flag (or white light or flare by night) or of the arms	**In general:** negative. Specifically : slack away - stop hauling

(9) Signals to be used to warn a ship which is standing into danger

International Code flag **'U'**

International Code signal **'U'** by light or sound · · —

or **'NF'**

(10) Signals used by Sub-Aqua divers

'I am OK'

'I need assistance'

Fig 4.26 *SOLAS search and rescue signals cont.*

The grab bag

Should you have to leave your sinking ship and take to the liferaft, there are a few extra things that might be useful to have with you. A waterproof bag kept where it can be grabbed quickly is the answer, and some bright spark has produced just such a bag – a 'Grab Bag' (Figure 4.27).

This bag could contain: a hand-held radio, thermal protective aids, ship's papers, passports, medication, spare spectacles, water, chocolate bars, pencil and paper, and some items to boost crew morale.

Fig 4.27 *A water-resistant bag.*

Man overboard

Prevention

1 When walking along the deck, try to lower your centre of gravity by stooping down. Drag heavy objects along the deck rather than carrying them at chest height.
2 Kneel or sit down to do a job on deck so that you do not topple over.
3 Men should use the toilet and not take 'a leak' over the side as many accidents have happened in this way, particularly at night after a pint or two.
4 Make sure that you save one hand for holding onto something secure.
5 Always wear a lifejacket and harness, and clip onto the jackstays when going on deck in rough weather, poor visibility and at night.
6 Practice the 'man overboard' drill as often as possible. When conducting drills, give the crew a different job each time so that all are familiar with the actions required.

Actions for returning to the man overboard

First we will look at methods for returning to the person with a yacht, and then with a power-boat or motor cruiser.

Sail and power

This is shown in Figure 4.28.

Fig 4.28 *Returning to the person in the water using both sail and power.*

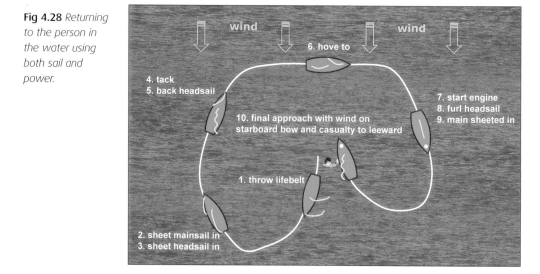

Diesel engines are far more reliable than they were in the past and can generally be relied upon to start when required, so the first tried and tested method is using a combination of both sail and power. Although it can be a matter of great personal pride to handle the boat under sail only, it is far more sensible to have additional help from a serviceable engine when it comes to saving a life.

When someone first goes into the water:

1 Shout 'Man overboard' – one crew member should keep pointing at the casualty.
2 Try to calm down by counting to 5.
3 *Crash tack* the boat, hauling both sheets in as the bow goes through the wind which will cause the headsail to back once the bow is round.
4 Start the engine.
5 When it has started, then furl (or lower) the headsail.
6 Continue to come round in the circle under power and approach the person with the wind at about 30° off the bow.
7 Ease the mainsheet on the final approach so that the mainsail flaps.
8 Stop the boat upwind of the casualty with the person on the leeward side level with the shrouds. Allow the yacht to drift towards the person.
9 Consider disconnecting the top guardrail to aid recovery.

Sail only

If Murphy's law makes itself felt and the engine does not start for some reason, the sails will be your only option. The method shown in Figure 4.29 has worked well for many but it is no good having your first go when it is for real! Practice, practice and more practice is the order here so that when you hear those dreaded words 'Man overboard' your drill takes over, not the stress.

1 Shout and throw the flotation to the person if possible.
2 Alter course as soon as is possible to put the wind about 30° aft of the beam.
3 Count to five.
4 Tack the boat without releasing the jib sheet and back the jib ('crash tack').
5 Point the boat to the windward side of the person in the water.
6 Furl the headsail.
7 Ease the mainsheet to slow the boat down. Use the mainsheet as the throttle – slacken to slow down and haul in to speed up.
8 If possible, stop the boat on the windward side of the man.

Fig 4.29 *Returning to a casualty in the water under sail only.*

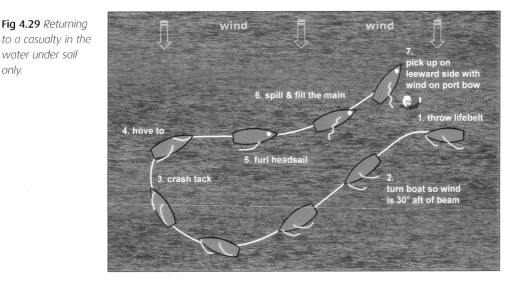

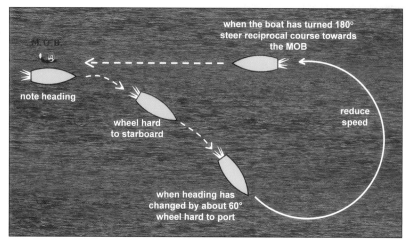

Fig 4.30 *The 'Williamson Turn' for powerboats and yachts under power.*

Power

A tested method for returning to a person, even in bad visibility, is known as the *Williamson Turn*. This method quickly gets you back onto a reciprocal course that leads to the casualty.

Figure 4.30 shows the method that relies on the helmsman noting the compass heading as the shout goes up. The wheel is then turned hard to starboard and kept there until the course has been altered by about 60°. As soon as this change has been achieved the helm is then put hard to port until the boat is heading on a reciprocal of the original course.

Signals from rescue craft

The rules introduced by SOLAS require all craft to carry a card showing the signals to be given to the casualty by rescue aircraft and ships. This information card (Figure 4.26, pages 40–41) may be included in an almanac or other book, or you could always mount it on the back of the toilet door where the crew may have some time to study it!

KEEPING SAFE: KNOWLEDGE CHECK

1 Describe the content of a flare pack suitable for use up to 7 miles off the coast.
2 When should the gas tap close to the stove be turned off?
3 What is the meaning of the term '150 Newton' when referring to lifejackets?
4 On which side of the boat should a liferaft be launched in the event of a fire?
5 Why is it important that life rings have a drogue attached to them?
6 What is meant by the term 'crash tack'?

CHAPTER FIVE

COMMUNICATIONS – USING THE VHF RADIO

Many people consider that the VHF radio telephone is the most important piece of safety equipment on the boat, but we must never forget that it is our responsibility to look after ourselves using a combination of good seamanship, good planning and common sense. We should not rely on the Coastguard or the RNLI to get us out of a mess of our own making.

Types of VHF Radio

There are two types of marine radio – *fixed* and *handheld*. The fixed sets (Figure 5.1) use the boat's power supply, have a permanently mounted antenna, and will be capable of transmitting at 25 watts – the maximum permitted from a 'ship station' afloat. The fixed antenna will usually be a lot higher than one attached to a handheld radio, so will give additional range. An upright sailing yacht with a 16-metre antenna should be able to speak to a rescue centre on shore from a distance of about 30 miles and the average motor cruiser with a 4-metre antenna will have a range of about 25 miles.

▲ **Fig 5.1** *A typical fixed marine VHF radio for talking ship-to-ship or ship-to-shore. The button on the fist mike is used to transmit.*

Handheld radios (Figure 5.2) have a maximum power output of just 5 or 6 watts, which greatly reduces the distance over which they may be heard. Even with the antenna held upright, the range will be no more than about 4 miles between two rigid inflatable boats.

Whichever type of equipment you choose, it has to be licensed. For details, log onto the Ofcom website: www.ofcom.org.uk.

◀ **Fig 5.2** *A handheld VHF radio.*

Whom We Can Talk To

We are most likely to talk to:

- Other ship stations.
- Marinas.

- HM Coastguard.
- Harbour masters and port controllers.

What We May Talk About

The maritime band is for 'ships' business', which could include:

- emergencies
- navigation
- pilotage
- berthing.

It does not allow (among other things):

- General chitchat about the state of the nation or a good restaurant for dinner.
- The broadcasting of music or the latest football scores.
- Swearing or other obscene language.
- Hoax distress calls.
- Using a handheld radio when ashore in the pub or in a shop.

The fine for these transgressions is large, and the radio or the whole boat may be confiscated if the offences are serious and proven.

The Channels We May Use

Important Channels	
1.	Ship to ship	6, 8, 72, 77
2.	UK Marinas (commercial & yacht club)	80 or M (37or 37A)
3.	UK Coastguard	16, 67
4.	Harbour masters and port controllers	Refer to Almanac

Fig 5.3 *UK Marine VHF channels*

Ship-to-ship

There are a great number of channels listed in the almanac – some are single-frequency channels and many are dual-frequency. The typical small-craft radio, found in a private or charter boat, uses just one antenna and can only be used on one frequency at a time. Choose a *simplex* (single frequency) channel if calling another boat – you will never make contact on a *duplex* channel. Ships with a more complex radio and large enough to mount two antennas a reasonable distance apart may use a dual frequency channel that allows them to speak and listen simultaneously.

UK Coastguard

HM Coastguard is responsible for the integrity of Channel 16 – the distress and calling channel. Coastguard stations maintain a continuous listening watch for Mayday calls and use the channel for working casualties. Once communication is established on Channel 16, the caller is directed to switch to Channel 67 which is designated as the UK small craft safety channel. The largest Coastguard rescue centre, sited at Lee on the Solent, allows direct calling on Channel 67 but other centres do not have sufficient operators to do this. Radio checks to HM Coastguard should be kept to a minimum – call the marina or another boat instead.

UK marinas

In the UK, commercial marinas use Channel 80 to allocate berths to visiting boats, but yacht clubs who own marinas mostly use Channel M, which on some sets is displayed as Channel 37 or 37A. Call direct on the working channel – not on Channel 16.

Port operations (harbour masters)

Large ports tend to use Channels 11, 12 and 14 for controlling traffic, but sometimes use others as well. The harbour information section of the almanac gives details of channels to monitor when entering a harbour. Again, call direct on these channels without establishing communications on Channel 16. (*Note*: This list of channels will give you an understanding of the marine band, but is by no means complete. The RYA 1-day Radio Operator's course covers the subject in much greater depth and is strongly recommended.)

The Controls of the VHF Radio

The set in Figure 5.4 consists of a bulkhead-mounted handset complete with control buttons and a remote power unit mounted away from damage.

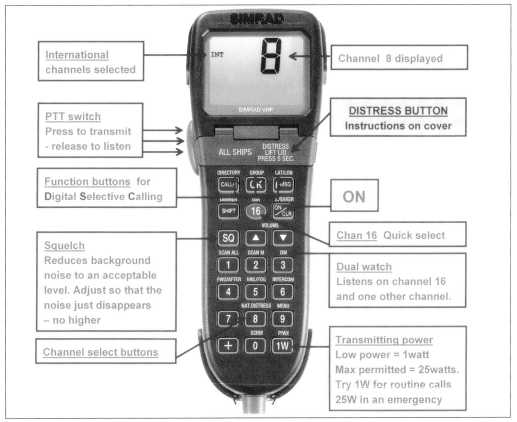

Fig 5.4 *Most marine radios will automatically select high transmitting power (25 watts) and the distress channel (Channel 16) at switch on.*

Switching on Many sets switch on with the volume control. The one in Figure 5.4 uses a clearly labelled 'On' button.

The 'press to transmit switch' This is situated on the side of the set. When it is depressed you may speak but cannot receive, and when you remove your hand from the switch you may listen but not speak. Remember to depress the mike button a second before you speak so that the first few words will not be lost.

The squelch This button controls any background 'hiss'. It should be adjusted so that the hiss just disappears – no higher, otherwise some messages may not be heard.

High/low Power The maximum permitted radiated power from ship stations is 25 watts, and it obviously makes sense to transmit on high power when in an emergency so that as many people as possible can hear your pleas for help. However, if making a routine call it also makes good sense to limit the range of your call to affect as few people as possible.

It is not within the brief of this book to teach what is normally learned on a full RYA 1-day Radio Operator's course. The aim here is that you learn enough to transmit a distress alert, distress call and message in the 'unlikely event' of some disaster. Figure 5.4 shows the controls of the VHF, most of which are common to all makes of radio.

When to Send a Distress Alert and Message

DISTRESS
When there is <u>grave and imminent danger</u> to a vessel, a life, an aircraft or other vehicle and immediate assistance is required

---

Fig 5.5 *A distress message is sent only when there is grave danger.*

Sending a Distress Alert

Digital Selective Calling (DSC) sets are fitted with a labelled distress button. When the skipper decides that a distress situation exists, the cover should be raised to reveal a red button. The button is pressed once to select the nature of distress, then pressed again for 5 seconds, until 'Distress sent' appears on the display.

The radio is connected to the ship's GPS receiver which gives the position of the casualty at the time the distress alert was sent. This will be received by rescue stations ashore and by other vessels fitted with DSC equipment. The boat's unique 9-figure number is also displayed. This shows its nationality and allows it to be identified from an international central register. This number, which is called an MMSI, is included in the Mayday voice message – an example of which is shown in Figure 5.6. The number 233 identifies the distressed craft as a UK vessel..

A strident alarm, which will continue until cancelled manually, will be sounded at receiving stations and all DSC radios within range will automatically be switched to Channel 16, high power ready to receive the distress message by voice.

The alarm will be automatically repeated every $3\frac{1}{2}$ to $4\frac{1}{2}$ minutes until it is electronically acknowledged by a shore rescue station or the power fails.

A craft that is on fire or is sinking is certainly in grave and imminent danger. A person who falls overboard and someone with unusual pains in the chest are also in jeopardy, making the issue of a Mayday quite justified. A simple grounding on mud or sand would not qualify unless the weather were extremely bad and waves were swamping the boat. Whether the call is sent or not is at the discretion of the skipper and must be a matter of judgement – don't hold back because you are afraid of getting into trouble. The rescue authorities are always willing to give sound advice to those in genuine need.

Running out of fuel in either a powerboat or a yacht would not qualify for lifeboat rescue – a commercial tow arranged with the Coastguard on Channel 67 would be more appropriate. The RNLI volunteer to save lives, not to risk their own because of stupidity.

The Spoken Distress Message

All ships and boats sending a Mayday give the message by voice even if they have sent a DSC alert. This will ensure that the message is received by as many craft as possible and additional information can be sent.

Distress call 3 times	**Mayday Mayday Mayday**
Name of casualty	**This is Motor Yacht Slimfish Slimfish Slimfish**
Distress message begins	**Mayday Slimfish**
Call sign or MMSI	**MMSI 233095762**
Position	**Position 50° 05'. 9N 5° 01'.2W**
	(just south of Falmouth entrance)
Nature of distress	**Serious fire onboard**
Assistance required	**Require immediate assistance**
Other information	**3 persons onboard. Abandoning to liferaft**
End of message	**Over**

Fig 5.6 *The unique MMSI number is issued to the boat when the radio is installed. The number 233 identifies it as a UK boat.*

Remember TO SPEAK SLOWLY AND CLEARLY because your life really does depend on someone being able to write down your position.

COMMUNICATIONS: KNOWLEDGE CHECK

1 For routine communication, should the radio be set to transmit on high or low power?

2 List three forbidden transmissions.

3 Name four inter-ship channels.

4 What is an MMSI?

5 Under what circumstances should a Mayday be sent?

6 Which channel is used for small craft safety by HM Coastguard?

CHAPTER SIX

AVOIDING A COLLISION WITH OTHER CRAFT

Having a collision with another boat will undoubtedly ruin the day for both parties! Worse still, if a small boat causes an emergency situation with a large ship in a narrow channel, there could also be injury or loss of life.

Despite the apparent chaos in a crowded harbour on a hot sunny weekend, collisions such as the one in Figure 6.1 are rare thanks to the International Regulations for Preventing Collisions at Sea which need to be studied before going out on the water to join in the fun.

These rules, which are under the control of the International Maritime Organisation, apply to all types of craft – ranging from small

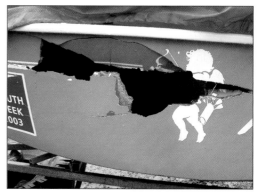

Fig 6.1 *A wet ending to the fun.*

canoes to large cruise ships – on navigable waters that are connected to 'the high seas'. Although lakes like Lake Windermere are not connected to the sea, local authorities usually adopt the rules in the local bye-laws and also impose speed limits.

These universally accepted rules do not give us a *right of way* and they state that the responsibility to avoid a collision lies with both parties. They speak of *the give–way vessel* and *the stand-on vessel* when establishing priorities, so it is necessary to watch converging traffic closely – you may have to alter course, even when you are the stand-on vessel, if the skipper of the other boat is slow to react.

Now we are going to look at the more important parts of the rules that are applicable to leisure craft and listed in the syllabus for the RYA Day Skipper qualification.

Conduct of Vessels in Any Condition of Visibility

THE LOOKOUT RULE – RULE 5

Every vessel shall at all times maintain a proper lookout by sight and hearing as well as by all available means appropriate in the prevailing circumstances and conditions so as to make a full appraisal of the situation and of the risk of collision.

Factors that may affect our ability to see other craft

1 When motor cruisers are being steered from the wheel house, the view astern is often obstructed by cabin superstructure. Other vessels coming up from behind could be missed unless particular effort is made to keep looking astern.

2 If sailing, a large deck-sweeping foresail will severely restrict the view to leeward, as it does in

Figure 6.2. Remember to appoint a crew member to keep looking for dangers behind the sail.

3 When the sea is choppy, spray hitting the fly-bridge or cockpit can affect the visibility. Nobody likes getting a face full of salt water and skippers should ensure that the crew look to windward as well as to leeward.

4 At night, careless use of torches on deck could destroy the helmsman's night vision for about 20 minutes.

5 A closing ship moving at 20 knots will move 2 miles every 6 minutes so don't put the autopilot on and go down below to put the kettle on – the ship may be too close when you return to the deck.

6 The rules say that a listening watch should also be kept and this will be essential in fog.

Fig 6.2 *This crew would be unable to see what is approaching from behind the sail.*

RISK OF COLLISION – RULE 7

a) Every vessel shall use all means appropriate to the prevailing circumstances and conditions to determine if a risk of collision exists. If there is any doubt such risk shall be deemed to exist.

b) Proper use shall be made of radar equipment if fitted and operational ...

c) Assumptions shall not be made on the basis of scanty information ...

d) In determining if risk of collision exists, the following considerations shall be among those taken into account:

i) such risk shall be deemed to exist if the compass bearing of an approaching vessel does not appreciably change.

ii) such risk may sometimes exist even when an appreciable bearing change is evident, particularly when approaching a very large vessel or a tow or when approaching a large vessel at close range.

Use the hand-bearing compass to take the bearings, as shown in Figure 9.9 on page 85. Bearings of an approaching ship will change quite slowly at first, then – as it gets closer – alter more rapidly when there is NO risk of collision. If the bearing remains constant, or is very slow to change, then consider what you should do next as it may be your job to alter course.

If your boat is fitted with radar and you are intending to use it for collision avoidance, make sure that you know how to use it correctly as this rule is very specific about the use of 'scanty' information. Going into a fog bank unexpectedly is highly stressful and it is very easy to misinterpret what you are seeing on the radar screen. A one-day radar course at an RYA Centre is worth every penny if it takes some of the fear and danger out of a situation later on.

If there is a risk of collision and you are the give-way vessel, alter course sooner rather than later and make a bold course alteration to show that you are taking evasive action. Small alterations may not be obvious – change heading so that the other skipper sees your boat from a different angle; at night alter to show him a different colour navigation light.

Never forget that you can also slow down – watchkeepers on commercial ships often look at sailing yachts to see whether they are slowing down by spilling wind out of the sails. A power craft slowing and coming off the plane is always very noticeable to others.

NARROW CHANNELS – RULE 9

a) A vessel proceeding along the course of a narrow channel or fairway shall keep as near to the outer limit of the channel which lies on her starboard side as is safe and practicable.

b) A vessel of less than 20 metres in length or a sailing vessel shall not impede the passage of a vessel which can safely navigate only within a narrow channel or fairway.

e) i) In a narrow channel or fairway when overtaking can take place only if the vessel to be overtaken has to take action to permit safe passing the vessel intending to overtake shall indicate her intention ...
ii) This Rule does not relieve the overtaking vessel of her obligation under Rule 13.

f) A vessel nearing a bend or an area where other vessels may be obscured by an intervening obstruction shall navigate with particular alertness and caution ...

g) A vessel shall, if the circumstances of the case admit, avoid anchoring in a narrow channel.

A channel that appears very wide to a small boat may be very restricted to a ship like the *Queen Mary 2*, but the rules do not define what is meant by 'a narrow channel'. The ferry in Figure 6.3 is finding it tight for space and the very manoeuvrable yacht is not keeping as far as he could to the starboard side of the channel. It is better for small craft to remain outside a big ship channel if there is sufficient depth of water.

Busy commercial harbours with narrow entrances, such as Portsmouth and Poole, often require leisure craft to use a special small boat channel or just one specific part of the main channel. Details of any restrictions may be found in a pilot book or nautical almanac. The photograph in Figure 6.4 was taken on a quiet day in poor weather when there were only a few small craft negotiating the entrance. Even so, the two ferries have a tight squeeze passing each other in the narrows.

◀ **Fig 6.3** *This large ferry has little space to manoeuvre.*

▶ **Fig 6.4** *Portsmouth Harbour entrance with two large commercial vessels about to pass each other in the narrow entrance.*

TRAFFIC SEPARATION SCHEMES – RULE 10

c) A vessel shall, as far as practicable, avoid crossing traffic lanes, but if obliged to do so shall cross on a heading as nearly as practicable at right angles to the general direction of traffic flow.

g) A vessel shall so far as practicable avoid anchoring in a traffic separation scheme or in areas near its terminations.

h) A vessel not using a traffic separation scheme shall avoid it by as wide a margin as is practicable.

j) A vessel of less than 20 metres in length or a sailing vessel shall not impede the safe passage of a power-driven vessel following a traffic lane.

Traffic schemes have been established to keep large commercial vessels from meeting each other head-on when rounding headlands and in areas heavy with shipping. Small boats may sometimes have to cross a scheme when on passage, but should generally stay well away from the lanes and their terminations. Figure 6.5 shows part of a scheme in the southern North Sea.

Ships are separated from each other by the purple shaded areas and must, by law, proceed in the direction of the arrows if using the lanes.

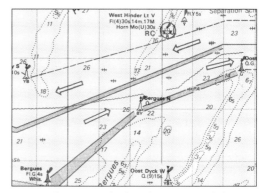

Fig 6.5 *This area is thick with commercial shipping and separation schemes are essential for safety.*

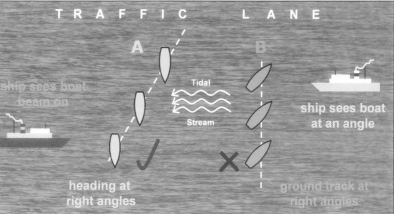

Fig 6.6 *A vessel crossing the lanes should head at right-angles to the traffic flow.*

Rule 10 c) tells us that, should we have to cross, we should head at right-angles to the lane. Figure 6.6 shows that, as we cross, this will present a beam-on aspect to large ships and will be quicker than crabbing across while correcting for tidal flow.

We shall now look at the rules for manoeuvring and it is worth remembering that Rules 12 to 18 are specifically for vessels in sight of one another, not where they can see one another by radar alone or just hear one another. You will see what happens in restricted visibility in Rule 19.

Conduct of Vessels in Sight of One Another

RULE 12 – SAILING VESSELS

a) When two sailing vessels are approaching one another, so as to involve risk of collision, one of them shall keep out of the way of the other as follows:

i) when each has the wind on a different side, the vessel which has the wind on her port side shall keep out of the way of the other;

ii) when both have the wind on the same side, the vessel which is to windward shall keep out of the way of the vessel which is to leeward;

iii) if a vessel with the wind on the port side sees a vessel to windward and cannot determine with certainty whether the other vessel has the wind on the port side or on the starboard, she shall keep out of the way of the other.

This rule talks about the wind being on either the port or starboard side, not the side that the boom is on. If the boom is on the starboard side the wind will be coming from the port side and will mean that you are the give-way vessel in many situations. If you are reefing when under way it is advisable to put the boat on the starboard tack so that you do not have to give way to all other yachts while you have the mainsail improperly set. Figures 6.7, 6.8 and 6.9 give diagrams for this rule.

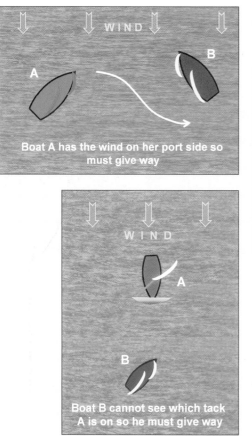

Boat A has the wind on her port side so must give way

WIND

Boat B cannot see which tack A is on so he must give way

◀ **Fig 6.7** *Rule 12 a) i) Boat A has given way and has eased the main and genoa sheets to pass behind Boat B.*

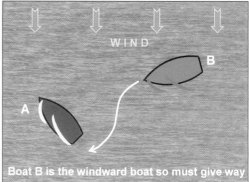

Boat B is the windward boat so must give way

▲ **Fig 6.8** *Boat B is further off the wind than close-hauled Boat A so he is the give-way boat.*

◀ **Fig 6.9** *Boat B must assume that Boat A has the wind on the starboard side.*

RULE 13 – OVERTAKING

Notwithstanding anything contained in the Rules of this section, any vessel overtaking another shall keep out of the way of the vessel being overtaken.

This rule applies to *all* vessels, however they are powered. A sailing yacht under spinnaker in a fresh breeze could well be going faster than a displacement motorboat, but must give way to the powerboat if overtaking. The yacht remains the give-way vessel until it is well clear of the other boat. At night it is easier to establish whether you are the over-taking vessel because you will see the white stern light of the other boat, not a red or a green. Figure 6.10 shows the overtaking arc and care

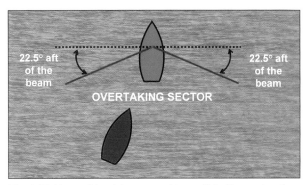

22.5° aft of the beam   **22.5° aft of the beam**

OVERTAKING SECTOR

Fig 6.10 *The red boat is approaching within the angle of the overtaking sector.*

should be taken not to hang fenders on the stern rail so as to obscure the light; a red ensign mounted near the stern light could lead other skippers to wonder why the stern light occasion-ally appears as a red flashing light!

HEAD-ON SITUATION – RULE 14 (POWER-DRIVEN VESSELS)

a) When two power-driven vessels meeting on reciprocal or nearly reciprocal courses so as to involve risk of collision each shall alter her course to starboard so that each shall pass on the port side of the other.
b) Such a situation shall be deemed to exist when a vessel sees the other ahead or nearly ahead and by night she could see the masthead lights of the other in a line or nearly in a line and/or both sidelights and by day she observes the corresponding aspect of the other vessel.
c) When a vessel is in any doubt that such a situation exists she shall assume that it does exist and act accordingly.

In theory, this rule is quite easy because *both* vessels are required to alter course, but it causes some problems in practice when yachtsmen forget that it is a rule for those under power – not sail.

Notice that the rule says 'ahead or nearly ahead'. Sometimes it is necessary to exaggerate your turn to star-board to remind others to do the same. The craft in Figures 6.11 and 6.12 will both have to alter to starboard.

Fig 6.11 *There is a risk of collision. Both boats should take action.*

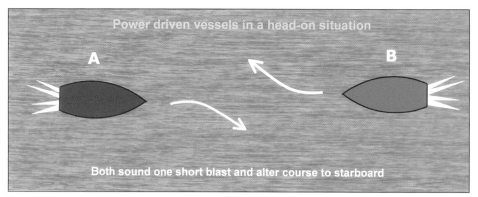

Fig 6.12 *Each vessel alters course to starboard to obey Rule 14.*

CROSSING SITUATION – RULE 15 (POWER-DRIVEN VESSELS)

When two power-driven vessels are crossing so as to involve risk of collision, the vessel which has the other on her own starboard side shall keep out of the way and shall, if the circumstances of the case admit, avoid crossing ahead of the other vessel.

In Figure 6.13 powerboat A has to either alter course to pass behind B or to slow down and allow him to pass ahead.

At night, the situation is again more obvious and the rhyme in Figure 6.13 is an excellent aide-mémoire.

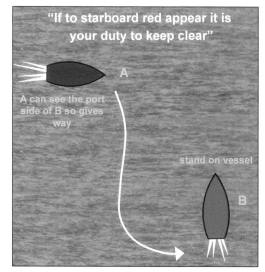

Fig 6.13 *A Crossing situation between two power-driven vessels.*

ACTION BY STAND-ON VESSEL – RULE 17

a) i) Where one of two vessels is to keep out of the way the other shall keep her course and speed.

ii) The latter vessel may however take action to avoid collision by her manoeuvre alone, as soon as it becomes apparent to her that the vessel required to keep out of the way is not taking appropriate action in compliance with these Rules.

b) When, from any cause, the vessel required to keep her course and speed finds herself so close that collision cannot be avoided by the action of the give-way vessel alone, she shall take such action as will best aid to avoid collision.

c) A power-driven vessel which takes action in a crossing situation in accordance with sub-paragraph (a) (ii) of this Rule to avoid collision with another power-driven vessel shall, if the circumstances of the case admit, not alter course to port for a vessel on her own port side.

d) This Rule does not relieve the give-way vessel of her obligation to keep out of the way.

Rule 17 requires that the 'stand-on' vessel keeps her course and speed, *but* if the 'give-way' vessel appears oblivious to the rules then action will have to be taken. It would be an unhappy ending were you to be sitting on your upturned wreck because you stood on to the bitter end!

If action has to be taken by the 'stand-on' craft the rules *prohibit a turn to port towards the other vessel.* Figure 6.14 shows the consequences of such an action.

▶ **Fig 6.14** *The result of a turn to port when not obeying Rule 17c).*

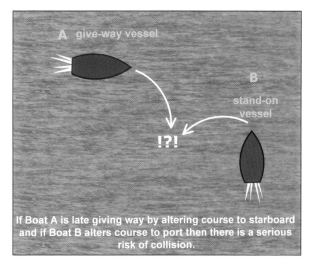

A give-way vessel

B

stand-on vessel

!?!

If Boat A is late giving way by altering course to starboard and if Boat B alters course to port then there is a serious risk of collision.

RESPONSIBILITIES BETWEEN VESSELS – RULE 18

Except where Rules 9, 10 and 13 otherwise require:

a) A power-driven vessel underway shall keep out of the way of:
   i) a vessel not under command;
   ii) a vessel restricted in her ability to manoeuvre;
   iii) a vessel engaged in fishing;
   iv) a sailing vessel.

b) A sailing vessel underway shall keep out of the way of:
   i) a vessel not under command;
   ii) a vessel restricted in her ability to manoeuvre;
   iii) a vessel engaged in fishing.

c) A vessel engaged in fishing when underway shall, so far as possible, keep out of the way of:
   i) a vessel not under command;
   ii) a vessel restricted in her ability to manoeuvre.

d) i) Any vessel other than a vessel not under command or a vessel restricted in her ability to manoeuvre shall, if the circumstances of the case admit, avoid impeding the safe passage of a vessel constrained by her draught, exhibiting the signals in Rule 28.
   ii) A vessel constrained by her draught shall navigate with particular caution having full regard to her special condition.

This rule lays down the order of precedence between vessels and we need to understand why some boats have priority over others.

The senior vessel is one that is *not under command.* But what does this mean? Is the skipper asleep? No, it means that because of some difficulty, such as the weather or a technical problem, it cannot obey the rules. For example, a high-sided cruise liner may have to follow the wrong side of a narrow channel to avoid being blown into shallow water – there is nothing wrong with the ship or crew; it is just the wind strength that prevents her from obeying the rules. During daylight hours she will display two black balls in a vertical line on her mast as in Figure 6.15 – the night signal is shown later in the chapter.

Fig 6.15 *This ferry is showing the 'not under command' shapes.*

Fig 6.16 *This motor yacht is preparing to launch a helicopter and is therefore restricted in its ability to manoeuvre.*

Fig 6.17 *This ship is displaying a cylinder at the mast to show that it is a deep-draught vessel.*

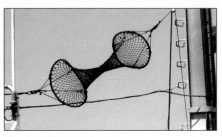

Fig 6.18 *Fishing shapes.*

Fig 6.19 *Sailing well.*

Fig 6.20 *Calm seas in the British Virgin Islands.*

Next, we have a vessel *restricted in its ability to manoeuvre*. In this case, it is the nature of its work that causes it to be hampered in some way. Vessels in this category are often called 'lame ducks' and are engaged in tasks such as towing another ship, laying cables or, in the case of the large motor yacht in Figure 6.16, launching a helicopter! It has hoisted three distinctive shapes consisting of a black ball, a diamond and another ball below. The moment it ceases this task, it will become an ordinary power-driven vessel and lose any priority.

A vessel that is *constrained by draught* is a special case and comes next. Large container ships have very little water under their keels in narrow channels like Southampton Water. The day signal is a black cylinder which is often very difficult to see. Small leisure craft should keep well clear of these ships and it is hoped that the yacht in Figure 6.17 will soon tack!

Third in the pecking order is a *vessel engaged in fishing or trawling*. Nets and trawls often extend more than 150 metres astern that hamper the craft, especially when hauling or setting nets, so keep well clear as they frequently turn unexpectedly. The shape hoisted to show that it is fishing is shown in Figure 6.18, two black cones with their points together. This slightly lop-sided shape was seen on a French fishing boat.

Almost last in the list comes the *sailing vessel*. Having some priority does not mean that there is an automatic right to short tack in a narrow channel or crowded harbour! Many harbours require that yachts proceed under power, although it is permissible to have sails hoisted so long as the engine is being used. A yacht that is motor sailing is classed as a 'power-driven vessel'.

Last in the list come the *power-driven vessels* both large and small (Figure 6.20). Being the most manoeuvrable they have to give way to all the 'lame ducks' unless they are being over-taken. Skippers of sailing vessels would prefer that powerboats overtake them on the leeward side so that the sails are not shielded from the wind and sailors should appreciate just how difficult it is to berth a high-sided motor cruiser with fly-bridge in a strong cross-wind.

CONDUCT OF VESSELS IN RESTRICTED VISIBILITY – RULE 19

a) This Rule applies to vessels not in sight of one another when navigating in or near an area of restricted visibility.

b) Every vessel shall proceed at a safe speed adapted to the prevailing circumstances and conditions of restricted visibility. A power-driven vessel shall have her engines ready for immediate manoeuvre.

d) A vessel which detects by radar alone the presence of another vessel shall determine if a close-quarters situation is developing and/or risk of collision exists. If so, she shall take avoiding action in ample time, provided that when such action consists of an alter-ation of course, so far as possible the following shall be avoided:

i) an alteration of course to port for a vessel forward of the beam, other than for a vessel being overtaken;

ii) an alteration of course towards a vessel abeam or abaft the beam.

e) Except where it has been determined that a risk of collision does not exist, every vessel which hears apparently forward of her beam the fog signal of another vessel, or which cannot avoid a close-quarters situation with another vessel forward of her beam, shall reduce her speed to the minimum at which she can be kept on her course. She shall if necessary take all her way off and in any event navigate with extreme caution until danger of collision is over.

This is an important rule to learn because all the manoeuvring rules we have looked at so far are for vessels in sight of one another and therefore do not apply in conditions of restricted vis-ibility. Rule 19 is more about what you should *not* do rather than what you should do!

Later in this section we shall look at the sound signals that vessels give in foggy conditions, but sound can become diffused in a blanket of fog and it is often very difficult to tell where the sound is coming from when you have no radar to pinpoint the other vessel's position. The rule assumes that radar is not available and one of the main instructions is to proceed at a safe speed for the conditions. Charging along at 25 knots on the plane in thick fog is definitely not recommended, but occasionally a slow-moving yacht may well need to go a little faster to clear a shipping channel in the shortest possible time.

Early action is also advised as this gives the radar operator on a merchant ship ample time to plot any alterations of course and speed you may make.

Apart from this general advice, the rule then tells us what we should avoid doing if:

1 a fog signal is heard forward of the beam, and
2 it is heard on the beam or aft of the beam.

If all else fails, we are told quite simply that we should reduce speed or, as a last resort, stop.

Sound Signals in Restricted Visibility

In fog it is necessary to make some sort of noise to announce your presence to others. If you are in a small boat under 7 metres in length you can make any noise you like – a lifejacket whistle or shouting would suffice. However, if the boat is larger, the signal will be different depending on the activity. There are two signals to be learned.

Fog signals that give a very deep bass tone are from the largest ships, and ones with the highest pitch are likely to be from a boat under 20 metres in length.

The signals are made up of a combination of short and/or prolonged blasts:

Short blast = A one-second blast.
Prolonged blast = A four- to six- second blast.

If making way under power in fog, the signal is:

One prolonged blast every 2 minutes (Figure 6.21).

Small boats mostly use horns powered by small compressed air cylinders, so it would be difficult to sound this signal for a number of hours. It is better to find a place to anchor that is well away from a channel and other traffic.

Sailing vessels give the same signal as a number of other vessels claiming some sort of priority (Figure 6.22). Remember that someone shut inside a large ship's bridge might find the horn difficult to hear but other small-boat users will find it extremely helpful when in close-quarters situations.

It sounds:

One prolonged and two short blasts every 2 minutes.

Power driven vessel making way

Fig 6.21 *This coaster is sounding one prolonged blast every two minutes when he is making way.*

Vessel under sail

Fig 6.22 *Sailing vessels and other 'lame ducks' sound the same signal.*

Sound Signals for Vessels in Sight of One Another

Power-driven vessels

Ships manoeuvring in tight spaces and entering crowded harbours often give sound signals to help other folk understand their intentions. It is worth noting that a large fast-moving ship who signals that his engines are going astern may well continue to go forwards for up to 2 or 3 miles before he finally stops. Ferries coming out of a berth stern-first in somewhere like Cowes, Isle of Wight, give this useful signal as a warning. Figure 6.23 gives all the manoeuvring signals.

All vessels

Often heard in narrow channels or crowded ports on a bank holiday is the 'Wake-up' signal. The Rules state that this should consist of a minimum of *five short and rapid blasts*. This is sounded when the skipper of one craft feels that the other boat is not taking sufficient action to avoid a collision. I have heard as many as 11 blasts from a ship with a very angry captain!

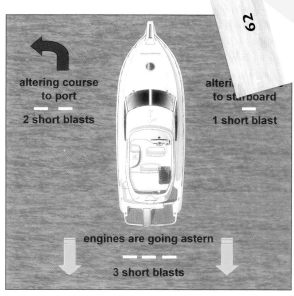

Fig 6.23 *Signals given by powerboats.*

The skipper of the tug in Figure 6.24 would have been justified in giving this signal.

◀ **Fig 6.24** *This tug was in a very narrow channel and could be forgiven for showing concern.*

Day Shapes

Figure 6.25 shows a yacht with mainsail hoisted. A black cone pointing down is displayed in the forward part of the vessel to indicate that it is under power and not sailing. Some harbour authorities are very keen that this shape is shown, particularly if a headsail is also hoisted.

Both powerboats and yachts need to carry a black ball on board to indicate when they are at anchor (Figure 6.26). This shape can

Fig 6.25 *No sailing breeze today.*

Fig 6.26 *At anchor in the Caribbean.*

be bought at the chandlery in flat pack form and is hoisted near the bow of the boat. It is necessary to let other boats know when you are anchored, especially when there is a tidal stream running and there is a small wave around the bow. At a quick glance this could suggest that the boat is under way and able to take avoiding action.

The ship in Figure 6.27 is flying the international code flag Alpha to announce that he has a diver operating close to the ship. This instructs other vessels to slow down, keep a good lookout, and pass well clear.

Fig 6.27 *A support ship with a diver working from the vessel.*

Lights

Venturing out at night for the first time is a great adventure and people are surprised that it is often easier to spot different types of vessels in darkness because of the specific light configurations they show.

Basic principles

Everyone *must* show some form of light. A small slow boat (under 7 metres and under 7 knots) may simply use a torch with a white light, so remember to take the torch with you when you go to the pub in the dinghy.

Boats with more sophisticated electrical systems are expected to show a variety of lights depending on their activity but all, whether sailing or motoring, must show a white light at the stern (Figure 6.28).

A white light on the mast showing forwards from 112.5° on one side to 112.5° on the other, and higher than the sidelights, indicates that it is a power-driven vessel. Figure 6.29 shows arcs of all the lights.

Fig 6.28 *All craft over 7 metres in length and faster than 7 knots will display a single white light on the stern.*

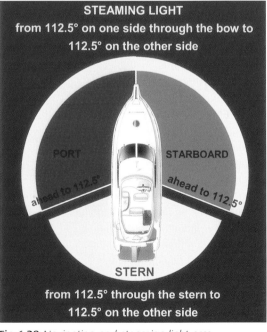

STEAMING LIGHT
from 112.5° on one side through the bow to 112.5° on the other side

PORT   STARBOARD

ahead to 112.5°   ahead to 112.5°

STERN

from 112.5° through the stern to 112.5° on the other side

Fig 6.29 *Navigation and steaming light arcs.*

Fig 6.30 *A power-driven craft under 50 metres in length carries one white light looking forward.*

Fig 6.31 *This yacht is under power and under 20 metres in length.*

Fig 6.32 *The side view of a power-driven vessel probably over 50 metres in length. The after light is carried higher than the one in the bow.*

Fig 6.33 *The bow view of the craft in Figure 6.32.*

Power-driven vessels

The boats in Figures 6.30 and 6.31 are both under power and show a white light on the mast. The yacht has his port and starboard lights combined in one lantern on the bow so that other craft will know that he is shorter than 20 metres because that is the maximum length allowed with this type of lantern. Any craft over 20 metres in length must have the side lights mounted, as on the motor cruiser in Figure 6.30.

When power-driven craft are longer than 50 metres in length they have a second mast for an additional steaming light – as shown in Figures 6.32 and 6.33.

Sailing vessels

Boats under sail display side lights and a stern light and, if less than 20 metres in length, have the choice whether to display them at the masthead or lower down.

The boat in Figure 6.34 is using the low lights which is the recommended configuration if sailing in close proximity to other craft in confined waters.

The yacht in Figure 6.35 is using a combined lantern at the masthead, known as a 'tri-lantern'. This light, which incorporates stern light and side lights, uses less power than separate lights and allows the yacht to be seen at a greater range when offshore. The tri-lantern is for sailing only and must not be used with a steaming light. Using the two together can make the yacht look like a trawler from one side and a vessel engaged in fishing from the other – not at all helpful to other boats!

Fig 6.34 *This yacht under sail is showing side lights and a stern light.*

Fig 6.35 *This 'tri-lantern' must only be used when the boat is under sail.*

Vessels at anchor

Craft under 50 metres in length at anchor show just one all-round white light near the bow, and anything over that length displays two as shown in Figure 6.36. Notice that the higher light on the large vessel is at the bow – a change from the configuration she shows when moving.

Small boats sometimes hoist a paraffin storm lantern in the rigging to save power, and so long as such a vessel displays an all-round light this is quite acceptable.

Fig 6.36 *A large and a small vessel at anchor.*

Distress Signals

When the unthinkable happens and you need help immediately, there are a number of signals you can make that will be instantly recognised as distress signals. The ones shown in Figure 6.37 are chosen as the most useful from the 15 listed in Annex 4 of the rules.

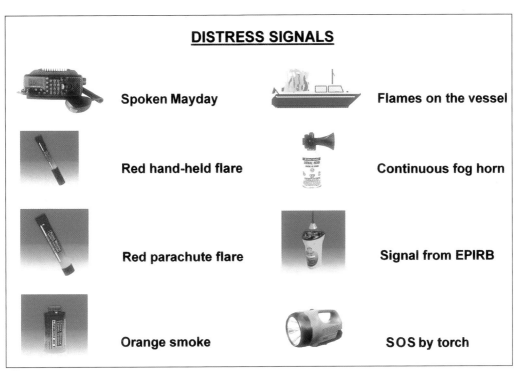

DISTRESS SIGNALS

Spoken Mayday

Flames on the vessel

Red hand-held flare

Continuous fog horn

Red parachute flare

Signal from EPIRB

Orange smoke

SOS by torch

Fig 6.37 *The distress signals most likely to be used on small craft.*

AVOIDING A COLLISION: KNOWLEDGE CHECK

1 Which shape should be hoisted by a craft to indicate that it is at anchor?
2 What is the fog signal for a power-driven craft making way through the water?
3 A craft is heard sounding one short blast on the ship's horn. What does this mean?
4 One sailing vessel is overtaking another. Who is the give-way vessel?
5 Which of the following is not a distress signal?
    a) a red hand flare   **b)** an ensign upside-down   **c)** spoken word 'Mayday'
6 Is it permissible to use a tri-lantern and the low navigation lights together?

CHAPTER SEVEN

THE ENGINE

On a powerboat the engines are the only source of power and, despite being fitted with a mast and sails, the average modern yacht is becoming increasingly dependent on its engine for instrumentation, lighting and all the other essentials of life in the twenty-first century. Mechanical failure is still the primary reason for lifeboat call-out, so it is important that you know how to perform daily engine checks and do some simple repairs to keep it running.

Most cruising boats have diesel engines, as the fuel is more economical and less explosive than petrol. Even rigid inflatable boats are now being fitted with inboard diesels, so we shall look at the diesel engine first.

The Diesel Engine

Most engines are installed into a bare hull and then the cabins and saloon are built around the engine. This results in virtually no space around the machinery and it is difficult to get a small hand into the engine box, let alone a spanner or a pipe wrench!

The principle behind the diesel engine is very simple, and the way that it works can be described in four words – *Suck, Squeeze, Bang* and *Blow*.

1. SUCK	Fresh air is sucked into each of the engine cylinders in turn.
2. SQUEEZE	The air is compressed enough to make it extremely hot.
3. BANG	Misted fuel is injected into the hot air and burns. This burning causes the air to expand, which moves the piston down.
4. BLOW	The exhaust valve opens to release the burnt gases through the exhaust pipe.

Fig. 7.1 *The diesel engine demands clean fuel and a fresh air supply.*

In order to perform these four tasks the engine has to have five systems:

1 Electrical.   **2** Fuel.   **3** Air and exhaust.   **4** Lubrication.   **5** Cooling.

We shall cover each of these five systems in turn, covering the routine checks and minor repairs.

1 Electrical System

The electrical system provides power to start the engine. The batteries need to be in good condition for this, so most boats have two or more so that one is kept fully charged for engine starting. Once started, the engine will use the alternator to charge the batteries, which will then provide power for running instruments, fans, pumps and lighting. In harbour, shore power can be used to supply electricity for domestic use and it will charge the batteries at the same time.

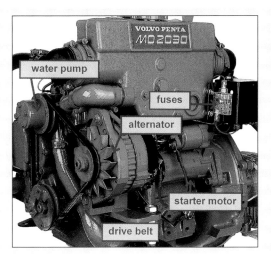

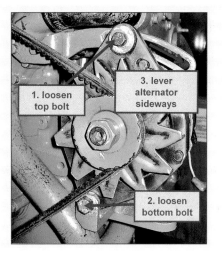

Fig 7.2 *Parts on the Volvo MD2030 engine.* **Fig 7.3** *Tensioning the drive belt.*

The alternator (Figure 7.2) is turned using a drive belt that should be checked daily as part of the pre-start check. If the drive belt is too loose or worn, the alternator will not turn and the batteries will go flat. If it is slipping there may be greasy, black powder covering the surrounding area or the teeth on the belt may look worn. An over-tight belt could damage both the alternator and the water pump.

The tension can be checked by twisting the belt. It should be able to twist through 90°, but not too easily. Should it feel floppy, it must be re-tensioned. For those who enjoy wielding a spanner, tighten the belt by levering the alternator sideways as shown in Figure 7.3.

If there is any vibration on the engine, the fuses (shown in Figure 7.2) occasionally shake loose; so if there is loss of power to instruments, it is worth checking the fuse box.

2 Fuel System

A diesel engine needs fuel that is free of water, dirt and air to allow it to run. We shall follow the diagram in Figure 7.4, starting at the tank and following through to the injectors:

Fig 7.4 *The fuel system for a diesel engine.*

The fuel tank

The tank should be kept as full as possible so that any condensation is reduced and every effort should be made not to fill the tank with water instead of fuel!

It has a breather pipe that allows air to escape while it is being filled, so do not over-fill the tank as it will leak from the breather pipe if the boat is heeled or rolling badly.

Shut-off valve

Close to the tank, there should be a valve to isolate it from the engine when the filters are changed. When taking over a charter boat it is always wise to check that this valve is open. From experience, I can tell you that the engine stops at the worst possible moment – just as you are emerging from the marina!

Pre-filter or water separator

From this valve, the fuel flows to the water separator where dirt and water drop to the bottom and the fuel floats above. Many pre-filters have the bottom section made of glass so that water and dirt can be seen with the aid of a torch. Most are fitted with a wing nut at the bottom so that waste can be drained into a small plastic cup. It is advisable to wear protective gloves for this job as diesel fuel can irritate the skin.

Fuel lift pump

The fuel now continues on its way to pass through the fuel lift pump, which is normally driven by the engine. The pump is fitted with a small lever, which may be operated manually to pump fuel from tank to fine filter when bleeding air out of the system.

The fine filter This filters very small particles of dirt and is the last defence before the injectors are reached. It should be changed at the annual service, but it is advisable to carry a few spares for each engine; if dirty fuel gets picked up; more than one filter may block.

Fuel injection pump This pump pressurises and measures the fuel so that a fine mist of fuel can be injected into the cylinders. The pressures involved are extremely high and the piping from injector pump to injectors is narrow but strong. This pump is a precision instrument so should be sent to a specialist for servicing – it is definitely not a 'do-it-yourself' job.

Injectors The injectors, one for each cylinder, convert the small quantities of fuel into an atomised spray at enormous pressure through a needle valve. Injectors are very expensive, precision instruments and, like the injection pump, not for the amateur to dismantle.

Bleeding the fuel system

A diesel engine will not run if it has air in the fuel line. Air can be sucked in from the fuel tank if the boat is in a rough sea and is running very short of fuel. It may run badly and then stop suddenly, and the only solution is to fill the fuel tank from your spare can and bleed the air from the system.

Working from the tank towards the injectors, locate the bleed screws – your instruction manual

Fig 7.5 A Lucas injector.

will tell you where they are located on your engine. Slacken each screw in turn and operate the lift pump until bubble-free fuel flows out. If the lift pump feels floppy and un-primed, the crank-shaft can be turned to prime it – a flick on the starter motor for about a second should do the job. Hopefully, when you get as far as the fine-filter bleed screw as shown in Figure 7.6, all the air will have been removed. If it still does not start, loosen the injector pipe unions about two or three turns, then turn the engine over with the starter motor until there are no air bubbles in the fuel. Tighten each nut in turn while the engine is being turned over. Take great care to keep clear of the drive belt and any other moving parts as the engine may start suddenly.

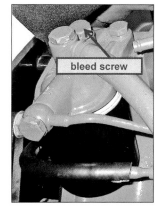

Fig 7.6 *The bleed screw on the fine filter.*

3 Air System

The fuel could not burn effectively if the engine could not suck in a quantity of clean, fresh air through a simple filter (Figure 7.7). Routine checks should be carried out to see that the fine sponge is not damaged or blocked. If there is a shortage of air there is likely to be unburnt fuel in the exhaust gases, which will give off unpleasant black smoke.

Fig 7.7 *This sponge filter prevents particles of dirt entering the engine.*

4 Lubrication System

Oil lubricates and protects the moving parts of the engine from wear and cleans small particles of carbon and metal from bearing surfaces. It also cools the pistons and bearings that cannot be reached by the cooling water, so running out of oil is certainly not recommended.

When you do the engine checks, always look under the engine to check that the well is not full of sump oil and a sump nut, although this will become obvious when you check the level with the dipstick.

Do not overfill above the maximum mark on the stick (Figure 7.8) as this puts added strain on the moving parts. *Do* push the stick right home after testing – or it will make a horrible mess as oil bubbles out over the engine.

Fig 7.8 *The oil filler cap and dipstick on a Volvo MD 2003 engine.*

5 Cooling System

An immense amount of heat is produced inside the engine when diesel fuel is burned and metal parts move against one another. Lorries and cars are cooled as air passes across a water-filled radiator but boat engines are not usually exposed to the air so sea water is used as a readily available alternative and may be used to cool the engine either *directly* or *indirectly*.

Direct cooling

In a directly cooled engine, sea water is pumped into the boat through the seacock, cools the engine and gearbox oil, then circulates inside the engine block before being discharged into the exhaust system and the sea. This very simple method of cooling was used for many small inboard diesel engines up until the end of the twentieth century, but had one great disadvantage – corrosion. Hot salt water is extremely corrosive and can damage the engine in the long term, which is why manufacturers are gradually phasing out directly cooled engines.

Indirect cooling

Both systems of cooling are similar until the salt water has cooled the gearbox oil. Instead of passing into the block, it is pumped into the 'heat exchanger' as shown in Figure 7.9. Here the salt water, running through in copper tubes, cools a mixture of fresh water and antifreeze stored in a header tank on top of the engine. Corrosion is greatly reduced and the engine temperature can be controlled more easily without the risk of salt crystals blocking narrow openings.

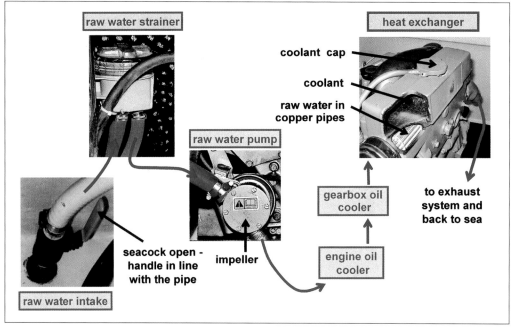

Fig 7.9 *The cooling system for an indirectly cooled marine diesel engine.*

Cooling system checks

1 *Raw water strainer.* Close the seacock before checking the strainer. This will stop the boat from flooding if the strainer is lower than the waterline and prevent an air lock if it is above it. Unscrew the top of the strainer and check to see that it is clear of seaweed and other rubbish. If necessary, remove the gauze filter and wash it. Re-assemble and screw the cap on with care. WARNING – they become cross-threaded in the twinkling of an eye! REMEMBER to open the seacock again.

2 *The coolant level in the header tank should be checked daily.* The tank has a pressure cap very similar to a car radiator, and great care should be taken not to remove this cap while the engine

is hot. If it is at all warm, place a large dry cloth over the top of the cap before unscrewing it. Do not over-fill the header tank, as the excess will flow into the bilges via the overflow pipe. (This is the yellow polythene tube shown in Figure 7.8.)

Changing the water pump impeller

If you forgot to open the seacock after checking for dirt in the strainer and the engine has over-heated, it is highly likely that the water pump impeller may have become damaged. It is normally cooled by the cold sea water but if it runs dry, the small arms will break off or disintegrate.

Figures 7.10 and 7.11 shows a cut-away section of the impeller housing and a new impeller.

Method

1 Close the seacock if it is not already closed.
2 Undo the screws holding the cover plate in place and re-move it.
3 Locate the remains of the paper gasket and remove them.
4 Prise the old impeller out of its housing without damaging the metal surrounds.
5 If some of the paddle blades are missing, you will need to find them before re-assembling. This may involve dismantling the rubber pipe-work between the pump and the heat exchanger. Try to piece the impeller together to check for missing parts.

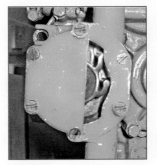 

Fig 7.10 *A cut-away section of an impeller and housing. The cover has a gasket.*

Fig 7.11 *A new impeller.*

6 Smear the new impeller with the lubricant supplied with it and slide it onto the shaft, making sure that the paddles are lying in the direction shown in the instructions.
7 Fit the new gasket to the cover with a little of the lubricant and then replace the cover.
8 Open the seacock!
9 Buy a new spare impeller.

Engine Spares

The spare belts and filters shown in Figure 7.12 are the minimum that should be carried by a small sailing yacht with an auxiliary engine. If you have a twin-engine motor yacht and are totally dependent on engine power, you may require a whole load of filters if you are unfortunate enough to pick up dirty fuel when away from your usual supplier.

For advice on fitting the filters and for winterisation, please consult your engine manual.

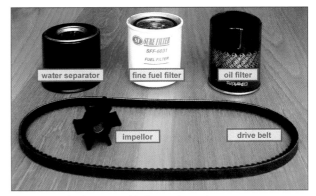

Fig 7.12 *A basic spares kit for each engine.*

Engine Controls

Combined gear and throttle lever

Figure 7.13 shows the combined gear and throttle lever for a single-engine sailing yacht. Once the engine has been started, the lever is pushed towards the bow to make the boat go forward and pulled backwards to drive the boat astern. The further the lever is pushed, the faster the boat will travel. The red button at the base of the lever disengages the drive when it is pushed in, which allows the throttle to be advanced for starting.

Fig 7.13 *This single lever is both throttle and gear change.*

Engine control panel

The panel in Figure 7.14 has a rev counter and warning lights for oil, temperature and alternator. There is no key, so the engine is started using the power and start buttons. 'Glow' plugs heat the combustion chambers and assist ignition when starting from cold – some engineers advocate that the glow plugs be used at every engine start.

Fig 7.14 *An engine control panel on a production yacht.*

Engine starting procedure

1 Check the engine battery is turned on.
2 Check there are no lines in the water that could foul the propeller.
3 Put the gear lever into neutral. (Note: Some engines require a small amount of throttle, so push the red button in when the lever is in the neutral position and move the gear lever forward a small amount.)
4 Press the 'Power' switch on the engine panel – the alarm indicators will light.
5 Hold the 'Glow' switch upwards for 10-plus seconds.
6 Press the 'Start' button with the glow switch depressed.
7 Release the glow switch after the engine has started.
8 Check that the water is coming from the exhaust pipe.

THE ENGINE: KNOWLEDGE CHECK

1 Which four words might describe how the diesel engine works?
2 What is the function of the fuel pre-filter?
3 What may happen if the drive belt breaks?
4 What colour will the exhaust smoke be if the engine is starved of air?
5 Why might the engine fuel system require bleeding?
6 Why should the seacock be closed when the raw water strainer is cleaned?

CHAPTER EIGHT

ABOUT CHARTS

A chart is just a maritime map. It is an essential part of the boat's equipment so that skippers can safely pilot their craft from harbour to harbour. It can be printed on paper or stored in electronic form for display on a chart plotter or PC. Charts can look a little baffling at first, but you will quickly realise just how much wonderful information they give.

If you are to have credibility as a navigator, remember to refer to them as 'charts'. Calling them 'maps' marks you out as a landlubber!

In the UK we are extremely fortunate that our Admiralty, since the days of Captain Cook, has conducted worldwide surveys and it is still the world's leading chart supplier. In recent years the Admiralty has also published chart packs for small craft, which are small enough to fit on the average chart table and are, in some cases, waterproof.

The Admiralty also sells survey information to other UK chart makers such as Imray and Stanford. These two companies have always specialised in producing high-quality, water-resistant charts for leisure boaters. Imray also offer pilot books and charts of the Caribbean, and other areas where there are bareboat charter fleets.

In most cases I have used Admiralty charts in this book.

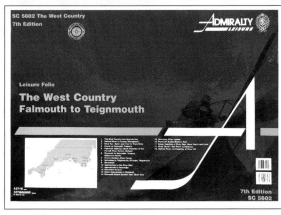

▲ **Fig 8.1** *An Admiralty chart folio of the West Country.*

▶ **Fig 8.2** *An Imray small-craft chart.*

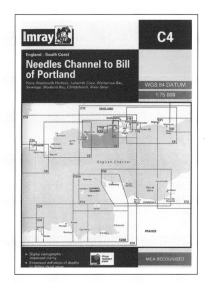

Latitude and Longitude

Before we learn how charts are made we need to revise some of the basic geography and geometry we learned at school.

Road maps and street plans are overlaid with a grid for pinpointing the position of a village or important features. Nautical charts are overlaid with a geometrical grid system, which uses parts of a sphere as its basis. The co-ordinates of this grid are called *latitude* and *longitude*.

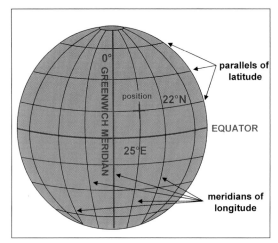

Fig 8.3 *Latitude and longitude graticule.*

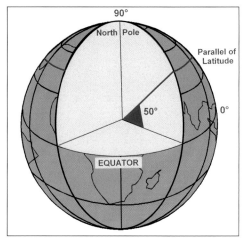

Fig 8.4 *Parallels of latitude.*

Latitude is measured as north or south of the Equator, and longitude is measured as east or west of the Greenwich Meridian. Figure 8.3 shows a grid position, which is 22° north of the Equator and 25° east of a north–south line that passes through the old Observatory in London's Greenwich Park.

Latitude

Notice that the position in Figure 8.3 gives positions as angles in degrees. Figure 8.4 shows how these angles are formed using the centre of the Earth as the reference point. The Equator is the 0° line and the Poles are at an angle of 90°.

Imaginary circles running parallel to the Equator encircle the Earth and are called *Parallels of Latitude*.

In Figure 8.4 the 50°N parallel, which runs through the English Channel, has been drawn in. Let's look at a few facts and figures to get the dimensions into perspective:

The circumference of the Earth at the equator	= 21,600 NAUTICAL MILES.
There are 360 degrees in a circle.	
A DEGREE is 1/360th of 21,600 miles	= 60 NAUTICAL MILES.
One NAUTICAL MILE	= 1, 852 metres.
A CABLE is 1/10th of a nautical mile	= 185 metres.

Fig 8.5 *A few facts and figures.*

Longitude

Longitude is measured either east or west of a half circle joining the Poles. This line is called a *meridian*.

The Equator, being the greatest circle on the globe, was the obvious choice as the reference for latitude. Selecting one for longitude was a lot more difficult as each maritime nation had its own zero line. It was not until 1884 that a line passing through the Greenwich Observatory was

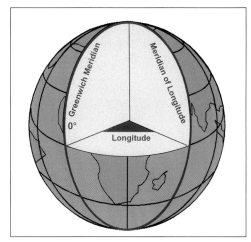

Fig 8.6 *Meridians of longitude.*

internationally accepted as the *prime meridian* (Figure 8.6).

The circle drawn around the Earth at the Equator has 360°, but it is divided into two half-circles of 180° for navigational purposes. Longitude is expressed as being east or west of Greenwich and the meridian at 180° would normally be the *International Date Line* except that it does a detour around islands in the same group so that it is not Saturday in one island and Sunday in the other. The Kiribati group of islands in the Pacific was the first to celebrate the new millennium in the year 2000.

A degree on the longitude scale is equivalent to 60 nautical miles, but only at the Equator as the meridians of longitude taper in towards the Poles the further north you go. This is why distance on a chart is always measured using the latitude scale up each side of the chart – never along the top and the bottom. However, when expressing our longitude position we read the figures from the top or bottom margins of the chart. Figures 8.7 and 8.8 demonstrate how to read the latitude and longitude positions.

Reading off latitude and longitude

Figure 8.7 shows the latitude scale of a chart. The position at the bottom of the picture shows a parallel of latitude that is 50° and 15 minutes north – that is, 3,015 nautical miles north of the Equator. Each nautical mile is one minute of latitude and we can see that each mile is subdivided into ten parts. One-tenth of a mile is called a cable and is 185 metres long. Notice that the minute symbol (') is placed immediately after the whole figure – not after the decimal point.

Figure 8.8 shows the longitude position being measured. The position is west of Greenwich so the longitude increases from right to left across the page – not in the direction of normal text. Extra care is needed when reading these positions as it is very easy to make mistakes. Notice that the minutes of longitude are a lot smaller than they are on the latitude scale. This is because the position is so far north of the Equator and the meridians of longitude converge at the Poles.

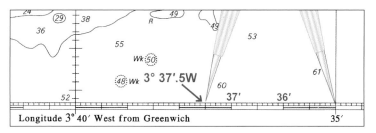

Fig 8.8 *The longitude scale.*

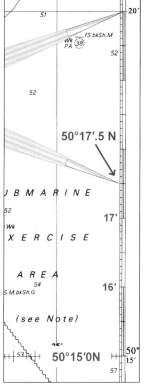

Fig 8.7 *The latitude scale.*

How Charts are Made

The history of chart making goes back many hundreds of years and some of the early efforts look very crude. Without the help of surveying instruments and satellite photographs, map making was extremely difficult – Scotland is almost unrecognisable in Figure 8.9. Projecting the round Earth onto a flat piece of paper was a major problem for cartographers and many different methods were devised.

Probably the most successful system was perfected by a sixteenth-century Flemish navigator, Mercator. His projection is still used nowadays for medium-scale charts – those that are typical of the passage chart we would use for crossing the Irish Sea or English Channel.

The way that the charts are made affects the way we measure distance, which is why we need to learn a little about *Mercator's projection* before we start plotting on a chart.

Fig 8.9 *An old chart of Scotland and the offshore islands.*

Mercator Projection

Using a light source in the centre of the globe, Mercator projected the lines of latitude onto a tube of paper wrapped around the sphere, as shown in Figure 8.10.

This meant that the latitude lines on the paper become further apart as distance from the Equator increases. Greenland and the northern part of Canada appear much larger than they are in reality. It is therefore important that, when using a Mercator chart, we measure distance on the latitude scale that is level with the boat's position.

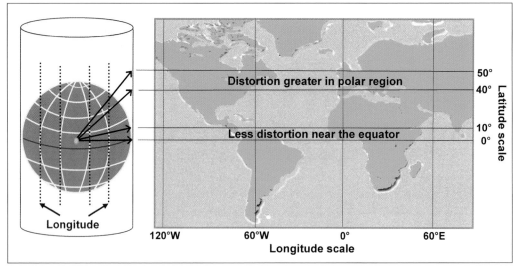

Fig 8.10 *Mercator projection*

Paper Charts

Title panel

Charts have a *title panel*, which tells us that Mercator projection has been used and that the depths are given in metres.

Harbour plans need to be 1:12,500 so that minute details may be included.

The chart in Figure 8.11 is one of 19 charts in the Admiralty West Country folio. Inside the pack are more detailed notes, an example of which is shown in Figure 8.12.

Positions

Satellite mapping is extremely accurate and the World Geodetic Survey of 1984 has been adopted internationally so that all chart makers have no discrepancies when marking the position of a danger. All Admiralty charts refer to this datum or one that is almost identical. The West Country chart folio of charts conforms to a compatible datum.

Depths and heights

Depths are measured from *chart datum*, a level to which the tide will seldom, if ever, fall.

Heights of lighthouses etc are measured above a level called *Mean High Water Springs* (MHWS).

Vertical clearances under bridges and cables are measured above *Highest Astronomical Tide* (HAT).

Do not worry too much about these levels now – we will look at them in detail in Chapter 11 on Tides.

Navigational marks

These are covered in Chapter 14 – Buoys, Beacons and Lights.

THE WEST COUNTRY
AND APPROACHES

DEPTHS IN METRES

SCALE 1:325 000 at lat 50°00′

Projection: Mercator

Notes: Refer to reverse of front cover for general charting notes and other information.

TIDAL INFORMATION

For details of Tidal Levels and Streams refer to the tables on the reverse of sheet 5602-17.

Fig 8.11 *A chart title from a folio-sized chart*

Positions are referred to the WGS84 compatible datum, European Terrestrial Reference System 1989 Datum (see SATELLITE-DERIVED POSITIONS note).

Depths are in metres and are reduced to Chart Datum, which is approximately the level of Lowest Astronomical Tide.

Heights are in metres: Underlined figures are drying heights above Chart Datum: all other heights are above Mean High Water Springs.

Navigational marks: IALA Maritime Buoyage System-Region A (Red to port).

SATELLITE-DERIVED POSITIONS

Positions obtained from satellite navigation systems, such as the Global Positioning System (GPS), are normally referred to the World Geodetic System 1984 Datum. Such positions can be plotted directly on these charts.

Fig 8.12 *Notes from the West Country folio of charts.*

Electronic Charts

Charts can also be carried in electronic form and displayed on either a dedicated chart plotter or laptop computer. The wise sailor will still have some paper charts in the chart table as a backup in the event of a power failure. Getting lost while frantically trying to sort out your technical problems is definitely bad for your blood pressure!

▲ **Fig 8.13** *Simrad combined chart plotter and radar.*

▶ **Fig 8.14** *Sea-Pro chart software displayed on a laptop computer.*

Dedicated chart plotter

Chart plotter screens are getting larger and larger and many yachts have a plasma or LCD screen mounted on a bulkhead (upright partition) with the computer box mounted under the chart table, well out of the way. Integrated systems allow the screen to be split or overlaid so that both chart and radar information can be displayed.

The great advantage of a chart plotter is that, when interfaced with the GPS receiver, the boat's position is displayed on the chart and progress across the chart may be monitored.

Laptop computer

Laptop computers (Figure 8.14) can be used to display charts on a large screen without spending a fortune on a big-screen plotter. GPS information can be received using a USB port and numerous software companies supply the charts and navigational programs.

Care should be taken with stowage, as even the strongest laptop is unlikely to survive salt water or being flung across a cabin.

Chart Symbols

Symbols used on marine charts are very similar to those on Ordnance Survey maps. There are too many to remember easily, so the Admiralty publishes a booklet, Chart 5011, which includes every symbol known to mankind. This booklet is a 'must' for both novice and experienced navigators, who require a ready reference when on board.

The booklet has a clever pictorial index at the back that makes it easy to find the section you need.

Imray charts use symbols similar to Admiralty charts, but have a more logical shading system – green for the land and yellow for the drying areas.

Symbols and Abbreviations used on Charts

LANDMARKS

⌘ Ch **Church**	**Castle, fort**	⚑ FS **Flagstaff**	«⋀» **Radio mast**	◣ **Slipway**

Overhead cables (with vertical clearance above highest astronomical tide)

●━●━●━● **Outfall**	● ◉ **Tanks**	✕ **Windmill**	**Water tower**	══════ **Track**

ROCKS, WRECKS AND OBSTRUCTIONS

depth unknown — awash at datum — covers and uncovers

+ ⁙ ∗

chart datum

Dangerous rocks

↘ (┼┼┼) **Dangerous wrecks**

56 : Wk ╫╫ **Non dangerous wrecks**

Obstn **Obstruction**

⌐Foul⌐ **Foul ground**

SEABED

S	Sand
M	Mud
Cy	Clay
G	Gravel
St	Stones
P	Pebbles
Sh	Shells
f	fine
m	medium
c	coarse
bk	broken

CURRENTS AND TIDAL STREAMS

Breakers	3kn → **Flood stream**	**Overfalls, races**	◉◉◉◉◉ **Eddies**

MARINAS & BERTHS

⚓ **Marina**   Ⓥ **Visitors' berth**

LIMITS & ANCHORAGE

Limit of area   ⟷ **Marine farm**   ⚓ **Anchorage**

LIGHTS

✦ **Major light**

◀ **Fig 8.15** *Some commonly used symbols and abbreviations used on charts.*

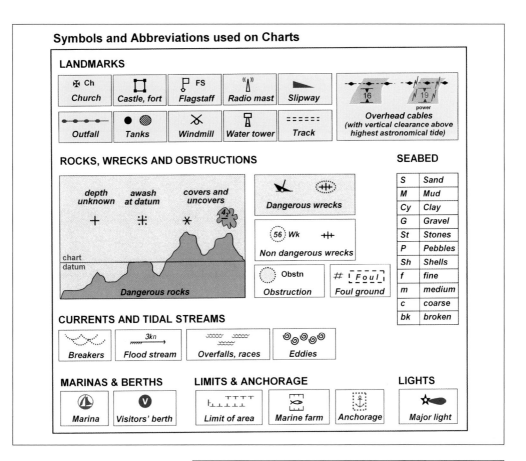

green shading = uncovered at chart datum

larger scale chart number

cliffs

blue shading = depths <10m

nature of seabed

charted depth

depth contour

▶ **Fig 8.16** *Some features found on Admiralty charts.*

Correcting Charts

Charts become out of date quite quickly, especially in areas where coastal erosion allows sand to shift and grow into sandbanks. Harbour authorities frequently change the buoyage in busy harbours and entering an unfamiliar harbour with an out-of-date chart can be quite daunting when buoys have been moved.

2979* ENGLAND – South Coast – Plymouth Sound Westwards – Whitsand Bay – Buoyage – Legend.

Source: Trinity House Notice 27/ 06

Chart 1613 [previous update 2571 / 06] ETRS 89 DATUM

Insert	Q.R	(a)	50° 19'.55N, 4° 15'.25W.
Delete	close W of:		(a) above
	legend, (buoyed), close N of:		(a) above

Fig 8.17 *A chart correction for the Plymouth area.*

The Admiralty issues chart corrections weekly in their Notices to Mariners (NMs), which can be downloaded from their website (www.ukho.gov.uk) and found in some monthly yachting and boating magazines. An example of these notices is shown in Figure 8.17.

Electronic charts can easily be updated electronically, but a fee is payable when your disk of charts is updated or your cartridge exchanged at the chandlery.

When you purchase a new paper chart you can quickly tell how recent it is by looking at the bottom left-hand corner of the chart. It is here that notes are added when a chart is corrected or updated.

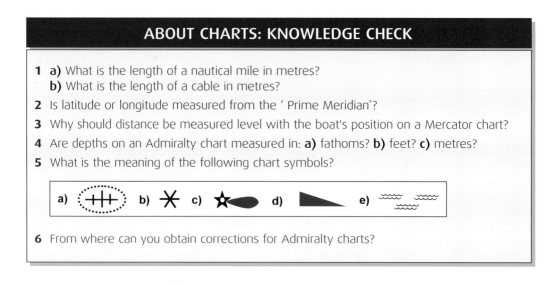

ABOUT CHARTS: KNOWLEDGE CHECK

1 **a)** What is the length of a nautical mile in metres?
   b) What is the length of a cable in metres?
2 Is latitude or longitude measured from the ' Prime Meridian'?
3 Why should distance be measured level with the boat's position on a Mercator chart?
4 Are depths on an Admiralty chart measured in: **a)** fathoms? **b)** feet? **c)** metres?
5 What is the meaning of the following chart symbols?

   a)   **b)**   **c)**   **d)**   **e)**

6 From where can you obtain corrections for Admiralty charts?

CHAPTER NINE
COMPASSES

Fig 9.1 *This compass installation is for a wheel-steered yacht. It is fitted with a light and a cover for protection.*
Photograph: www.stephenrichard.co.uk

Fig 9.2 *A bulkhead-mounted magnetic compass for a tiller-steered boat.*

Direction

North is at the top of the circle at 000° – experienced navigators never call it '360°'. You will remember from Chapter 8 that the top of almost all maritime charts is north.

South is 180°, east is 090° and west is 270°. When giving a heading to the helmsman to steer due east we say all three numbers, ie 'Steer zero, nine, zero'. This number is then repeated back to you by the person at the helm

If the boat is going to travel over the open sea and enter the correct harbour, it will be necessary to use a compass to keep it pointing in the desired direction. A small boat is most likely to have a magnetic compass close to the helm position and an electronic one to direct the auto-pilot and radar.

If the boat is wheel–steered, the compass will be mounted just forward of the wheel where it is in constant view of the helmsman as shown in Figure 9.1.

Tiller-steered craft usually have two compasses mounted on the bulkhead (an upright wall-like partition) either side of the companionway so that the helmsman has a good view whichever tack the boat is on.

Notice that both the compasses illustrated (Figures 9.1 and 9.2) have a circular card that is numbered from 000° to 359°, so before we explore compasses further we shall see how these numbers tie up with north, east, south, west and the chart.

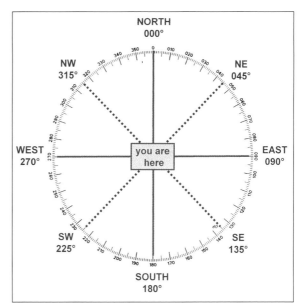

Fig 9.3 *If the boat is on a northeasterly heading, the compass will read 'zero four five degrees'.*

so that there is no confusion or ambiguity. If an object is seen on the starboard beam when you are heading south, it is described as being 'on a bearing of two seven zero'.

A tip when plotting a course is to work out its rough direction first. If, for example, you are drawing a line in a direction of 202°, the line must lie in a direction that is between south and southwest. You may hear this direction referred to as 'sow sow west' by some skippers.

The Magnetic Compass

Inside the liquid-filled compass bowl (Figures 9.1 and 9.2) you will see a card mounted on a pivot. Some vertical posts can be seen inside the bowl, the centre one of which is aligned with the fore-and-aft line of the vessel. This is called the *lubber line* and is lined up with the heading when steering a compass course. A magnet is attached to the card and this will always point towards the *magnetic North Pole*. Remember that it is the boat that moves under the compass card; the card itself does not move.

The Magnetic North Pole

The Earth has a molten core so that ferrous metal deposits move around under the Earth's mantle. Unfortunately, the magnetic North Pole also moves about 50 kilometres a year, which means that the compass needle is always pointing at a slowly moving target!

However, this movement can be forecast reasonably accurately for a few years ahead and, as the Pole is in their territory, the Canadians take responsibility for tracking its movement.

Maritime charts are based on the geographical North Pole and not the magnetic Pole so we have to apply a correction to bearings and headings. This correction is called *variation*; it is angular and is labelled as being 'east' or 'west'.

Refer to Figure 9.4 where you will see two positions, A and B. If you stand at position A and look at the two Poles, the magnetic Pole will be to the east of the true Pole and the variation will be labelled as *east variation*.

Now stand at position B and the opposite will be true – magnetic is to the west of true and will be *west variation*.

When the two Poles are directly in line, there is no variation and therefore no correction is applied to the calculations when a plot is put on the chart.

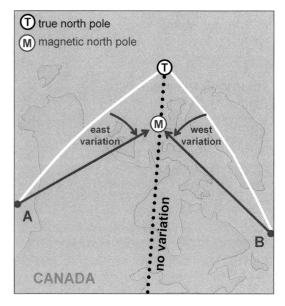

Fig 9.4 *When the two Poles are directly in line there will be no correction.*

The Compass Rose

All good charts are overprinted with a compass rose that gives details of the variation. The value given is for a position at the centre of the rose.

Looking at Figure 9.5, we see that the variation in 2004 was 6 degrees and 40 minutes west (6°40'W). The number in brackets tells us that this value is decreasing 8 minutes annually.

In 2008, the variation will therefore be 32 minutes less then it was in 2004, to become 6 degrees and 8 minutes (6°8').

Practically, we cannot possibly steer the boat to a fraction of a degree, so we round this figure to the nearest whole degree. In this case, down to 6°west.

Converting from Magnetic to True

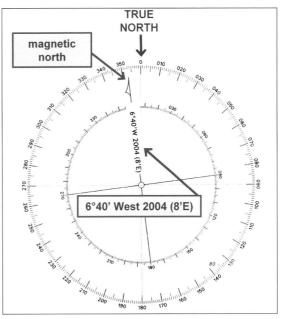

Fig 9.5 *A large chart is likely to be overprinted with several compass roses. Each rose will show the magnetic variation for the immediate area. Here the variation is 6°40' west.*

As the chart is based on true north, we plot true bearings and headings onto the chart, not magnetic ones. It will be necessary to convert the magnetic bearings we take with our hand-bearing compass to true and to convert headings to magnetic when we give the helmsman a compass course to steer.

The UK will have westerly variation for the next quarter of a century, so to begin with we shall concentrate on converting for a westerly error.

We can use various mnemonics so that we apply the correction properly – choose the one you find easiest to use. As you work through Mnemonic example 1, look at Figure 9.6 to check that the rhyme works:

Mnemonic example 1

For westerly variation only:

MAG TO GRID (Chart) = **GET RID** (subtract)
GRID TO MAG = ADD

Example: a) 084° **MAGNETIC** -16°W = 068° **TRUE**
b) 068° **TRUE** + 16°W = 084° **MAGNETIC**

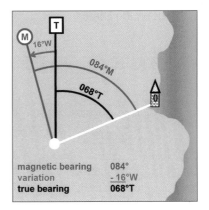

Fig 9.6 *When the variation is towards the west, the compass will measure the greater angle. To convert to true, subtract the westerly variation.*

magnetic bearing	084°
variation	- 16°W
true bearing	**068°T**

Mnemonic example 2a

If the error is WEST then magnetic will be BEST (ie greater than true).

Mnemonic example 2b

If the error is EAST then magnetic will read LEAST (less than true).

Deviation

Care is needed to ensure that the compass is not adversely affected by ferrous metals, other magnets and wires carrying direct current. The humble mobile phone can cause chaos if it gets lodged in the very convenient gap between the binnacle and its protecting rail – the compass reading could be deflected up to 50° due to the magnets in the speaker. If you were offshore, such a hefty error could mean that you were steering for the USA instead of France without being aware of it!

Any deflection by permanent installations – such as an engine and cast iron keels – is unavoidable, but it is necessary to know just how much 'deviation' there is. Fortunately, glass-fibre boats do not usually have the excessive deviation experienced by steel hulls, but when a boat is commissioned from new, the supplier will most likely persuade you to have the compass 'swung' and corrected by a compass adjuster.

As the deviation changes with the heading of the vessel, this professional will take the boat into the local area and check the deviation on headings about 20° apart. Once this is done he

Fig 9.7 *Lodestar's owner has had his compass swung and a deviation card has been prepared.*

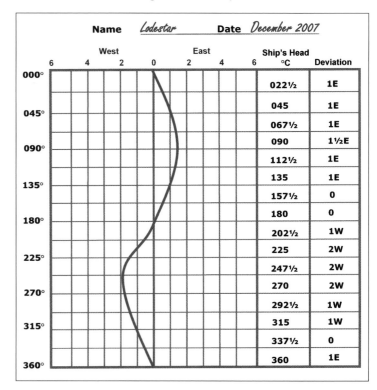

| Name | Lodestar | Date | December 2007 |

Ship's Head °C	Deviation
022½	1E
045	1E
067½	1E
090	1½E
112½	1E
135	1E
157½	0
180	0
202½	1W
225	2W
247½	2W
270	2W
292½	1W
315	1W
337½	0
360	1E

will correct any gross error with some very small magnets, and then prepare a deviation card similar to the one in Figure 9.7.

The rest is up to you; even though you have a deviation card, it is always wise to check that that compass remains accurate and that no one has left the odd screwdriver near the compass. This check can be done quickly and easily when in sight of land or as you enter harbour. If you know what your heading should be from the chart, you can compare it with the actual reading.

Calculating for variation and deviation

Let us assume that the variation is 4°west and that the course we wish to steer = 245°True:

Course	**245° T**
Variation	**+ 4°W** (Grid to Mag = Add)
Magnetic	**249°M**

Now look at the deviation card in Figure 9.7 and find the heading closest to 249°. 247° is closest, which gives a *deviation of 2°W*.

Using the mnemonic we used for variation, we get a course of *251° Compass*.

Notice that we label this course with a °C to show that heading has been adjusted for both variation and deviation.

The Hand-bearing Compass

A small portable compass is used to take bearings of approaching ships and conspicuous objects on the shore. The one in Figure 9.8 is focused on infinity, fitted with a light, and has a robust rubber cover. Remember to put the lanyard round your neck, as it will bounce over the side with amazing ease when dropped!

Hand-bearing compasses do not normally have deviation cards; when taking bearings, try to stand well away from outboard engines and loudspeakers – near the mast of a yacht is often best, as there is always something to hold onto. Although the mast is metal, neither aluminium nor stainless steel rigging cause deviation as they are non ferrous.

Fig 9.8 *Small and robust, this magnetic compass is fitted with a lanyard and a light for use at night.*

Fig 9.9 *Using the hand-bearing compass to take a bearing of a ship in the English Channel.*

Fig 9.10 *A Raymarine fluxgate compass sensor.*

Fig 9.11 *A Raymarine ST40 compass display.*

Electronic Compasses

An electronic or fluxgate compass measures the relative strength of magnetic fields passing through two coils of wire. Using sophisticated electronics, this sensor can deduce the direction of the Earth's magnetic field and magnetic north.

It is still affected by local magnetic fields from steel components and speaker magnets, but will compensate electronically if it is calibrated when installed. This calibration is done afloat while the boat completes two circles at a slow speed.

These compass sensors are small, reasonably robust, and can be mounted away from the usual magnetic influences in a locker. Just remember not to stow your largest mole wrench in the same locker!

One sensor can provide heading information to a number of instruments such as radar, autopilot and chart plotter. Some instruments such as the ST40 display, have their own fluxgate sensors.

COMPASSES: KNOWLEDGE CHECK

1 You were heading 135°M. Are you heading:
   a) northeast? b) southwest? c) southeast? d) northwest?

2 You are facing southwest. Would the compass be reading:
   a) 025°? b) 225°? c) 310°? d) 145°?

3 Convert the following TRUE bearings to MAGNETIC:
   a) 126°T Variation 4°W b) 358°T Variation 6°W c) 180°T Variation 10°E

4 Convert the following MAGNETIC bearings to TRUE:
   a) 324°M Variation 3°W b) 002°M Variation 10°W c) 270°M Variation 5°E

5 Using the deviation card in Figure 9.7, what will be the deviation on a heading of 045°M?

6 Variation 5°W. No deviation card.
   The heading should be 045°T, but your compass is reading 055°C.
   Is the deviation 5°W or 5°E?

Day skippers gather to plan a passage.

CHAPTER TEN

CHARTWORK – FIRST STEPS

Before we can begin work on the chart, we need to assemble a few tools of the trade.

Equipment

Dividers

Dividers can either have straight or bow-shaped arms (Figure 10.1) – both are suitable. Whichever pattern you choose, make sure that there is an adjustment screw because the riveted ones work loose and cannot be tightened. They should be as long as possible so that measurement may be taken from larger-scale charts – preferably 18 centimetres or longer.

Pencils

2B pencils are soft and, although dark, the chart does not suffer damage when the lines are erased. Purchase at least four, because 2B pencils wear down quickly. It is a good idea to keep them in a case, as pencils always seem to vanish on boats.

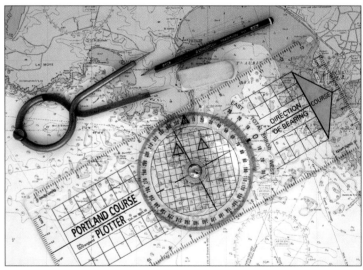

Eraser

A good-quality plastic eraser is best – the ones on the end of a pencil always leave black marks on the chart.

Fig 10.1 *The tools of the navigator's trade.*

A4 notebook

Small notebooks are seldom adequate when preparing passage plans or calculating the height of the tide. A large A4 pad is perfect for the job. Write in pencil so that all your errors can be corrected easily and there is no risk of using a ballpoint pen on the chart by mistake. Many skippers ban pens on the chart table, and even the ship's logbook is kept in pencil.

A navigational plotter

The traditional large-ship navigator uses a parallel or roller rule. These work well on the vast chart tables of a reasonably stable ship, but are of limited use on small boats.

The plotting instrument in Figure 10.1 is of the Portland (or Breton) type, which was originally designed so that it could be used on the lap of an airborne navigator. It is compact, easy to use and has the great advantage that any bearings that are set on the central dial remain set until they are manually changed. It also has an adjustment for magnetic variation, which can be used as an aide-mémoire until the calculation becomes second nature.

You may have noticed that the dial at the centre of the plotter bears a remarkable similarity to the compass rose illustrated in Chapter 9. The plotter is really just a portable compass rose, which can be used wherever there is a need to measure the angle of a bearing.

It may be used for measuring the angle of a line drawn on the chart, drawing a line at a given angle and for drawing parallel lines.

Measuring the Angle of a Line Drawn on the Chart

Step 1

Place the plotter on the chosen part of the chart. Make sure that the large green arrow points to your destination or to the feature whose bearing you wish to determine. Draw a pencil line (Figure 10.2).

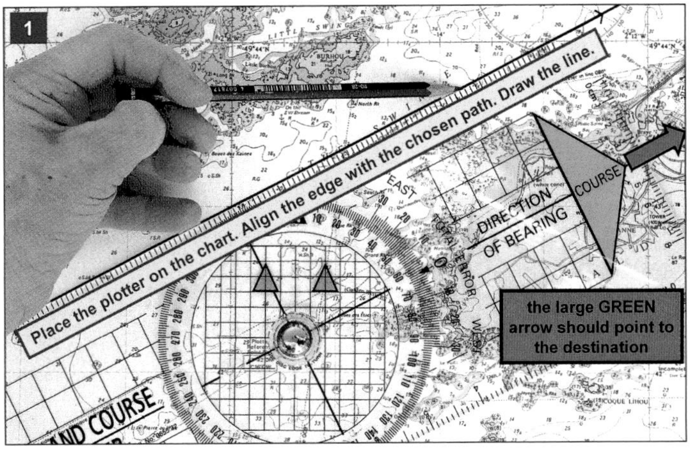

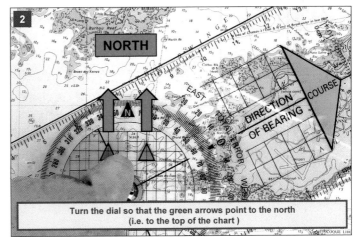

Fig 10.2 *Step 1: Drawing on the chart.*

Step 2

Keeping the instrument on the line, twist the dial of the rose until the two small green arrows point approximately north (the top of the chart) (Figure 10.3).

Fig 10.3 *Step 2: Aligning the green arrows.*

Step 3

Now fine tune so that the grid lines on the rose are parallel to a parallel of latitude or to a meridian of longitude on the chart, making sure that the edge of the plotter remains on your drawn line (Figure 10.4).

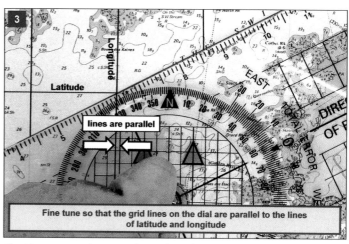

Fig 10.4 *Step 3: Lining up the grid on the rose.*

Step 4

Read the true bearing from the *direction of bearing* line (Figure 10.5).

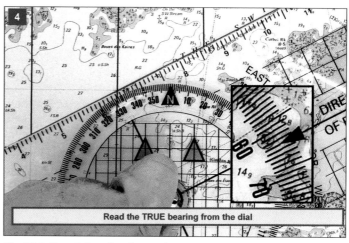

Fig 10.5 *Step 4: Reading the angle.*

Step 5

The final task is to convert the true bearing to magnetic, so we must first establish the local variation using the information from the centre of the nearest compass rose on the chart. Assume 5°W for the example in Figure 10.6. Make a mark on the 5°W graduation with a pencil or coloured pen. The true bearing is shown under the zero line and the magnetic bearing under the red line.

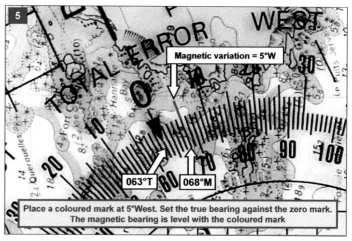

Fig 10.6 *Step 5: Converting from true to magnetic.*

Drawing an Angle for a Given Bearing

Let us now assume that we have used the hand-bearing compass to take a magnetic bearing of a headland on the Devon coast and find that it bears 335°M. Before we can plot anything on the chart, we will have to convert the bearing to true.

Assuming the variation of 5°W for this example, we will apply the rhyme we used in Chapter 9 to help with the conversion:

'Mag to grid – get rid' = 335°M – 5°W = 330°T

Step A

Turn the rose until 330° is level with the zero line (Figure 10.7).

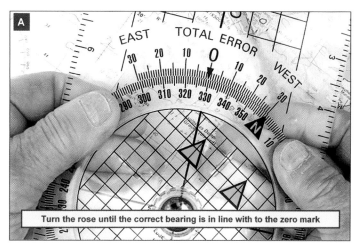

Turn the rose until the correct bearing is in line with to the zero mark

Fig 10.7 *Step A: Setting the true bearing level with the zero line.*

Step B

Place the plotter on the chart and swivel the whole instrument until the grid lines on the rose are parallel to the latitude or longitude lines on the chart, with the two small green triangles pointing to north. Do not be tempted to turn the rose, which you have fixed at 330°T (Figure 10.8).

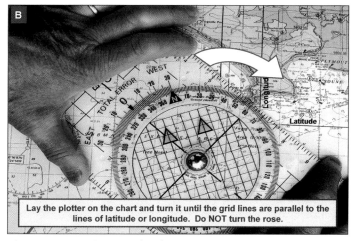

Lay the plotter on the chart and turn it until the grid lines are parallel to the lines of latitude or longitude. Do NOT turn the rose.

Fig 10.8 *Step B: Lining up the plotter.*

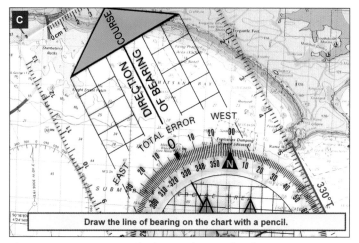

Draw the line of bearing on the chart with a pencil.

Fig 10.9 *Step C: Drawing the bearing line on the chart.*

Step C

Once the plotter is aligned, check that the edge of the instrument is on the headland, and then draw the line. If you are in any doubt about which side of the headland you should draw the line, remember that you are at sea looking towards the northwest, and therefore could not be on a line that is on the northern side of the headland (Figure 10.9).

Measuring Distance

In Chapter 8, you may recall that we learned about Mercator charts and how distortion increases with increase in latitude.

Now that we are doing some practical navigation, it is important to remember that when measuring distance we should always use the latitude scale level with the boat's position – never on the longitude scale along the top or bottom of the chart.

Use the dividers to measure the distance – the scale on the side of the plotter may not be to the same scale.

Try not to have a chart of a different scale lying underneath the chart you are currently using. It is all too easy to use the edge of the wrong chart when measuring how far it is from A to B.

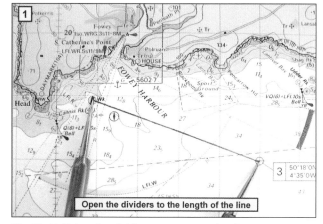

Open the dividers to the length of the line

Fig 10.10 *Using the dividers to measure the distance.*

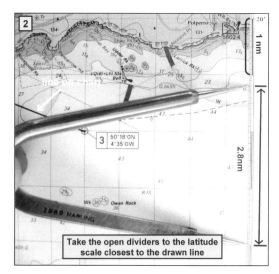

Take the open dividers to the latitude scale closest to the drawn line

Fig 10.11 *Measuring distance on the latitude scale.*

The Distance Log

In order to plot our position on the chart we need to have information about the distance we have travelled through the water. Most small-production boats are fitted with a mechanical distance log, which is mounted through the hull. A small paddle wheel revolves as the water passes across it and counts the number of revolutions within a given time. This information is sent to an LCD display box that shows speed through the water, distance travelled since the log was turned on, and accumulated mileage – very much like the milometer in a car. The one in Figure 10.12 is part of the ST 60 Range from Raymarine, which also gives a depth sounder reading – a piece of vital information in pilotage situations.

Fig 10.12 *A Raymarine Tridata display.*

On a long passage, this log reading will be recorded in the ship's logbook each hour and when there is any alteration of course.

Ship's Logbook

The ship's logbook is a legal document and you are required, under the Safety of Life at Sea rules (Solas V), to keep a navigational record and to show that you have planned your passage. Figure 10.13 shows a typical extract from a logbook.

Passage from Dartmouth To Salcombe			Crew Mark, Judy, Claire, Henry					
Date 15 September 2007								
			Time	Comments	Log	C'se	Baro	Vis
Weather SW to West 3 or 4. Fair. Good vis. becoming SW 2 to 3 sunny periods. Good vis			1330	Slipped under engine	0.0	Pilot	1022	G
			1355	Main + full genoa	2.7	190°		G
			1430	Red can buoy to S/B	4.3	190°	1023	G
Tidal Information HW Plymouth 0835 BST 5.2m LW " 1450 " 1.1m Range 4.1m HW " 2045 " 5.2m								
Tidal Streams Stream setting west from 1400 to 1830								

Fig 10.13 *An extract from a ship's logbook.*

Symbols used for Chartwork

Now that you are beginning to do serious chartwork, you will need to know some of the conventional symbols, which are readily understood by navigators worldwide. If you sail with others on a long passage and someone takes over from you in the middle of the night, it is important that they can decipher what you have drawn on the chart. Confusion could put the boat into danger and cause bad feeling between watchkeepers.

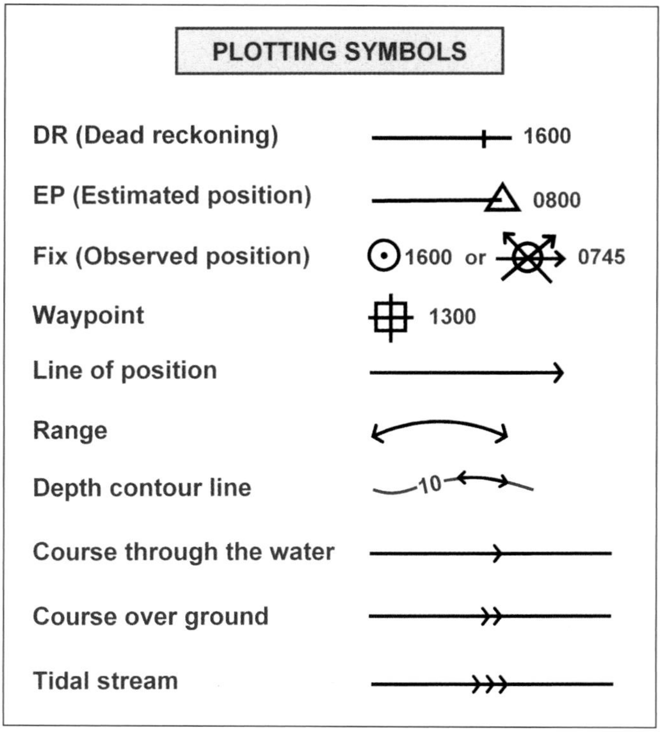

PLOTTING SYMBOLS	
DR (Dead reckoning)	———+— 1600
EP (Estimated position)	———△ 0800
Fix (Observed position)	⊙ 1600 or ⊗→ 0745
Waypoint	⊞ 1300
Line of position	————→
Range	↤⌣→
Depth contour line	—10⟷
Course through the water	————→
Course over ground	———≫——
Tidal stream	———⋙——

Fig 10.14 *Symbols used when plotting on a chart.*

CHARTWORK – FIRST STEPS : KNOWLEDGE CHECK

Use the chart in Figure 10.15 to answer questions 2–5.

1 Why is it advisable to use a 2B pencil for chartwork?

2 What is the distance between the radio mast at Bolberry Down and the radio mast close west of Salcombe entrance?

3 What is the true bearing from a position 50° 12'.0N 3° 55'.0W to the edge of Bolt Tail?

4 What is the true bearing and distance from the 6.8m charted depth off Salcombe entrance to a position 50° 10'.0N 3° 43'.0W?

5 a) Using 5°W variation, what is the magnetic bearing from the Mewstone (off Salcombe entrance) to a position 50° 10'.2N 3° 50'.0W?

   b) What is the distance?

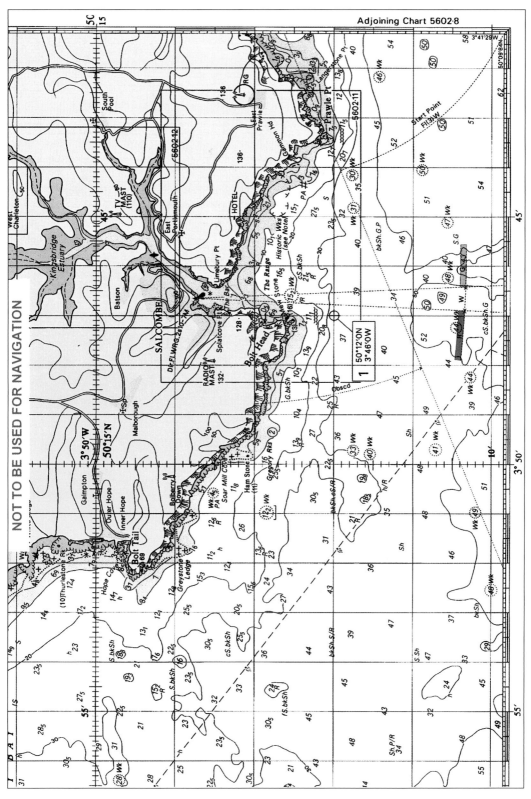

Fig. 10.15 *Plot your answers on this chart.*

CHAPTER ELEVEN

TIDES AND TIDAL STREAMS

The waters around Northern Europe, and in particular the British Isles, are known as *tidal waters*. The ebb and flow of the waters govern whether a boat will float or be hard aground – like the yacht in Figure 11.1. Her skipper will have to wait a good few hours for the water to float her.

It is all very well sitting on the bottom when we are on a mooring or at anchor, but when we wish to move around safely, we need to know how much water is under the boat. If the seabed is rocky, it could be catastrophic to hit the bottom at speed in a powered craft with vulnerable propellers.

In this chapter we will learn a little tidal theory, how to calculate the height of the tide, and how to work out whether we have sufficient water for a safe passage.

Fig 11.1 *This mooring at Emsworth is high and dry at low water.*

The Moon and the Earth

Both the Moon and the Sun have a gravitational effect on the waters surrounding the Earth, but it is the Moon that has the greatest influence as it is held in close orbit around the Earth.

The Earth completes a rotation every 24 hours, and the water on the side of the Earth facing the Moon is pulled up into a bulge – a high tide. You might think that this would cause a 'low tide' everywhere else, but it doesn't. The waters on the surface facing away from the Moon are less affected by the pull, and the movement of water is delayed. The result is therefore two high tides and two low ones within the 24-hour period, as shown in Figure 11.2.

Things get a bit more complicated because while the Earth is orbiting the Sun, the Moon is on the move as well. It takes about 27½ days to orbit the Earth, which means that the tide cycle is lengthened from 24 hours to approximately 24 hours and 48 minutes.

This means that the duration between the high and the low water is approximately 6 hours and 12 minutes.

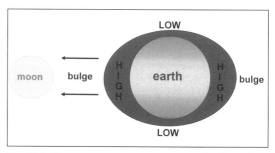

Fig 11.2 *The Moon exerts a gravitational pull on the waters facing the Moon. The waters on the far side are not affected and the level remains high.*

The Sun

While the Moon and the Earth are moving in relation to each other, they are also orbiting around the Sun. At certain stages during the Moon's orbit, the Sun can either increase or decrease the Moon's gravitational pull, which gives larger or smaller tides – called 'spring' and 'neap' tides.

Spring Tides

When the Sun, the Earth and the Moon are in line with one another, there is maximum pull on the waters, giving big tides that we call *spring tides*. This name has nothing to do with the season of the year because spring tides happen every fortnight throughout the whole year, giving high, high waters and low, low waters.

The highest spring tides happen when the Moon is full because the Sun is pulling on the waters facing away from the Moon – as they are in picture A of Figure 11.3.

When the Moon is new we still have a spring tide, but the *range* (the numerical difference between high and low water) is not so great.

Neap Tides

When there is a half moon it is the sign that the Moon and the Sun are pulling the water in different directions – a situation we call *neap tides* (Figure 11.4). At these times, again at fortnightly intervals, we have high tides that are not quite so high and low tides that are not quite so low. In other words, there is a smaller range.

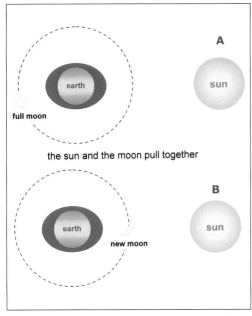

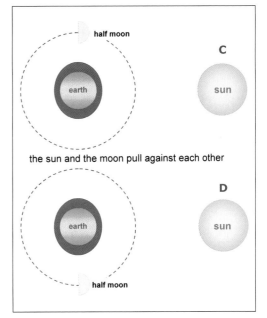

Fig 11.3 *Spring tides occur when the gravitational effect of the Sun and Moon are at their greatest.*

Fig 11.4 *At neaps the gravitational forces of the Sun and the Moon oppose each other.*

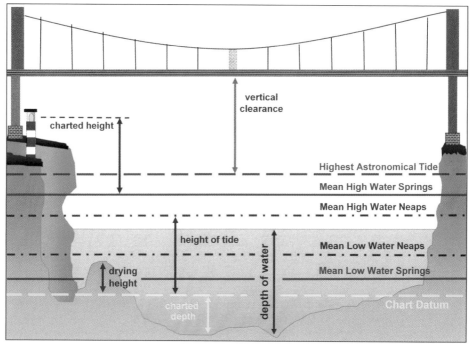

Fig 11.5 *Tidal levels.*

Tidal Levels and Definitions

Now is the time to learn some of the terms that are associated with tides. We will work through the levels shown in Figure 11.5 that appear horribly complicated at first glance, but are well worth studying before we proceed any further. A quick glance back to this illustration may be required should you forget something later on in the chapter.

Chart Datum (CD)

Chart Datum is the level to which the tide will seldom if ever fall when astronomical factors are taken into consideration and corresponds to the Lowest Astronomical Tide (LAT). Bad weather and gales may give higher tides, and prolonged periods of fine weather may cause all tides to be lower than forecast. Any height mentioned in a tide table is normally above Chart Datum, so a High Water (HW) of 5.0 metres can be added to the depth shown on the chart. Figure 11.6 shows that there is a charted depth of 1.2 metres, so the depth of water will be 6.2 metres at high water.

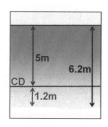

Fig 11.6 *The depth of water is 6.2 metres.*

Highest Astronomical Tide (HAT)

This is the level above which all vertical clearances under bridges and electrical cables are measured. It corresponds to the highest predicted sea level that should occur with any astronomical situations and average weather conditions. See Figure 11.5.

Mean datum levels

The average tidal levels for many ports are shown on some charts, in the almanac, and in pilot books. This data will help us to calculate the depth of water when visiting other ports:

Fig 11.7 *This extract from a UKHO chart shows the mean spring and neap tidal heights at ports to the west of Plymouth.*

Place	Lat N	Long W	Heights in metres above datum			
			MHWS	MHWN	MLWN	MLWS
Cape Cornwall	50°08′	5°42′	6·0	4·3	2·0	0·6
Sennen Cove	50 04	5 42	6·1	4·8	–	–
Penzance	50 06	5 33	5·6	4·4	2·0	0·8
Porthleven	50 05	5 19	5·5	4·3	2·0	0·8
Lizard Point	49 57	5 12	5·3	4·2	1·9	0·6
Coverack	50 01	5 05	5·3	4·2	1·9	0·6
Helford R Entrance	50 05	5 05	5·3	4·2	1·9	0·6
Falmouth	50 09	5 03	5·3	4·2	1·9	0·6

Tidal Levels referred to Datum of Soundings

MHWS = Mean high water springs
MHWN = Mean high water neaps
MLWS = Mean low water springs
MLWN = Mean low water neaps

Remember that the levels shown in Figure 11.7 are all in metres above Chart Datum.

Charted depth

This is the amount of water at a given place if the tide level falls to zero. The purple triangle in Figure 11.8 shows a charted depth of 1.5 metres.

Charted height

The height of a feature such as a lighthouse, church tower or height contour is measured above MHWS. The tower in Figure 11.8, highlighted in red, is 44 metres above that level.

Drying height

This is an area that would be uncovered if the tide falls to zero, but completely covered when the tide rises to the MHWS level. A drying height of 2.7 metres is circled in yellow in Figure 11.8. This means that Blackstone Rocks would be 2.7 metres above the level of the water if the tide were to fall to the zero level.

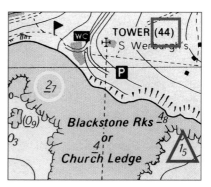

Fig 11.8 *Features near the River Yealm entrance.*

Tide Tables

Tidal height predictions for the year ahead are published in nautical almanacs, Admiralty tide tables and leaflets distributed by some harbour authorities. Plymouth is considered to be a

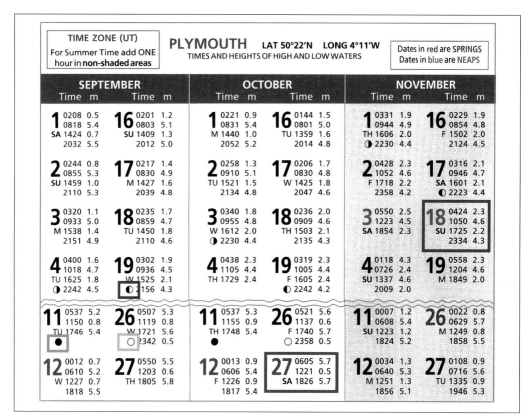

TIME ZONE (UT) For Summer Time add ONE hour in **non-shaded areas**	**PLYMOUTH** LAT 50°22'N LONG 4°11'W TIMES AND HEIGHTS OF HIGH AND LOW WATERS	Dates in red are SPRINGS Dates in blue are NEAPS

SEPTEMBER		OCTOBER		NOVEMBER	
Time m	Time m	Time m	Time m	Time m	Time m
1 0208 0.5 0818 5.4 SA 1424 0.7 2032 5.5	**16** 0201 1.2 0803 5.1 SU 1409 1.3 2012 5.0	**1** 0221 0.9 0831 5.4 M 1440 1.0 2052 5.2	**16** 0144 1.5 0801 5.0 TU 1359 1.6 2014 4.8	**1** 0331 1.9 0944 4.9 TH 1606 2.0 ◐ 2230 4.4	**16** 0229 1.9 0854 4.8 F 1502 2.0 2124 4.5
2 0244 0.8 0855 5.3 SU 1459 1.0 2110 5.3	**17** 0217 1.4 0830 4.9 M 1427 1.6 2039 4.8	**2** 0258 1.3 0910 5.1 TU 1521 1.5 2134 4.8	**17** 0206 1.7 0830 4.8 W 1425 1.8 2047 4.6	**2** 0428 2.3 1052 4.6 F 1718 2.2 2358 4.2	**17** 0316 2.1 0946 4.7 SA 1601 2.1 ◐ 2223 4.4
3 0320 1.1 0933 5.0 M 1538 1.4 2151 4.9	**18** 0235 1.7 0859 4.7 TU 1450 1.8 2110 4.6	**3** 0340 1.8 0955 4.8 W 1612 2.0 ◑ 2230 4.4	**18** 0236 2.0 0909 4.6 TH 1503 2.1 2135 4.3	**3** 0550 2.5 1223 4.5 SA 1854 2.3	**18** 0424 2.3 1050 4.6 SU 1725 2.2 2334 4.3
4 0400 1.6 1018 4.7 TU 1625 1.8 ◑ 2242 4.5	**19** 0302 1.9 0936 4.5 W 1525 2.1 ◑ 2156 4.3	**4** 0438 2.3 1105 4.4 TH 1729 2.4	**19** 0319 2.3 1005 4.4 F 1605 2.4 ◑ 2242 4.2	**4** 0118 4.3 0726 2.4 SU 1337 4.6 2009 2.0	**19** 0558 2.3 1204 4.6 M 1849 2.0
11 0537 5.2 1150 0.8 TU 1746 5.4 ●	**26** 0507 5.3 1119 0.8 W 1721 5.6 ○ 2342 0.5	**11** 0537 5.3 1155 0.9 TH 1748 5.4 ●	**26** 0521 5.6 1137 0.6 F 1740 5.7 ○ 2358 0.5	**11** 0007 1.2 0608 5.4 SU 1223 1.2 1824 5.2	**26** 0022 0.8 0629 5.7 M 1249 0.8 1858 5.5
12 0012 0.7 0610 5.2 W 1227 0.7 1818 5.5	**27** 0550 5.5 1203 0.6 TH 1805 5.8	**12** 0013 0.9 0606 5.4 F 1226 0.9 1817 5.4	**27** 0605 5.7 1221 0.5 SA 1826 5.7	**12** 0034 1.3 0640 5.3 M 1251 1.3 1856 5.1	**27** 0108 0.9 0716 5.6 TU 1335 0.9 1946 5.3

Fig 11.9 *Tide tables for Plymouth. September and October are in the non-shaded area, so an hour has to be added to the times.*

standard port as it is used by warships, ferries and commercial shipping, so it has a full tide table for the year. Almanacs are probably the most used source, so we are going to concentrate on entries in *Reeds Nautical Almanac*.

Figure 11.9 shows part of the tide table for Plymouth, which has been annotated with colours to highlight features worth a mention.

The *orange* square in Figure 11.9 highlights the *new moon* symbol and the *turquoise* one shows the *full moon*, with the slightly larger range.

The *brown* square shows a *half moon*, the symbol for neaps.

The *red* and the *blue* squares are explained in Figure 11.10.

On 18 November we see that a LW of 2.3 metres (above CD) occurs at 0424 and a HW of 4.6 metres at 1050.

On 27 October, the date is shaded in *red*, emphasising that it is a spring tide with a much greater range. In October, the clocks are still set to BST so we must add an hour to the almanac time.

The LW is not given for the evening of 27 October, as it will be after midnight.

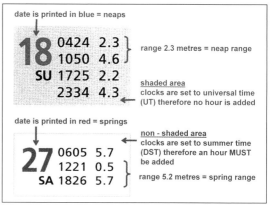

date is printed in blue = neaps

18 0424 2.3
1050 4.6 } range 2.3 metres = neap range
SU 1725 2.2
2334 4.3 ← shaded area
clocks are set to universal time (UT) therefore no hour is added

date is printed in red = springs

27 0605 5.7 ← non - shaded area
clocks are set to summer time (DST) therefore an hour MUST be added
1221 0.5
SA 1826 5.7 } range 5.2 metres = spring range

Fig 11.10 *Features of the tide table.*

The Rise and Fall of the Tide

When the tide begins to rise from LW, it starts off quite slowly for an hour and then gains height a lot more quickly during the middle hours of its six-hour rise. Towards the end of the period, it slows down again for the hour before HW. The rate of flow will depend on the geography of the coastline and on how deep the harbour is. Where there is silting and mud flats over a large area, the rise may be much slower as the mud is being covered.

The Admiralty publishes diagrams called *Tidal Curves*, which show the rate of tidal rise and fall for the hours either side of HW. We are going to use the one for Plymouth and the calculator on the left-hand side of it to work out how high the tide is at any given time. Don't worry! It is far easier than it looks!

How to calculate the time that the tide will reach a given height

Let us imagine that it is November and we have decided to have one last long weekend on the boat before she is laid up for the winter. We decide to return home to our drying mooring in Plymouth on the morning of Monday 26 November, but realise that it will be LW at lunchtime. We know from past experience that we have to be back on the mooring before the tide falls to 3.7 metres, so we use the Plymouth curve, shown in Figure 11.11, to calculate the latest time to arrive there.

Using the curve and the tide table in Figure 11.9, follow the steps through to the answer.

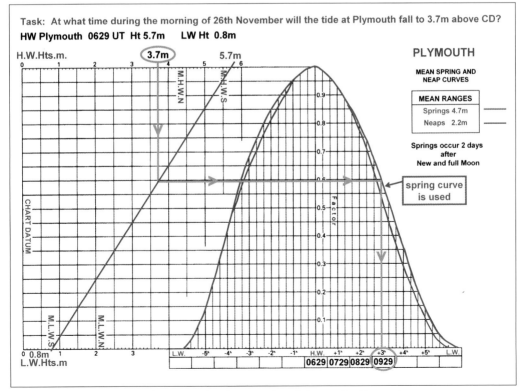

Fig 11.11 *Calculating a time for a given height using the tidal curve for Plymouth.*

Method

1 Look at the tide table and find the entry for 26 November. As we are arriving back during the morning we choose the early morning HW at 0629 UT and the lunchtime LW for our calculations. We do not have to add an hour, as it is no longer summer time.

The table shows: **HW 0629 5.7m LW 1249 0.8m**

HW	5.7m
LW	0.8m
Range	4.9m Sp

Fig 11.12 *The spring range.*

2 Next, we work out the range to see whether it is a spring or a neap tide. To do this, subtract the LW height from the HW height and compare the answer with the mean range data shown on the right-hand side of the curve.

The range is 4.9 metres, which is slightly above the mean spring range. This means we will be using the red spring curve for our calculations.

3 Now, we find a 2B pencil and write the time of HW in the centre box at the bottom of the curve – 0629. Mark the subsequent hours in the boxes.

Because the curve is based on the HW time, we do not enter the time of LW.

4 Enter a mark against the height of HW on the top horizontal line of the graph and the LW height on the bottom line. Join these two points.

5 Next, make a mark against 3.7 metres on the HW line and draw a perpendicular line down to the sloping line you drew previously.

6 As it is a falling tide, draw a horizontal to the red line on the right-hand side of the curve.

7 Lastly, draw a perpendicular down to the time box at the bottom.

8 The answer should be exactly **3 hours after HW at 0929**, so we will have to make an early start if we are to be in time.

Calculating the height of tide for a given time

In the next situation it is 1835 on the evening of 18 October when we anchor for the night in a sheltered part of Plymouth Sound. A member of the crew asks, 'What is the height of tide at the moment?'

We use the Plymouth curve again, and work out the answer with the help of Figure 11.14, page 103.

Method

1 Look at the tide table in Figure 11.9 and find the entry for 18 October. We are anchoring in the evening, so we choose the HW at 2135 and the earlier LW height.

The entry reads: **LW 2.1m HW 2135 4.3m**

The clocks are still set to summer time so we must add the hour, making **HW 2235 BST.**

HW	4.3m
LW	2.1m
Range	2.2m Np

Fig 11.13 *The neap range.*

2 The next question is 'Is it springs or neaps?' Look at the range – it is 2.2 metres, which is exactly the mean neap range.

3 Enter the new HW time in the box at the bottom and work backwards an hour at a time until you get to 1835.

4 Now enter the heights of HW and LW on the left-hand side of the graph and join the two points. Notice that the line passes through the MHWN and the MLWN captions – another way of telling whether it is neaps or springs.

5 Follow the arrows up from the minus 4 hours box to the red line of the curve. Note that the curve does not have a red and blue line for this state of the tide. Now draw the horizontal to the diagonal line and then another line upwards as you did in the last exercise.

6 The answer of 3.0 metres is circled on the top line.

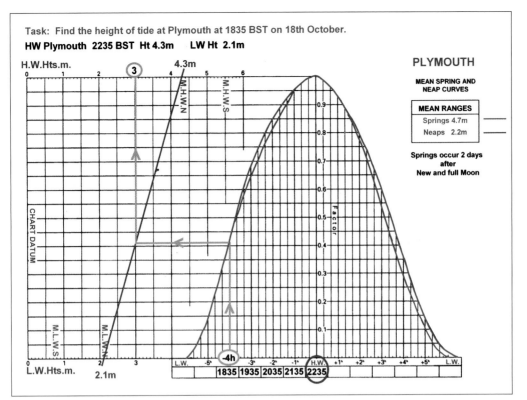

Fig 11.14 *Calculating the height of tide for a given time using the Plymouth tidal curve.*

What will be the clearance under the keel at LW?

Now that we know how to calculate the height of the tide at any time between HW and LW we can also solve further problems with little extra effort.

Going aground in the middle of the night while at anchor means a rotten night's sleep and possible damage to the hull and propellers during the process. Far better that we do a few simple sums to avoid a miserable time.

The situation We anchor during the late morning, intending to have lunch and an afternoon kip in a quiet cove. Our boat has a draught of 1.5 metres and we would like to have a 1-metre clearance under the keel when the water falls to its lowest point. The question is 'What clearance, if any, will we have at LW?'

The first thing we need to do is to calculate the height of tide on anchoring using the tide table and tidal curve for the closest harbour.

Having done this, we find that the **height of tide is 3.0 metres** as the anchor goes down and that the **LW height is 0.8 metres**. We also need to know the actual depth on anchoring. Our echo sounder or lead line will give us this information; in this case, the **depth is 4.0 metres**.

We can see from Figure 11.15 that if the depth is 4.0 metres and the height of tide is 3.0 metres then the charted depth must be 1.0 metre. We can also see that we have 2.5 metres of water under the keel when we anchor.

Looking at the situation at LW, we see that the tide has dropped from 3.0 metres to 0.8 metres – a fall of 2.2 metres. As we only had 2.5 metres under the keel when we anchored, this leaves us with only 0.3 metres under the keel at LW – not really enough if there is a swell.

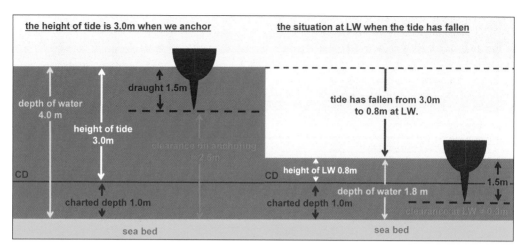

Fig 11.15 *The tide falls 2.2 metres between anchoring and LW. A theoretical clearance of 0.3 metres is not sufficient for peace of mind.*

Never forget that the data in the Almanac is a prediction, not a certainty.

It would have been better if we had worked out the amount of water we required before anchoring as this simply requires that three figures be added together as shown in Figure 11.16:

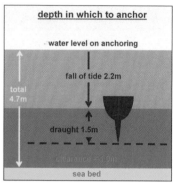

Fig 11.16 *The fall of tide, the draught and the clearance are added to determine the depth of water required.*

1 The fall of tide to LW	= 2.2m
2 The draught	= 1.5m
3 The clearance required	= 1.0m
Total depth required	**= 4.7m**

Secondary Ports Heights

Each standard port has a cluster of smaller ports in close proximity. Looe in Cornwall, for example, is just a few miles to the west of Plymouth and has mean tidal heights that are only 0.2 metres lower than those at Plymouth. The River Yealm, to the east, is also one of Plymouth's satellite (secondary) ports and has HW times that are just a few minutes later than those at the major port.

These *secondary ports* are often small and shallow, so before entering the harbour we should check the differences and apply corrections to the times and the heights of HW and LW at the standard port; these corrections may be found in the (ever useful) nautical almanac.

Figure 11.17 includes an extract from the Plymouth tide table that shows that *Friday 2 November* has been marked with a BLUE square for our chosen date.

The RED rectangle gives the corrections for the River Yealm that are very simple. We will start with this easy port first and graduate to the more complex ones later on.

One particular point to remember is that these time corrections are applied to the *time printed in the almanac (UT time)* – the extra hour for summer time is NOT added until AFTER the corrections have been applied.

Let us look at the time differences first using the two daytime tides.

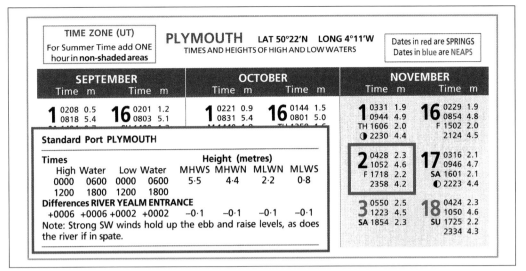

TIME ZONE (UT) For Summer Time add ONE hour in **non-shaded areas**	**PLYMOUTH** LAT 50°22'N LONG 4°11'W TIMES AND HEIGHTS OF HIGH AND LOW WATERS	Dates in red are SPRINGS Dates in blue are NEAPS

SEPTEMBER		OCTOBER		NOVEMBER	
Time m	Time m	Time m	Time m	Time m	Time m
1 0208 0.5 0818 5.4	**16** 0201 1.2 0803 5.1	**1** 0221 0.9 0831 5.4	**16** 0144 1.5 0801 5.0	**1** 0331 1.9 0944 4.9 TH 1606 2.0 ◑ 2230 4.4	**16** 0229 1.9 0854 4.8 F 1502 2.0 2124 4.5

Standard Port PLYMOUTH

Times				Height (metres)			
High Water		Low Water		MHWS	MHWN	MLWN	MLWS
0000	0600	0000	0600	5·5	4·4	2·2	0·8
1200	1800	1200	1800				

Differences RIVER YEALM ENTRANCE

+0006	+0006	+0002	+0002	−0·1	−0·1	−0·1	−0·1

Note: Strong SW winds hold up the ebb and raise levels, as does the river if in spate.

2 0428 2.3 1052 4.6 F 1718 2.2 2358 4.2	**17** 0316 2.1 0946 4.7 SA 1601 2.1 ◑ 2223 4.4
3 0550 2.5 1223 4.5 SA 1854 2.3	**18** 0424 2.3 1050 4.6 SU 1725 2.2 2334 4.3

Fig 11.17 *Tidal differences for the River Yealm – a secondary port in Devon.*

The time differences In the RED square, you will see two headings – HW and LW with some times underneath. Below that, there is a further heading 'Differences RIVER YEALM ENTRANCE'. The two +0006 entries below the HW heading mean that 6 minutes should be added to the time of Plymouth HW. Similarly, 2 minutes are added to the LW time.

The corrected times for the Yealm are:

HW 1052 UT + 6 minutes = 1058 UT
LW 1718 UT + 2 minutes = 1720 UT

The height corrections The mean heights for Plymouth are also given in the RED box. We know it is neaps, so we will use the neap corrections and apply them to Plymouth's heights for 2 November.

The corrected heights are:

HW 1052 UT 4.6m – 0.1m = 4.5m
LW 1720 UT 2.2m – 0.1m = 2.1m

More complex secondary port calculations

Secondary ports that are a greater distance from the standard port often have corrections that are not as simple as those for the River Yealm. Newlyn, in Cornwall, approximately 100 miles to the west of Plymouth, is also a Plymouth secondary and experiences its HW up to an hour earlier.

We will now work slowly through an example to apply the necessary corrections to a date in October.

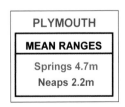

PLYMOUTH
MEAN RANGES
Springs 4.7m
Neaps 2.2m

Fig 11.18 *Plymouth mean ranges.*

Example
Plymouth Tuesday 16 October
Step 1
Look up the morning HW and the afternoon low times and heights from Figure 11.9 and calculate whether it is neaps, springs or mid range, using Figure 11.18.
The result should be:

> **Plymouth (UT)   HW 0801 5.0m   LW 1359 1.6m   Range 3.4m – mid range**

Step 2
Look at Figure 11.19 and ORANGE BOX A.

The figures in this box tell us that if HW Plymouth is at 0000 (midnight) or 1200, then Newlyn HW will be 40 minutes before Plymouth. Alternatively, if HW Plymouth is at 0600 or 1800, then Newlyn HW will be 1 hour and 10 minutes before Plymouth.

On 16 October, Plymouth HW is not at any of these times, but at 0800 (forgetting the odd minute). This means that we will have to do some interpolating to get the difference for our chosen date. One way to do

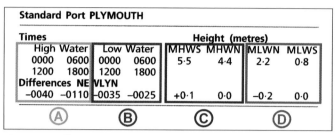

Standard Port PLYMOUTH							
Times				**Height (metres)**			
High Water		**Low Water**		MHWS	MHWN	MLWN	MLWS
0000	0600	0000	0600	5·5	4·4	2·2	0·8
1200	1800	1200	1800				
Differences NEWLYN							
−0040	−0110	−0035	−0025	+0·1	0·0	−0·2	0·0
Ⓐ		Ⓑ		Ⓒ		Ⓓ	

Fig 11.19 *Differences for Newlyn.*

Differences for Newlyn							
Times	0600	0700	0800	0900	1000	1100	1200
Mins	-70	- 65	- 60	- 55	- 50	- 45	- 40

Fig 11.20 *If Plymouth HW is at 0800, then Newlyn HW will be 60 minutes earlier.*

this is to draw a linear graph like the one in Figure 11.20 in which I have converted the minus 1 hour and 10 minutes to 70 minutes for ease.

By interpolation, Newlyn HW is exactly 1 hour earlier than HW Plymouth.

Step 3
Now we will look at GREEN BOX B and use a similar graph to calculate the correction for LW which is at 1359 (1400) at Plymouth.

Differences for Newlyn LW							
Times	1200	1300	1400	1500	1600	1700	1800
Mins	-35		- 32½	- 30	- 27½	- 25	
			- 32 mins				

Fig 11.21 *LW differences at Newlyn for Tuesday 27 October.*

Summary for times

Plymouth (UT)	HW 0801	5.0m	LW 1359	1.6m
Diffs Newlyn	−0100	????	−0032	????
NEWLYN +1 hr (BST)	0800	????	1427	????

Step 4
Look at PURPLE BOX C in Figure 11.19.

For the height, there is no need to draw a graph as we have such a small correction. The secret here is to glance at the height of HW Plymouth on the 16th to see whether it is closer to the spring or neap mean. At 5.0 metres, it is marginally closer to the spring correction, so we will simply **add 0.1 metres**.

Step 5
Look at PINK BOX D in Figure 11.19.

Following the procedure we used in step 4, we see that the LW height on the 16th (1.6 metres) is exactly halfway between the spring and neap mean values, so we **subtract 0.1 metres** from the LW height.

The answer
The times for Newlyn on 16 October are:

Plymouth (UT)	HW 0801	5.0m	LW 1359	1.6m
Diffs Newlyn	− 0100	+ 0.1m	− 0032	− 0.1m
NEWLYN +1 hr (BST)	**0800**	**5.1m**	**1427**	**1.5m**

Height of Tide Using a Chart Plotter or Pocket PC

At this stage of the chapter, you may be forgiven if you utter a deep groan and say with gritted teeth, 'Why didn't you tell us this before we learned the hard way'!

I make no apologies for this – just remember how often you rely on a computer and it fails to deliver!

Most chart plotters include a tidal height element and Figure 11.22 shows one displayed on a Simrad CP33 plotter. Most plotters are menu driven – just a few clicks and the tidal heights will be displayed in graphic form.

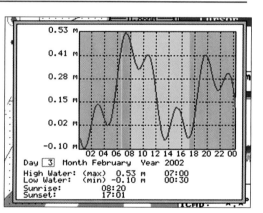

Fig 11.22 *Tidal height graph from the Simrad CP33 chart plotter.*

Tidal Streams

We have talked about the vertical movement of the tide, and we saw that the water in the Plymouth area rises and falls by about 5 metres at springs. Now we are going to discuss the horizontal movement that must happen as the tide falls. After all, those 5 metres of water have to go somewhere – they cannot vanish!

This horizontal movement, known as *tidal stream*, mostly runs parallel to the coast and in and out of large river estuaries and harbours, but there are many exceptions. The rate of the stream will be increased if the water is diverted around a headland or squeezed through a narrow gap, and be weaker in large bays such as Torbay and Weymouth Bay. The stream may not change direction at either HW or LW – off Guernsey it changes about halfway through its rise and fall, just to surprise us!

Fig 11.23 *The tidal stream flowing past a Solent buoy.*

When passage making we need to use these streams to advantage – if we are moving forward at 6 knots with a 6-knot stream moving against us, then we are going nowhere; with 6 knots of stream going our way, we shoot forward at 12 knots and reach our destination a lot earlier. Fast power craft would have no trouble making progress against such a stream, but may be unable to cope with the rough seas that can occur when the wind is against the stream, so it is equally important that skippers of both power and sail craft have tidal stream information to hand.

The information we require is published on charts, in almanacs and in tidal stream atlases. All the data comes from the same source, but it is presented in a more 'user friendly' form in the tidal atlas, as directional arrows are used instead of a numerical table.

Tidal Stream Atlas

The Admiralty tidal stream atlas has 13 charts showing the flow from 6 hours before to 6 hours after HW at a standard port. The one in Figure 11.24 uses Dover as the base port because it is considered the national standard port, but any major port could have been chosen.

The page shown is of the Channel Islands area for 2 hours after HW Dover, with the tidal stream setting towards the west.

The strongest streams are represented by heavy black arrows and the weakest by short lighter ones. There are strong streams around the Cherbourg peninsula as the water is diverted around the headland and funnelled by the island of Alderney. This happens around many prominent headlands, and it is wise to go around them in moderate winds and with a slack stream.

The numbers circled in RED show the rates at neaps and springs. The decimal point is omitted so the rates are **1.4 knots at neaps** and **3.2 knots at springs**. If it were a mid-range tide we would average the numbers to give a rate of **2.3 knots**.

The direction of the stream is found by placing the course plotter on the atlas, lining up the grid with the edge of the page, and then transferring the angle to the chart.

Tidal Diamonds

In Chapter 8 we had a look at chart symbols and found that diamond-shape symbols were placed at regular intervals on the chart. These symbols show the same information as the tidal stream atlas, but in a more compact form.

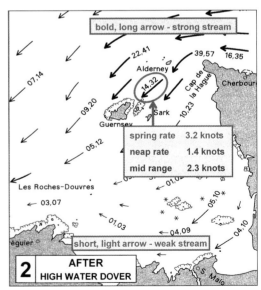

Fig 11.24 *An extract from a tidal stream atlas showing the streams 2 hours after HW Dover.*

Tidal Streams referred to HW at PLYMOUTH

	Ⓐ 49°59'·4N 6 24·8W		Ⓑ 49°54'·7N 6 22·1W		Ⓒ 49°54'·1N 6 19·0W		Ⓓ 49°55'·8N 6 13·3W	
−6	252	1·0 0·5	320	0·4 0·2	300	0·4 0·2	007	0·9 0·4
−5	318	0·5 0·3	042	0·3 0·1	020	0·1 0·0	011	1·1 0·5
−4	034	0·9 0·5	097	0·6 0·3	109	0·7 0·3	017	1·6 0·8
−3	055	1·6 0·8	116	1·0 0·4	110	1·2 0·5	022	1·7 0·8
−2	062	1·9 0·9	121	0·8 0·4	111	1·5 0·7	027	1·4 0·7
−1	066	1·6 0·8	125	0·7 0·3	111	1·6 0·7	035	0·9 0·4
HW	072	0·9 0·5	161	0·2 0·1	111	1·7 0·8	110	0·2 0·1
+1	102	0·4 0·2	224	1·0 0·4	125	1·5 0·7	201	2·0 0·9
+2	206	0·7 0·4	233	1·1 0·5	190	0·1 0·0	188	2·9 1·4
+3	227	1·3 0·6	241	1·2 0·5	275	1·3 0·6	202	2·2 1·0
+4	239	1·7 0·8	262	1·5 0·7	272	1·7 0·8	227	1·1 0·5
+5	240	1·7 0·8	262	1·2 0·5	265	1·0 0·4	326	0·4 0·2
+6	245	1·2 0·6	296	0·5 0·2	292	0·7 0·3	000	0·7 0·3

4 hours before HW Plymouth the stream at diamond A is 034°True.

0.9 knot at springs 0.5 knot at neaps 0.7 knot at mid range

Fig 11.25 *Tidal diamond table for the Isles of Scilly.*

The illustration in Figure 11.25 shows streams around the Isles of Scilly off Land's End and we notice that the standard port used is – once again – Plymouth, and that the streams are much weaker than in the Alderney Race.

There are 13 rows of data in the table covering the hours from 6 hours before HW to 6 hours afterwards. The rates are given in a different order to the tidal stream atlas – here the spring rate is shown first and the neap second.

Remember that the tide sets towards the direction shown – a stream setting 034° True is flowing in a northeasterly direction.

The Tidal Hour

Looking at the table in Figure 11.25 for diamond A we can see that the stream 1 hour after HW is running towards the east at 0.4 knot and that 1 hour later it has picked up speed and altered direction by 100°. In reality, the change in both direction and rate would have been very gradual – it does not do a smart right turn and march in the other direction like a squad of soldiers. This is all very well, but does not help us when we are attempting to plot a course to counteract the tide! We therefore have to assume that it has a uniform rate for the period half an hour either side of the stated hour. If, for example, the HW is at 1800, the HW rate and direction for navigational purposes will be valid from **1730 to 1830**.

Figure 11.26 shows a method for laying out the information neatly when calculating the stream. Use a notebook to keep a tidy record of your calculations, so that others can read what you have written.

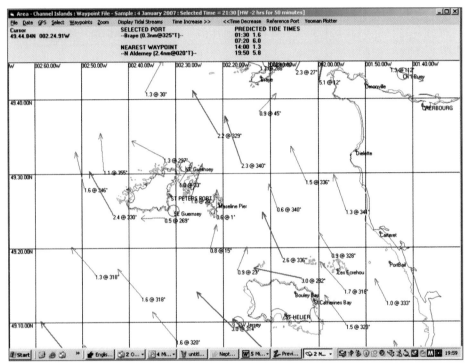

Plymouth HW 1800 Springs

⟨B⟩

	HW hour	1730 - 1830
	HW + 1	1830 - 1930
233°T 1.1 knots	HW + 2	1930 - 2030

Fig 11.26 *One method for recording the times of the tidal hour.*

Fig 11.27 *Tidal stream information displayed on a laptop computer using the Neptune program.*

Calculating the Stream Electronically

Some chart plotters or an onboard laptop computer can be used to give tidal stream information when using a software package, such as the Neptune tidal stream and passage planning program. Figure 11.27 shows streams around the Channel Islands at 2130 on 7 January 2007.

Checking the Tidal Stream Visually

Information about streams is often scanty inshore, in river estuaries and small creeks. All is not lost, because there are pointers that can help us establish the direction of the stream. Small pick-up buoys attached to moorings float downstream of the main buoy. In Figure 11.28 the weak stream is flowing from left to right.

Fig 11.28 *A pick-up buoy floating downstream of a mooring.*

Fig 11.29 *Boats secured to moorings lie head-to the stream.*

Boats attached to moorings also give a good indication of stream direction, as they will lay head to stream unless there is a strong cross-wind. Even swinging to the wind, the way they lay will help you to choose an angle of approach. The powerboat in Figure 11.29 is swinging to the tide at Langstone Harbour entrance.

TIDES AND TIDAL STREAMS: KNOWLEDGE CHECK

1 Do tides with the greatest range occur at springs or neaps?

2 Above which level are clearance heights measured?

3 What will be the depth of water over a drying 0.8 metre shoal if the height of tide is 2.6 metres?

4 Should the time corrections for UK secondary ports be added to UT or BST?

5 Using the information given in Figure 11.25, what is the direction and rate of the tidal stream 3 hours before HW Plymouth at tidal diamond C at springs?

6 'The tidal stream always changes direction at high and low water.' True or false?

CHAPTER TWELVE

FINDING OUR POSITION

Until you gain familiarity with your local area, it will be necessary to keep a very close eye on the position of the boat and its proximity to hidden dangers and shallow water. The Rolls-Royce solution to the problem is an electronic chart plotter, which shows the boat's position at a glance. Most skippers, though, are on a budget and use a basic GPS set before transferring the position to a paper chart. The traditional method of fixing position is to use a hand-bearing compass to take bearings of prominent landmarks, but whichever method is used it will always be wise to make a visual check to ensure that the position has feasibility. Offshore, the GPS position may be checked by plotting an estimated position on the chart. We shall be looking at all these methods in this chapter.

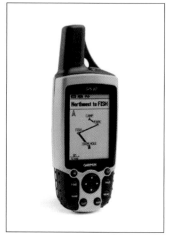

Fig 12.1 *A Garmin GPS60.*

Using the GPS to Fix Position

GPS background and functions

The basic GPS system consists of 20-plus satellites, which orbit the Earth and use an atomic clock to transmit perfectly synchronised time data. Depending on the range of the boat, these signals reach the boat at slightly different times, which enables the GPS receiver to calculate the distance from each satellite. If the data from a number of satellites is used, a very accurate calculated position will be given in *latitude and longitude* on the GPS screen.

As this geographical position is updated every few seconds, the receiver can track the boat's progress and calculate its *course over the ground* (COG) and *speed over the ground* (SOG). It is therefore possible for it to predict an *estimated time of arrival* (ETA) at a nominated latitude and longitude, called a *waypoint*. The GPS will also calculate the *bearing and distance* to that waypoint.

A number of waypoints may be entered into a directory and then used to form a route to the destination. The *cross-track error* screen will show you whether you are on or off track on each leg of the route and indicate the direction in which the helmsman should steer to regain track.

An additional function on many sets is the *man overboard button*. If this is pressed the

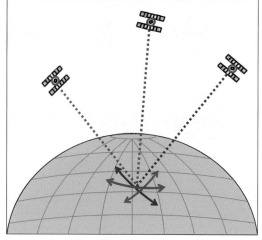

Fig 12.2 *Three satellites fixing the boat's position. A fix using a greater number of satellites will give a more accurate position.*

moment the person enters the water, the bearing and distance to his or her position will be given.

Finally, the GPS may be interfaced with other navigational equipment, such as a chart plotter, DSC VHF radio, radar and AIS.

Navigating at speed – plotting bearing and distance to a waypoint

Navigating in a small fast boat such as a semi-rigid inflatable has always been a problem, as the chart has to be used on a surface that is never still. The GPS displays the bearing and distance to a waypoint and this is the quickest type of fix to plot. We can make the job even easier by drawing a 'spider's web' radiating out from the waypoint at the destination.

Figure 12.3 shows that a boat is approaching a harbour, which has drying rocks close to the entrance. A waypoint has been entered into the GPS, and range markers at half-mile intervals have been drawn on the chart in the safe approach arc. Bearing lines radiating out from the waypoint are drawn every 10°.

In the illustration (Figure 12.3), the GPS display shows that the bearing to the waypoint is 315°M and the distance 2.5 nautical miles. As long as the navigator can get the pencil to the chart, plotting this position is simplicity itself.

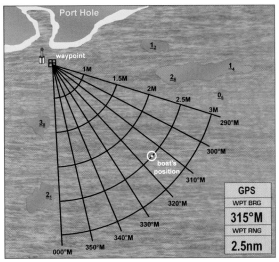

Fig 12.3 *The 'spiders web' is useful when plotting position at high speed.*

Range and bearing to the centre of a compass rose

When plotting latitude and longitude it is very easy, for even the most experienced navigator, to make a mistake by transposing numbers. Plotting a bearing and distance to the centre of a convenient compass rose seldom leads to errors, and on Admiralty folio charts the latitude and longitude of the compass rose is always given for just this purpose.

It also makes for ease if the GPS is set to give the true bearing to the waypoint – not the magnetic. This adjustment is quickly made – often by going to the 'set up' menu.

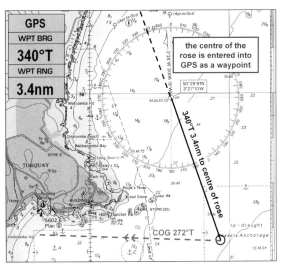

Fig 12.4 *Bearing and distance to the centre of a compass rose.*

In Figure 12.4 the GPS screen gives the bearing and distance to the centre of the rose as 340°T 3.4 nautical miles. Lay the edge of a ruler through the middle of the compass rose to the 340° graduation and draw a line out from the centre as shown in the illustration. Measure 3.4 miles on the latitude scale, then mark the distance on the line.

Try to remember that it is the bearing and distance **TO** the waypoint – not the other way around.

Visual checks

Every time an electronic fix is plotted, there should be some visual check to see whether it is correct. Take a depth sounder reading and, if land is in sight, look at the chart to find a significant feature. If the plot is correct, it should be within view. In Figure 12.4, we would expect to see a pronounced headland and a large, 32-metre rock about 2 miles away on the starboard bow.

Position Lines – Transits

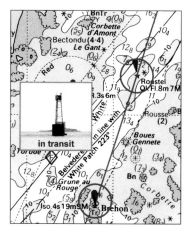

When two charted objects are kept in line, one behind the other, they are said to be 'in transit', which means that the observer must be somewhere on the 'position line' that extends from the two objects. Transits are a very powerful pilotage tool as the position of the boat can quickly be checked visually from the cockpit. Figure 12.5 shows two beacons off the coast of Guernsey, Roustel and the Brehon tower, which are frequently used in transit for pilotage in an area of strong cross-tides.

It is comforting to know that the boat is travelling down a line devoid of dangers on either side, but there is no indication how far along the line we are. In order to get a definite fix we need additional bearings from other landmarks in the area before we can confirm the position.

Fig 12.5 *Roustel beacon and the Brehon Tower in transit.*

Using the Compass to Take a Three-point Fix

Choosing the landmarks

If three or more features can be identified on the shoreline, it should be possible to use them to take compass bearings for an accurate position fix. Castles, chimneys and monuments are usually prominent, but extra care is needed with churches, as there is often more than one in even the smallest town. Steep headlands are often seen in silhouette and can be used for bearings if they are not too far away; the closer the object, the more accurate the fix will be. If the feature is large or wide, like the Brehon tower in Figure 12.6, the bearing should be taken on one of its sides, and a record of which edge has been used entered in the navigator's notebook.

The landmarks chosen for the fix should have a good 'angle of cut' for accuracy. In Figure 12.6, the boat is again off the coast of Guernsey where there are numerous beacons. The navigator has chosen the three features in the photographs, as the angle between them is about 40° or more – perfect for a good fix.

Fig 12.6 *The navigator has chosen three charted features in the Little Russel channel off Guernsey.*

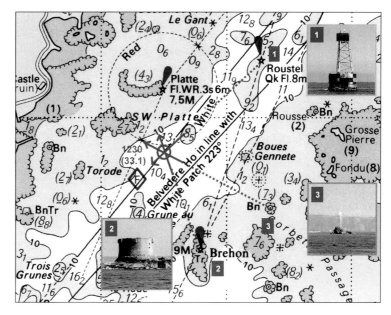

Taking the bearings

Try to stand in a position well away from magnetic influences when you take the bearings. The main engine, radio loudspeakers and outboard engines will all deviate the hand-bearing compass if you stand within 1 metre of them, so wedge yourself in a safe place and remember to keep one hand on a shroud or rail for safety. Wait for the compass needle to stop swinging around and call out the bearings to a willing helper, making clear whether it is a true or magnetic bearing.

Notice that the beacon on the rock in Figure 12.6 was the third and last bearing to be taken. This is because, being beam-on to the boat, it will change most rapidly as the boat moves forward. The distance log was read as this last bearing was taken.

Plotting the fix

In Figure 12.6, the following bearings were taken at 1230 when the log read 33.1. The magnetic variation is 3°W:

Roustel beacon	050°M = 047°T
Right-side Brehon tower	163°M = 160°T
Corbette beacon	120°M = 117°T

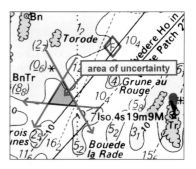

The fix was a good one because, when plotted, the bearings all pass through one point, but this will not always be the case if it is choppy and the boat is moving around a lot. Sometimes a large triangle, known as a *cocked hat*, is formed. The one shown in Figure 12.7 probably means that one of the bearings is wrong – they should be taken again to check which one is in error.

Fig 12.7 *A poor fix with a large 'cocked hat'.*

Dead Reckoning and Estimated Position

On some shorelines there are no noticeable features on the chart for fixing position, but we still need to keep track of our likely position for safety reasons. We can plot either a *dead reckoning* position or a more accurate *estimated position*.

Dead reckoning

A dead reckoning position (DR) considers just two factors: course steered and distance run through the water. It therefore gives only an approximate position in an area where there are tidal streams or wind-driven currents, but works well in areas like the Baltic and the Mediterranean.

The distance run through the water is easy to calculate – the distance log reading at the start is simply subtracted from the one taken at the end of the run.

Course steered is a little more complicated because we have to adjust from magnetic to true and also assess how much we have been pushed off course by the wind (leeway).

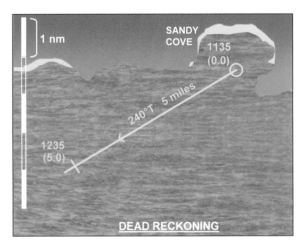

Fig 12.8 *A plot for a dead reckoning position at 1235.*

Look at Figure 12.8 and imagine that it is 1135 BST on the morning of 19 October and that you are the skipper of the yacht *Goodwill*. You have set sail from Sandy Cove and are steering a course of 243°M. About an hour later you decide to check on your approximate position and plot a dead reckoning position on the chart.

You do the following tasks:

1 Plot the start position and enter a time and log reading on the chart.
2 Check the compass deviation card for an error on a 243° heading = none found.
3 Confirm the variation is 3°W. Convert to true 243°M – 3°W = 240°T.
4 Consider whether the boat is making leeway. The wind is from astern and very light = no leeway.
5 Take a log reading and record the time = 1235 BST. The log reads 5.0 nautical miles.

The results of your labours are shown in Figure 12.8. The DR position is marked with a short line at the 5-mile mark. This plotted line is often called *the water track*.

Estimated position

You realise that there is some tidal stream running and that the DR position you have plotted can only be approximate. Therefore you delve into the almanac for details of the tidal stream so that you can add a tidal stream vector onto the end of your dead reckoning plot.

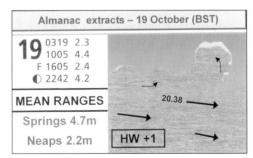

Fig 12.9 *Tide times and tidal stream information for 19 October.*

You need to know the following information from the almanac (Figure 12.9):

1 The time at the beginning and at the end of the run = 1135 to 1235 BST
2 The time of the closest HW. Add an hour for BST? = 1005 UT+1 hr = 1105 BST
3 The range of the tide. Spring or neap rate? = Range 2.0m. Neaps
4 The HW hour = 1035 to 1135 BST
5 Chartlet to use (1135 to 1235). = HW +1 hr

The direction is measured with the plotter as: = 097°T
                               Rate = 2.0 knots

This now means that all known factors have been taken into account – compass deviation, magnetic variation, leeway and tidal stream.

You now plot the tidal vector at the 5-mile point on your 1135 to 1235 line, as shown in Figure 12.10, making sure you add three arrows to the tidal stream and a triangle to indicate that you have plotted an estimated position.

Finally, you draw a line joining the point of departure to the end of the tidal vector so you can measure your actual *speed over the ground* and the angle of your *course over the ground* (Figure 12.11).

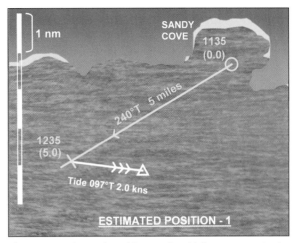

Fig 12.10 *Estimated position 1: The tidal stream vector is added at the end of the water track.*

On measuring the angle, you find that it is 220°T and that your speed over the ground is just 3.6 knots!

Perhaps it may have been better to wait until the stream was west-going and in your favour!

Allowance for leeway

Leeway is covered fully in Chapter 13 ('Course to steer'), but Figure 12.12 shows how we deal with it when plotting a dead reckoning or estimated position.

A craft is steering 240°T in a northerly wind, which is pushing the boat off to port by 10°. This means that the actual course through the water is 230°T – the angle that is plotted on the chart.

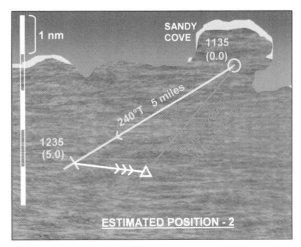

Fig 12.11 *Estimated position 2: The line is drawn joining the start point to the end of the tidal stream vector.*

Avoiding Dangers

If a boat is intending to pass close to an area of danger when a tidal stream is running, it is wise to know the angle of the course over the ground so that progress may be monitored and the dangers avoided. For this, we plot a *projected EP*. In effect, we are saying to ourselves, 'What will be the course over the ground if we continue to sail in this direction at this speed?'

The method is the same as the estimated position except that we plot the triangle before the passage begins – not at the end when it may be too late.

Projected estimated position

It is 1430 on Wednesday 12 September and you are skippering the traditional motorboat, *Silver Dawn*, which is on passage to Cod Creek. En route, you have to pass to the east of Dolphin Island, which has a large patch of rocks at its eastern end. Your aim is to have a good dinner ashore tonight, not become a shipwreck statistic, so you decide to work up a projected EP to check whether your present course will pass safely clear of the rocks. You consult your almanac, an extract from which is shown in Figure 12.13:

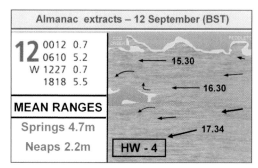

Almanac extracts – 12 September (BST)

12 0012 0.7
0610 5.2
W 1227 0.7
1818 5.5

MEAN RANGES

Springs 4.7m

Neaps 2.2m

15.30

16.30

17.34

HW - 4

Fig 12.13 *Almanac extracts for 12 September.*

1 The HW is at 1918 BST.
2 The range is 4.8m. Springs.
3 The HW hour is from 1848 to 1948.
4 The HW-4 chartlet is valid from 1448 to 1548 – the one to use.
5 You measure the tide angle with the plotter = 270°T, rate 3.0 knots.
6 Using your present boat speed of 10 knots and the average course of 304°T, you plot the dead reckoning position and add the tidal vector to the end of the line. (See Figure 12.14.)
7 Lastly, you join the 1448 position to the end of the tidal stream vector to determine your course over the ground.

Fig 12.14 *A DR is plotted and the tidal vector added at the end.*

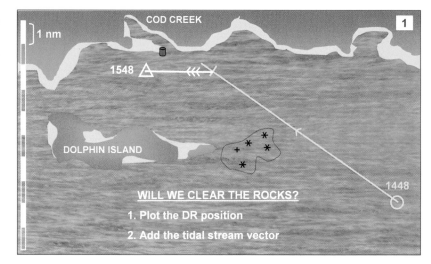

COD CREEK

1

1 nm

1548

1448

DOLPHIN ISLAND

1448

WILL WE CLEAR THE ROCKS?

1. Plot the DR position

2. Add the tidal stream vector

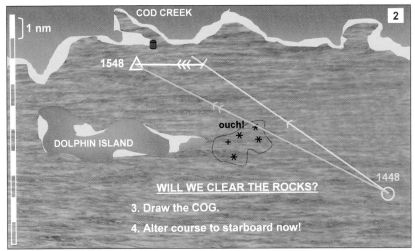

Fig 12.15 *The course over the ground is drawn. Unless an alteration to starboard is made, the boat will hit the rocks.*

You were certainly wise to plot the projection, and an alteration of course to starboard should allow *Silver Dawn* to pass to the east of both the rocks and the red can buoy in the harbour entrance. Your dinner looks more likely now!

Safely moored in the Morbihan, south Brittany.

FINDING OUR POSITION: KNOWLEDGE CHECK

Use Variation 3°W and plot your answers on the chart provided in Figure 12.16, page 128.

1 At 1145, the following bearings were taken from a boat (just west of Plymouth) when the distance log read 17.5M:

Rame Head	113°M
Beacon on 128-metre hill	058°M
Chimney	023°M

Plot the position on the chart and give the latitude and longitude.

2 At 1215, when the distance log read 20.2, the following bearings were taken near Portwrinkle:

Hotel at Portwrinkle	038°M
Two beacons in line (west of Portwrinkle) 330°M	

Plot the position and give the latitude and longitude.

3 At 1850, when the distance log reads 0.0M, a powerboat is in position 0.5M due south of the Fl WR light on the western end of Plymouth breakwater. From this position, the boat is steered on a course of 135°M for 10 minutes. At 1900, the log reads 3.0M. The tidal stream is slack.
   a) Plot the dead reckoning position at 1900 and give latitude and longitude.
   b) What is the boat speed in knots

4 At 0930, a boat is anchored over the 12.8-metre charted depth south of Downderry. The skipper weighs anchor and steers a course of 140°M for 30 minutes at a speed of 14 knots. The tidal stream between 0915 and 1015 is calculated as 085°T 2.2 knots.
   a) Plot the estimated position at 1000.
   b) Did the boat pass to the east or to the west of the Military wreck?

5 At 1430, a boat is in position 50° 15'.0N 4° 06'.0W. The helmsman is steering a course of 330°M and the boat speed is 5 knots. The tidal stream has been calculated as 270°T 1.3 knots.
   a) Plot the estimated position at 1530.
   b) Will the boat pass safely to the east of Penlee Point if the helmsman continues on the same course?
   c) What is the angle of the course over the ground?

6 a) Plot a waypoint (WP1) on the chart in position 50° 17'.0N 4° 21.0W.
   b) At 0500, the bearing and distance to WP1 is shown on the GPS as 285°T 2.4M. Plot the 0500 position on the chart and give the latitude and longitude.

▶Fig 12.16 *Plot your answers on this chart.*

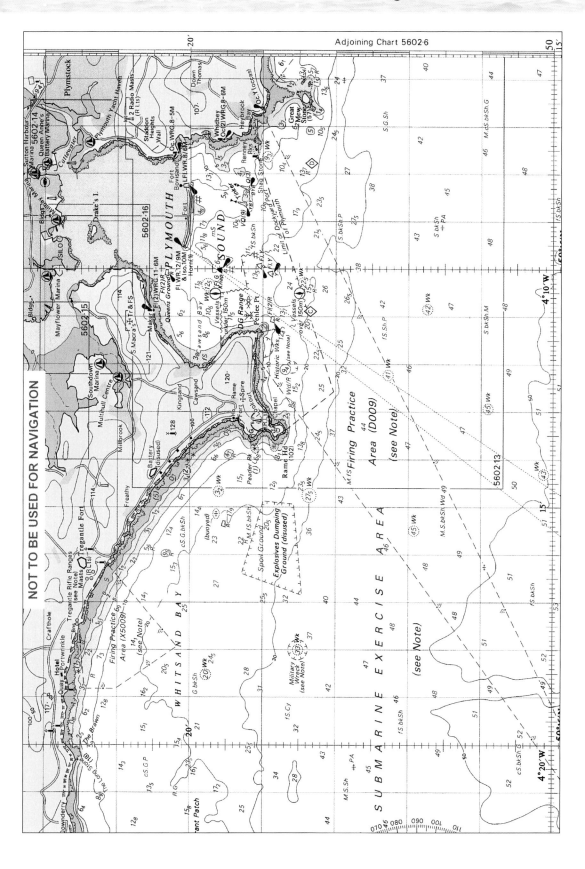

Adjoining Chart 5602·6

NOT TO BE USED FOR NAVIGATION

CHAPTER THIRTEEN

COURSE TO STEER

When we were plotting an estimated position in the last chapter, we saw how the tidal stream affects the course over the ground. Streams can run at over 5 knots where the water is funnelled into a narrow gap, around headlands and in rocky or shallow areas. It is therefore vital that the boat maintains a ground track that will keep it in safe water.

The craft in Figure 13.1 are both attempting to reach the inlet on the other side of the tidal channel, but have adopted different tactics to get there.

The purple boat has steered a course at right-angles to the stream, but has been swept to the right and onto a dangerous patch of rocks. The green boat has turned into the tide to compensate so that the course over the ground takes him safely to the inlet. In this chapter, we learn how this was achieved.

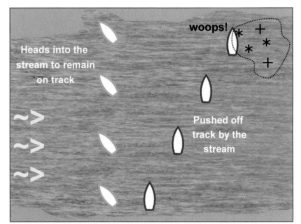

Fig 13.1 *The purple boat has been swept onto the rocks, but the green one has compensated for the stream to reach the haven safely.*

Plotting a Course to Steer to Compensate for Tidal Stream

In order to calculate the correct angle for crossing the river we must do a bit of simple geometry and plot a triangle of velocities on the chart. Before we can do this, we need to have the necessary information to construct it, a well-sharpened 2B pencil, and a good-quality eraser.

Boat speed

In a motor cruiser, it is easy to set the engine revs for the speed we would like, but it is a lot more difficult to keep a steady speed in a yacht with fluctuating wind strength. The sailing-boat skipper will therefore have to estimate the probable average speed, which is usually lower than you would expect – just as it is on a long car journey.

For our first plot, we will use a speed of *6.5 knots* – quite fast for a sailing yacht, but slow for a power craft.

Direction and rate of the tidal stream

Creekhaven is a standard port and the present time is 1030 BST on 1 June.

HW 1101 UT 9.7m LW 3.4m Range 6.3m

The range is close to the spring range so we will use spring rate from the stream atlas.

HW 1201 BST
HW hour   = 1130 – 1230 (rounded)
HW minus 1 hr = 1030 – 1130 spring rate

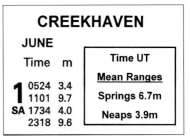

CREEKHAVEN

JUNE

Time	m	Time UT
		Mean Ranges
1 0524	3.4	
1101	9.7	Springs 6.7m
SA 1734	4.0	Neaps 3.9m
2318	9.6	

Fig 13.2 *Tidal information for Creekhaven shows that it is springs.*

Plotting – Step 1

Now we shall begin plotting on the chart and will follow the instructions given in Figure 13.3. Once we have plotted the start and finish positions, we measure the distance between the two using the scale down the left-hand side of the chart. We find that it should take very roughly 1 hour to get there at a speed of 6.5 knots, so we shall draw a 1-hour triangle using 1 hour of tide and 1 hour of boat speed.

Fig 13.3 *Step 1: The starting position and destination are joined with a line and the distance from A to B is measured.*

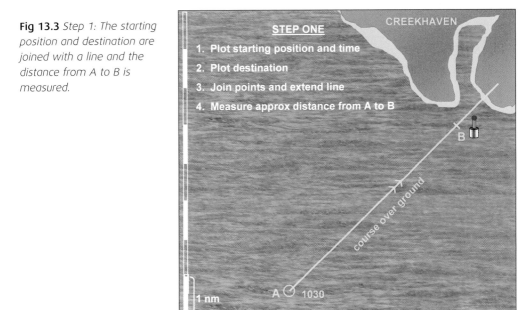

CREEKHAVEN

STEP ONE

1. **Plot starting position and time**

2. **Plot destination**

3. **Join points and extend line**

4. **Measure approx distance from A to B**

B

course over ground

1 nm

A 1030

Plotting – Step 2

Now we have to look at the tidal stream atlas extract, which is shown in Figure 13.4. We decide to use the figure near the middle of the picture, as this is the area we are going to be in during the next hour. It shows that the spring rate for the HW −1 hour is 2.0 knots with a northwest-going stream. We measure the angle accurately with the Portland plotter and find that it is 335°T.

This tidal vector is plotted at the point of departure because we have to correct for the stream before we start – a good way of remembering which end of the line to plot it.

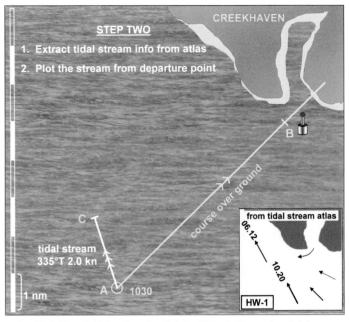

Fig 13.4 *Step 2: Using the chartlet for HW −1, the spring tidal stream is plotted at point A.*

Plotting Step 3

Having plotted the tidal vector we can see that if our boat were not driving through the water between 1030 and 1130 it would drift to point **C** on the tide during that time. We can think of point **C** as the new starting point and plot our 1-hour run at 6.5 knots from this position.

To do this, open up the dividers and use the scale down the left-hand side of the illustration (Figure 13.5). Place one point of the dividers on **C** and the other on the line **AB**. Make a light pencil mark and label it point **D**.

Lastly, we join the end of the tide to **D** and measure the angle with the plotter. It should read 062°T.

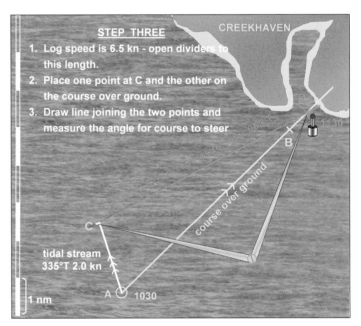

Fig 13.5 *Step 3: The third side of the triangle is drawn and the angle is measured.*

Plotting – Step 4

All that remains now is to determine how fast we are moving over the ground. We know we are moving through the water at 6.5 knots, but the tide is giving us a push forward. This should speed us up over the ground. By measuring **A** to **D** (our distance travelled in 1 hour), we find that we are moving at 6.85 knots. We also see that we will reach point **B** before the hour is up – by eye, it looks as if it will take about 55 minutes.

Fig 13.6 *Step 4: The speed over the ground is measured from point A to D.*

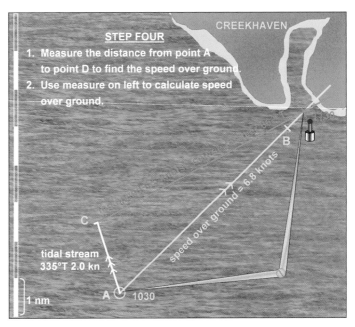

Summary

Remember that the aim is to keep the boat on the intended course over the ground. The bow of the boat will not be pointing at the destination; the heading will be 062°T and we will crab down the line as illustrated in Figure 13.7. The triangle we have drawn is for 1 hour and we will get to a position just past the buoy in that time. We will arrive at point **B** in just under the hour.

Had we been travelling a lot faster we could have plotted a half-hour triangle, which would have looked just like the hourly one, but with all dimensions scaled down. The course to steer would have been the same angle.

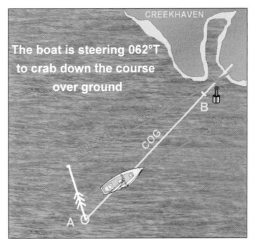

Fig 13.7 *The boat crabs down the course over the ground, but heads 062°T to remain on it.*

Making Allowance for Leeway

Once we have drawn the 'course to steer' triangle there is one more factor to consider – the effect that the wind will have on the boat, known as *leeway*. Yachts are pushed downwind when they are heeled since the keel is angled and slips more easily through the water; motor cruisers are more affected as they have a lot of superstructure above the waterline (freeboard) and much less under the water to stop them being pushed sideways by the wind. In order to remain on the intended course over ground, we have to steer into the wind a few degrees to compensate. The tricky bit is deciding just how much leeway we are likely to make.

If the wind speed is above about 7 knots then the following rough guide works well. If the wind is forward of the beam, assume that you will be blown 2° off course for each Beaufort wind force. A Force 3 will give 6° of leeway and Force 5 will give you about 10°. This is a slight over-estimation for some fast yachts, but do not worry – over-estimation will always put you a little upwind of your destination, which is a far better position to be in than struggling against the wind to make up lost ground.

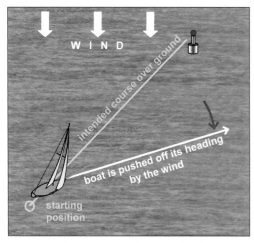

Fig 13.8 *The yacht is sailing close to the wind and is heeled over. It is pushed off its heading by the wind.*

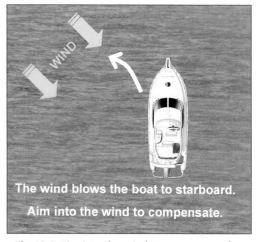

Fig 13.9 *Aim into the wind to compensate for leeway.*

Using GPS or a Chart Plotter for Course to Steer

Remember that our course to steer triangle was drawn using tidal predictions and an estimation of leeway and boat speed. In a motor cruiser, the boat speed may have to be changed to cope with sea state and, if sailing, the progress will vary with the wind shifts so we must always check that the course we have calculated is effective.

Offshore, we either have to resort to traditional navigation and work up an estimated position, as we did in the previous chapter, or use a GPS or chart plotter to monitor progress.

The GPS measures the course over the ground, not the course being steered, so it is ideal for checking whether we are on, or off, our track. If we enter a waypoint at or near our destination, it will tell us the bearing to the waypoint, the distance to go (DTG) and our course over the ground (COG). As a bonus, it also works out the time it will take to get there (TTG).

If we modify our course to keep the COG as close as possible to the bearing to waypoint, we will slide down the intended track – simplicity itself! Figure 13.10 shows an approach to Plymouth Sound where the boat's position is symbolised by a red circle and the waypoint by a red diamond.

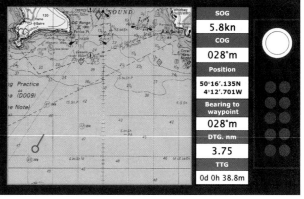

SOG
5.8kn
COG
028°m
Position
50°16'.135N **4°12'.701W**
Bearing to waypoint
028°m
DTG. nm
3.75
TTG
0d 0h 38.8m

Fig 13.10 *Notice that the data panel is showing the bearing to waypoint is the same as the course over the ground. This means that the boat is tracking nicely to the waypoint.*

Plotting a Course for a Longer Passage

When a passage involves a leg that will take longer than 1 hour, we can plot two or more tidal vectors at once. This keeps us reasonably close to the intended track, but not necessarily on it for the entire passage, so this method should only be used when there are no dangers adjacent to the track.

Figure 13.11 shows a 3-hour plot. Notice that the boat is logging 5 knots, so will travel 15 miles through the water in 3 hours.

Fig 13.11 *The 3 hours of tide are all plotted at the point of departure. Remember that the boat will not necessarily remain on the line.*

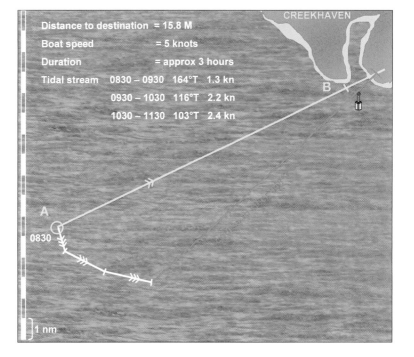

Distance to destination = 15.8 M
Boat speed = 5 knots
Duration = approx 3 hours
Tidal stream 0830 – 0930 164°T 1.3 kn
0930 – 1030 116°T 2.2 kn
1030 – 1130 103°T 2.4 kn

CREEKHAVEN

B

A
0830

1 nm

COURSE TO STEER : KNOWLEDGE CHECK

Use the chart in Figure 13.12, page 129 to plot the answers to the following questions. Variation = 3°W.

1 At 1400, a yacht is in position 50° 14'.0N 4° 27'.0W.

a) What is the magnetic course to steer to Polperro harbour entrance if the boat speed is 5.5 knots and the tidal stream is setting 280°T 1.3 knots?

b) Will the passage take more or less than 1 hour?

2 At 1000, a small sea angling boat is at the south cardinal buoy near Udder Rock (centre top of chart).

a) What is the magnetic course to steer to the 8.8 metre charted depth close to Fowey entrance? The boat speed is 3 knots and the tidal stream is 255°T 1.1 knots.

b) What is the speed over the ground?

3 At 1830, a motor cruiser is in position 50° 15'.0N 4° 33'.0W.

a) What is the magnetic course to steer to the south cardinal buoy to the southwest of Fowey if the boat speed is 12 knots and the tidal stream is setting 090°T 2.4 knots? *Clue: Could this be a half-hour triangle?*

b) What is the speed over the ground?

c) What will be the magnetic course to steer to correct for 10° of leeway in a south-westerly wind?

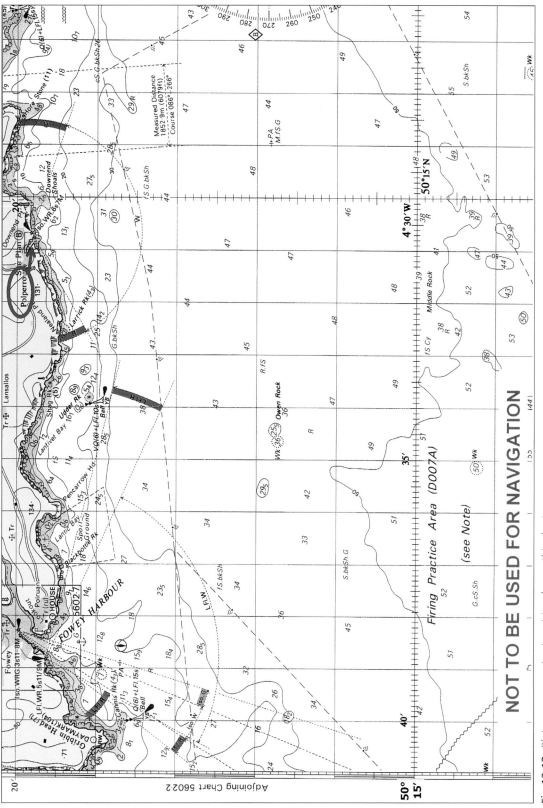

NOT TO BE USED FOR NAVIGATION

Fig 13.12 *Plot your course to steer triangles on this chart.*

CHAPTER FOURTEEN

BUOYS, BEACONS AND LIGHTS

Finding your way into an unfamiliar harbour for the first time can either be enormous fun or a stressful epic, depending on whether you prepared well enough before embarking on the adventure. You may remember the quote from G K Chesterton in Chapter 4 about adventures – they need to be 'rightly considered' to turn out well.

Your first few trips will almost certainly be made in coastal waters, where there are numerous buoys and beacons marking safe channels to use and the dangers to avoid.

Buoys and Beacons

At one time, each country had its own buoyage system, which was both confusing and dangerous to seafarers. In the 1970s, the International Association of Lighthouse Authorities (IALA) attempted to introduce one system for all, but agreement was hard to reach. As a result there are now two systems, *IALA A* for the majority of countries including Europe, and *IALA B* for North and South America, the Philippines and Japan.

Some of the buoys are common to both buoyage schemes, so we shall look at these first.

Cardinal marks

Buoys marking points of interest are called *cardinal marks* because they are placed either North, South, East or West of the feature – in other words the cardinal points of the compass.

The cardinal marks use a distinctive colour combination, together with triangular topmarks, which follow a very logical pattern and are easy to remember.

Triangular top marks The top of the chart is usually North, so the mark which is placed on the north side of the danger has triangular shapes which *point up*; the bottom of the chart is South, so the triangles *point down*, leading us to the south of the buoy – so far so good.

The Eastern triangles look like the shape of an egg – '**Easter Egg**'.

The Western mark is pinched in at the middle – '**Western Women have Wasp Waists**'.

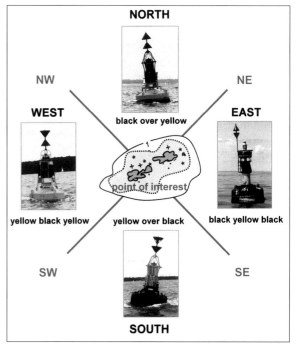

Fig 14.1 *The cardinal marks guard the point of interest from North, South, East and West.*

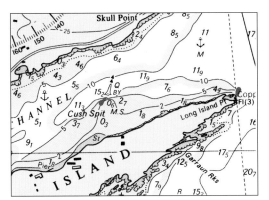

Fig 14.2 *Just one cardinal mark is used to guard the shoal patch to the south of the buoy.*

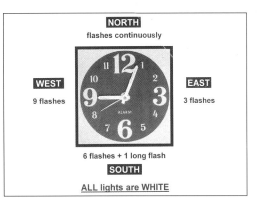

Fig 14.3 *Cardinal marks use the clock face when determining the sequence of the light.*

Colours The north cardinal mark is painted black at the top and yellow at the bottom – the points of the triangles point upwards to the top where the black paint is. Follow this argument through using Figure 14.1 and you will see that it works for all the buoys. Eureka!

All four cardinal marks are used if the danger covers a large area; for a danger close to a coastline, just one may be used – as in Figure 14.2 where a single north cardinal marks Cush Spit.

Lights All cardinal marks have WHITE LIGHTS.

The light sequences use the clock face, as shown in Figure 14.3. The East and West are easiest to remember, but the South mark has an additional long flash so that it cannot be confused with the nine flashes of the West mark. Later in the chapter, we will learn what is meant by a *flashing light*.

Isolated danger mark

If an isolated obstruction or rock needs to be buoyed then another type of mark is used.

Figure 14.4 shows a beacon with red and black horizontal bands and two black balls as a topmark. There is clear water all around this mark, but do not pass too close because the post often stands on the obstruction itself.

There is an isolated danger post marking a wreck in Figure 14.5. Notice the letters BRB (black red black) written under the post. We know that this mark is lit because it has a white 'teardrop' and the light sequence added to the icon.

Light WHITE LIGHT. Flashing in groups of two.

Fig 14.4 *An isolated danger post marking an obstruction.*

Safe water mark

Approaching a harbour there is often a *safe water mark*, sometimes called a 'fairway buoy', which marks the beginning of a buoyed channel. There is a safe water mark outside Langstone Harbour entrance, near Portsmouth (Figure 14.5). You will notice the letters RW under the post, denoting that it has red and white stripes. The beacon is very similar to the one in Figure 14.6.

Light WHITE LIGHT. Long flash, isophase or occulting (see later in this chapter).

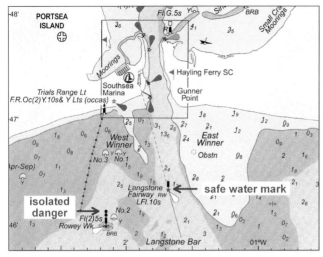

Fig 14.5 *The chart of Langstone shows the safewater mark and an isolated danger beacon outside the entrance.*

Fig 14.6 *A safewater mark.*

Lateral marks

Buoys or posts that mark a channel into a harbour or the navigable part of a river also have a distinctive colour and shape so that no mistakes will be made should the paint wear off. These are lateral marks. In a river such as the Beaulieu (Figure 14.8) where posts mark the extremities of the navigable channel, it is impossible to stray outside the posts without going aground. In areas where large ships operate it is advisable for small craft to remain outside the channel provided that there is sufficient water.

▲ **Fig 14.7** *A port-hand post with a can topmark.*

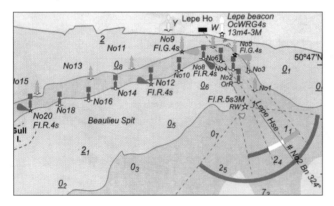

◄ **Fig 14.8** *Navigation marks into the Beaulieu River.*

Colours When entering the harbour from the sea:

Port side of channel – RED (Figures 14.7 and 14.10).
Starboard side of channel – GREEN (Figures 14.9 and 14.11).

Shapes Port hand-mark = Can shaped. Starboard-hand mark = Conical.

Fig 14.9 *A starboard-hand post with a conical topmark.*

Fig 14.10 *A port-hand buoy marking a large-ship channel.*

Fig 14.11 *A large channel buoy. The colour does not show up well, but the shape of the topmark is in silhouette.*

Special marks

Buoys that mark areas of special interest, racing marks and large data collection buoys, are painted yellow. Although these buoys are not, strictly speaking, navigational marks, they mark the boundary lines around water-skiing areas and offshore gunnery ranges. Keep a good lookout for them if you wish to avoid being mown down or having a shell through your hull!

Figure 14.12 shows a racing mark in the Solent, and Figure 14.13 is a mark just outside St Peter Port, Guernsey.

Fig 14.12 *A typical Solent racing mark.*

Fig 14.13 *A special mark off St Peter Port.*

Preferred channel marks

Rivers often split into two arms where each arm is navigable and buoyed, but the major channel needs to be marked. In this case, the posts are both red and green with the predominant colour for the preferred channel.

These markers are not very common in the UK, but the Solent has one at the entrance to the River Hamble where it would be easy to pass down the wrong side of the long visitor's

▶ **Fig 14.14** *The predominantly red post acts as the port-hand mark for the major channel and the starboard-hand mark for the minor one.*

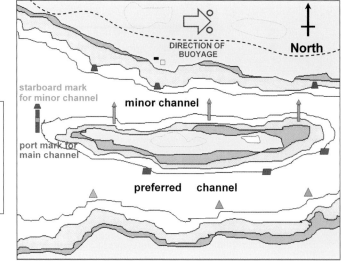

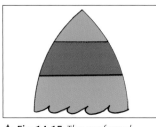

▲ **Fig 14.15** *The preferred channel to the left.*

pontoon. Figure 14.14 shows a channel either side of an island, with the major channel to the right as the river is entered from the west.

The buoy in Figure 14.15 would have been used if the main channel had been to the left.

Lights Red flashing 2 + 1 for Figure 14.14, and Green 2 + 1 for Figure 14.15.

Temporary wreck marks

Trinity House has recently introduced a very noticeable buoy to mark new wrecks that are close to busy shipping lanes. It is blue and yellow in colour, with an alternating amber and blue light – the first time that blue has ever been used for the light on a navigational mark.

Fig 14.16 shows THV *Alert* laying such a mark in the Harwich area. Some later models are fitted with a yellow St George's cross topmark.

▶ **Fig 14.16** *THV* Alert *laying a temporary wreck buoy. Photograph by kind permission of Trinity House*

IALA Region 'B' Buoyage

System B buoyage is very similar to System A as it is only the lateral buoys that differ. When entering the harbour, the conical buoys are left on the starboard side and the can-shaped ones to the port side, just as they are with IALA A, but the colours are reversed: the cans are green and the cones are red.

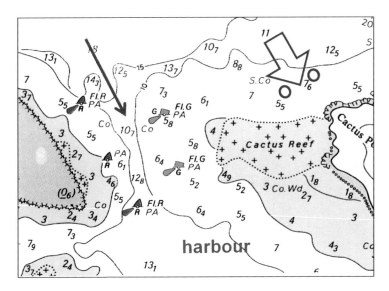

Fig 14.17 *IALA B lateral marks are red conical to starboard and green can-shaped to port when entering the harbour.*

The mnemonic 'RED RIGHT RETURNING' is a good one to remember. Figure 14.17 shows buoys in the Caribbean that mark a channel through a reef.

Light Characteristics

The three most commonly found light characteristics are:

Flashing (Fl) = The period of darkness is longer than the period of light.
This characteristic is used for cardinal marks and channel buoys. Where there are two cardinal marks close to each other then one may have a light that is quick flashing at 50–79 flashes a minute, and the other a very quick flashing light at 80–159 per minute so that each can be identified. A light that is labelled as flashing 5 seconds (Fl 5s) is on for less than 2½ seconds out of every 5 seconds.

Occulting = The period of light is longer than the period of dark.
A light with a characteristic of **Oc 3s** will be lit for 2 seconds and dark for 1 second.
Figure 14.18 shows the occulting light at Looe, in Cornwall, that has a white and a red arc. Vessels remaining in the white sector will clear the rocky ledges on either side of the entrance.

Isophase (Iso) = Equal periods of light and dark.
This is mostly used for leading lights and lighthouses; a light labelled **Iso 4s** is lit for 2 seconds and dark for 2 seconds.

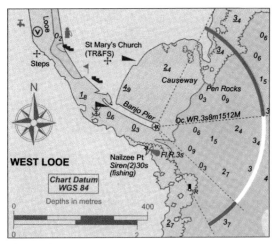

Fig 14.18

*Fig **14.19** This isophase light has a white, red and green sector.*

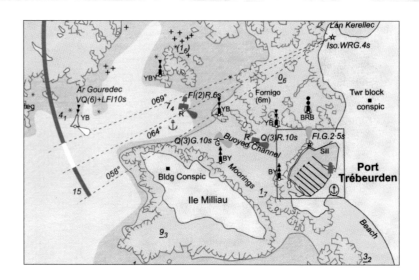

The light at Trébeurden, in Brittany, (Figure 14.19) has an isophase light to lead boats safely through the rock-strewn approach.

Note the cardinal marks and the isolated danger post.

Fixed lights

Fixed lights are used for lighting piers and marina pontoons that are connected to the shore, so it is definitely a bad idea to pass on the wrong side of them! Two lights are mounted one above the other with the notation **2FR (vert)** or **2FG (vert)** – the River Dart chart extract in Figure 14.20 shows these clearly.

Lighthouses

The brightest lights around our coast come from the lighthouses that have helped sailors for hundreds of years. Once manned by light-house keepers, they now have automated lights and fog horns.

The light on Caldey Island in South Wales is shown on the chartlet in Figure 14.21. The caption next to the light reads:

Fl(3)WR.20s 14/12M

This means that it has a flashing light that has a white sector and a red sector. The letters **W** and **R** have been added to the dotted circle over which the arcs can be seen. It is common for a red sector to guard a rocky or shallow area as it does here.

The white light, which flashes three times within a 20-second period, has a nominal range

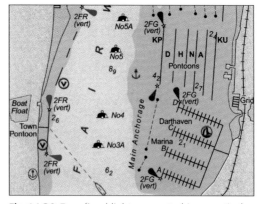

*Fig **14.20** Two fixed lights mounted in a vertical line are used to illuminate the extremities of piers and pontoons.*

of 14 nautical miles and the red has a range of 12 nautical miles. 'Nominal range' assumes that the Earth is flat and that the visibility is 10 miles or more. In other words, the optical system can project the light to a distance of 14 miles. We are not told how high the light is, so we have no idea exactly how far we could see it above the curvature of the Earth.

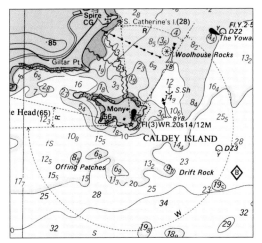

Fig 14.21 *Caldey Island light has a white and red sector.*

BUOYS, BEACONS AND LIGHTS: KNOWLEDGE CHECK

1 What colour is a special mark? For what purposes is this mark used?

2 What is the light characteristic of an isophase light?

3 What is the shape of the topmark on a west cardinal mark?

4 You see a buoy that is painted black over yellow. On which side of the point of interest is it placed?

5 When entering a UK harbour, should a green conical buoy pass down the port or starboard side of the boat?

CHAPTER FIFTEEN

PILOTAGE – FINDING YOUR WAY INTO CREEKS AND HARBOURS

When a boat is well offshore and cannot see the coastline, a position to the nearest half-mile is probably good enough, but once near land and close to a rocky shore like the one in Figure 15.1, we need to change our tactics – we must now use our eyes, a pilot book and a large-scale chart to remain in safe water. We have changed from navigator to pilot and, with the aid of a pair of good binoculars and a hand-bearing compass, we can use some of the powerful tools in the pilotage armoury to find our way into creeks and harbours with confidence.

Fig 15.1 *A good pilotage plan is necessary when entering Trébeurden on the Brittany coast.*

Pilotage Tools

Leading lines

Many of the most sheltered harbours have sand bars or rocky outcrops guarding their entrances, and laying buoys to mark the dangers has often been too expensive or just too difficult for small communities. As a result, generations of sailors have been using prominent structures such as church spires or monuments to assist them with a safe passage into, and out of, harbour. If no suitable features were available, then beacons were erected as a substitute.

Most harbours have permanent leading marks such as the two beacons that lead craft safely into Keyhaven, at the western end of the Solent (Figure 15.2). When these two beacons remain in line with each other, they are said to be *in transit*.

The bearing of 283°T is given on the chart as a check that the correct beacons are being used. The boat may have to crab down the line to counteract the tidal stream, but will nevertheless remain in safe water as long as one post is directly behind the other.

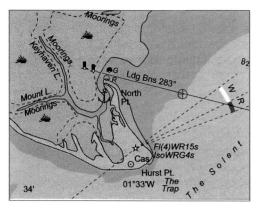

Fig 15.2 *The leading beacons into Keyhaven.*

Keeping them in line can sometimes appear difficult, but the secret is to concentrate on the closest object. Figure 15.3 shows a beacon and a tower close to Guernsey that are frequently used when approaching St Peter Port, so it is the latticed beacon that demands our attention.

In photo 1 (Figure 15.3) it is to the right of the tower, so a turn to starboard will be needed to align them.

In photo 2 they are in perfect transit.

In photo 3 the beacon is to port of the tower, so this time we move left to regain the transit.

Fig 15.3 *Roustel beacon and the Brehon tower off Guernsey are being used for this transit.*

Transits may be homemade ones – a significant tree may be lined up with a fixed feature, as in the series of photos in Figure 15.4. Had the vessel continued on the same course, it would have hit the platform, which is used to start yacht races off Lymington.

Tracking in to a destination on a visual transit saves us from having to draw a course-to-steer triangle on the chart – we can correct for a cross tidal stream visually from the cockpit or fly-bridge rather than remaining below while the boat is in a close-quarters situation.

Fig 15.4 *A home-made transit using a high tree and a race-starting platform.*

Leading lights

Transits are also used for leading lights when it is dark. In Figure 15.5, two occulting lights lead craft directly between the channel markers at Barfleur. As the lights are higher than the channel markers and are shown as having a nominal range of 10 nautical miles, they will be seen from a far greater distance than the red and green channel markers. The lights are white as no colour is given in the description.

▲ **Fig 15.5** *Leading lights at Barfleur.*

Using GPS

GPS can be used to great advantage when piloting into a harbour and, when combined with a chart plotter, a visual running plot can be kept as the boat tracks down the leading line.

In Figure 15.6, a waypoint has been placed just outside the breakwater at Barfleur. The boat is in the position of the cursor, marked by a cross.

The plotter display shows:

- The speed over the ground as 5.5 knots. (*Note: Not* speed through the water.)
- The course over the ground as 225°M.
- The cursor latitude and longitude position.
- The magnetic bearing to the waypoint.
- The distance to the waypoint.

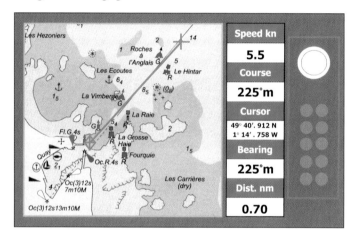

Notice that the boat is being steered to keep the bearing to the waypoint and the course over the ground the same – 225°M. If this is achieved, then the craft will continue to track down the leading line to enter the harbour safely.

◀ **Fig 15.6** *The craft is shown as being on track to enter Barfleur.*

Using local features to clear a danger

When there are no formal leading marks, chart makers will often name any features that could be considered useful for pilotage, so the first step is to study the chart to see what is available.

Let us say we wish to enter Coostrawvarra in Southern Ireland where a rock lies across the entrance. The chart in Figure 15.7 shows that there is a yellow ruin at the head of the creek, which we could keep on a steady compass bearing as we enter. As long as the bearing remains constant at 325°T, the boat will track along the drawn line into the anchorage missing Cotton Rock.

Clearing bearings

We can develop this method further if it is necessary to pass between a reef or shallow areas to enter a secluded cove, or a yacht wishes to tack into the bay. Again, looking at the chart in Figure 15.8 for a useful charted landmark, we can see a conspicuous hotel at the head of the cove, which looks ideal. However, this time we will draw two bearings to clear the dangers on

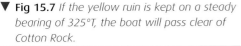

▼ **Fig 15.7** *If the yellow ruin is kept on a steady bearing of 325°T, the boat will pass clear of Cotton Rock.*

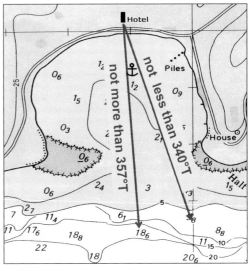

▲ **Fig 15.8** *Bearings are drawn to clear the dangers on either side of the cove entrance.*

each side. As the water is shallow quite a distance from the reef the resulting 'cone of safety' is quite narrow.

As we enter, a member of the crew will use the hand-bearing compass to take frequent bearings on the hotel. It must not bear less than 340°T or more than 357°T until we are abeam the house on the right-hand side of the entrance.

When leaving, the process will be identical with bearings taken looking astern.

Depth contours

The depth sounder is an instrument, which is almost always turned on while under way and unobtrusively does its job bouncing sound waves off the seabed. It is almost always situated within view of the helm and screeches in pain when it feels the boat is running out of water in which to float! What a valuable tool it is to have during pilotage situations, and often so under-used.

Figure 15.9 shows an area just east of Cowes where the depths change significantly within a short distance. There are numerous unlit buoys off the coast that are difficult to see at night, but depth contours can be used to avoid them. Notice that all the obstructions are in less than 15 metres below chart datum – if we calculate the height of tide at the time we pass through the area, we can pilot so that the boat remains north of the 15-metre depth contour.

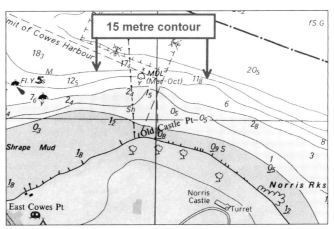

Fig 15.9 *Using the 15-metre contour line for pilotage.*

International port entry signals

Large commercial ports frequently use light signals to control the flow of traffic in and out of the harbour (Figure 15.10). Small craft under 20 metres in length are often exempted on the condition that they remain well away from commercial traffic and outside a narrow channel.

Restricted areas

In areas heavy with both commercial traffic and leisure craft, small vessels are often excluded from narrow channels while a large ship is in the vicinity. Figure 15.11 shows such a restriction, a marked precautionary area, at the entrance to Southampton Water. Even outside the channel, a good lookout for fishing pots has to be kept if a fouled propeller is to be avoided.

Preparing a pilotage plan

A well-prepared pilotage plan is vital for a stress-free entry into an unfamiliar harbour, and for this we shall need an almanac, a pilot book and an up-to-date chart. I have chosen Fowey, in Cornwall, for this exercise and have shown port information from *Reeds Nautical Almanac* (Figures 15.12 and 15.13).

When studying this information there are a number of questions we shall ask:

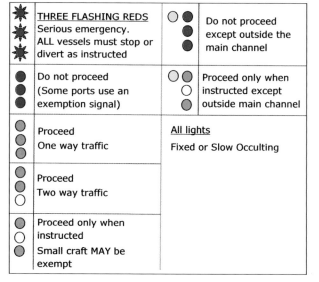

	THREE FLASHING REDS Serious emergency. ALL vessels must stop or divert as instructed		Do not proceed except outside the main channel
	Do not proceed (Some ports use an exemption signal)		Proceed only when instructed except outside main channel
	Proceed One way traffic	**All lights** Fixed or Slow Occulting	
	Proceed Two way traffic		
	Proceed only when instructed Small craft MAY be exempt		

▲ **Fig 15.10** *International port entry signals.*

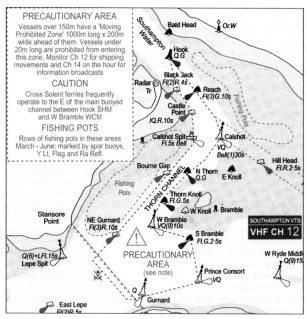

▲ **Fig 15.11** *The precautionary area at the entrance to Southampton Water.*

- Can the harbour be approached at any state of the tide or is the entrance restricted?
- Is the entrance dangerous in bad weather or if the wind is in a certain direction?
- Are there any dangers on the approach or inside the harbour?
- Are there leading marks and leading lights for the harbour or special channels for small craft?
- Does the harbour give adequate shelter and is there berthing for visitors?
- What is the speed limit in the harbour?

- Are there any conspicuous landmarks on the approach and inside
the harbour that would assist with
the pilotage?
- What facilities does the harbour offer?
Can we pick up fresh water and fuel?

Next we need to draw lines on the chart
that will give us a heading and distances
on the approach but, most important of
all, *brief the crew well* so that they can
help and join in the fun.

This list is not exhaustive. It is just an
example of the many things we must
think about.

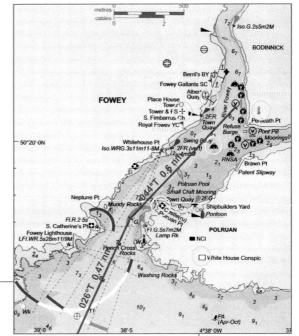

▲ Fig 15.12
*A chart of
Fowey Harbour.
Significant
landmarks are
highlighted in
yellow.
Headings and
distances aid
pilotage.*

FOWEY   Cornwall 50°19'.65N 04°38'.54W

CHARTS AC *1267*, 148, 31, *5602*; Imray C6, 2400.7/8;
Stanfords 2, 23; OS 204

TIDES −0540 Dover; Duration 0605; Zone 0 (UT)

Standard Port   PLYMOUTH

Times				Height (metres)			
High Water		Low Water		MHWS	MHWN	MLWN	MLWS
0000	0600	0000	0600	5.5	4.4	2.2	0.8
1200	1800	1200	1800				
Differences FOWEY							
−0010	−0015	−0010	−0005	− 0.1	− 0.1	−0.2	− 0.2

SHELTER   Good but exposes to winds from S to SW. Gales from thee directions can cause heavy swell in the
lower hbr and confused seas, especially on the ebb. Entry at any tide in any conditions. Fowey is a busy clay port.
Speed limit 6kn. All visitors' pontoons are marked 'FHC VISITORS'

Craft should berth/moor as directed by Hbr Patrol. Visitors' pontoons are in situ May-Oct. Pont Pill, on the E side,
offers double-berth fore and aft visitors' moorings and alongside in 2m on two 36m floating pontoons; there is
also a refuse barge. Opposite Albert Quay, on the E side of the channel there is another 36m pontoon. At
Albert Quay the 'T' shaped landing pontoon is for short stay (2 hrs), plus Fresh Water. A visitors' pontoon
(double-sided) is off the E bank, midway between - Bodinnick and Mixtow Pill. At Mixtow Pill (5ca upriver)
is a quieter 135m, shore-linked pontoon in 2·2m, visitors on S side. Showers, landing slip and boat
storage ashore.

NAVIGATION WPT 50°19.33N 04°38'.80W, 027°/7ca through hbr ent to Whitehouse Pt Dir Lt in W sector. Appr in
W sector of Fowey Lt ho. 3M E of ent beware Udder Rk marked by SCM Lt buoy. From SW beware Cannis Rock (4ca
SE of Gribbin Hd) marked by SCM Lt buoy. Entering hbr, keep well clear of Punch Cross Rks to stbd. Give way to the
Bodinnick-Caffa-Mill ferry.

LIGHTS AND MARKS See chartlet. An unlit RW tower 33m on Gribbin Hd (1.3M WSW of hbr ent) is conspic from
all sea directions, as is a white house 3 cables E of hbr ent. Fowey Lt ho is conspic. The W sector (022°-032°) of
Whitehouse Point directional light leads safely through the 200m wide hbr entrance.

R/T Call *Fowey Hbr Radio* **Ch 12** 16 (HO). Hbr Patrol (0900 - 2000LT) Ch 12. Water taxi Ch 06.

TELEPHONE (01726) HM 832471; MRSC (01803) 882704; NCI 870291 @ Polruan; Marinecall 09068

FACILITIES   Overnight fees on visitors' pontoon: average £1.13/m,but £1.37/m on pontoon in Mixtow Pill.
Reductions for 3 or 7 days. From seaward: Polruan Quay Pontoon, Slip, landing, fresh water, Crane (3 ton), Diesel:
Note this is the only fuel available by hose at Fowey/Polruan.

Royal Fowey YC, FW, R, Bar, Showers.   **Albert Quay** HM's Office, landing , fresh water.
Fowey Gallants SC Showers, Bar, R.   **Berrills BY** pontoon, fresh water, oil disposal.
Mixtow Pill, Visitors on S side of 135m shore-linked pontoon; Slip, hoist (8.4 ton), fresh water, showers.
Services: M, Gas, Gaz, CH, ACA, BY, Slip, ME, El, Crane (7 ton).
Town EC Wed/Sat; R, Bar, Post Office, Rail Station (bus to Par), Airport (Newquay).

◀ Fig 15.13
*Edited Fowey
Harbour infor-
mation taken
from* Reeds
Nautical
Almanac. *Many
abbreviations
are used, but
an explanatory
page is always
included.*

Summary

1 The harbour is plenty deep enough at all states of the tide, but we will not go into Fowey if the wind is blowing strongly from the south or southwest as it may be uncomfortable at the berth.

2 There is a lighthouse and a white house on the approach and numerous conspicuous features inside the harbour; these have been highlighted on the chart.

3 We must keep our speed down to 6 knots or less.

4 A pontoon berth or a fore-and-aft mooring is available in the river and a water taxi will take us to and from the shore.

5 Fuel and water are best picked up from Polruan Quay pontoon, as this is the only fuel by hose in the river. As there are no marinas, shore power is unlikely to be available, so the engine will need to be run during socially acceptable hours if the battery requires a charge.

   Finally, we must remember why we came to Fowey in the first place – to enjoy visiting this very attractive town, have a great meal out, and to sleep comfortably at night!

PILOTAGE: KNOWLEDGE CHECK

1 If you were leaving the transit in Figure 15.14 astern which way would you alter course to bring the two objects into line?

Fig 15.14 *The transit for Knowledge Check: Question 1.*

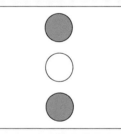

Fig 15.15 *Knowledge Check: Question 2.*

2 What is the meaning of the international traffic signal in Figure 15.15?

3 Does the GPS give your course over ground or course through the water?

4 Which charts would cover Fowey?

5 Which VHF channel would you use if you wished to speak to the Fowey Harbour Patrol?

6 When entering the harbour, are there any dangers you need to avoid?

CHAPTER SIXTEEN

LOOKING AT THE WEATHER

When a skipper is planning a passage, the first thought is usually about the weather and how strong the wind will be. Luckily, we no longer have to rely on a piece of seaweed or granny's aches and pains to tell us what is going to happen to the weather because it is relatively easy to obtain a good forecast before setting out and while at sea.

Obtaining a forecast is all very well, but it is necessary to have some idea what it all means.

This chapter gives an explanation of pressure systems, fronts and isobars to give you a head start.

Getting a Forecast

Met Office Shipping Forecast

The Met Office (www.metoffice.gov.uk) issues a shipping forecast for the following 24 hours, updated four times daily. HM Coastguard give relevant parts of it in their Maritime Safety Information broadcasts (MSI) on marine VHF radio and on Navtex, a dedicated text service, for weather and navigational warnings. The BBC also broadcast the shipping forecast on Radio 4 (LW 198 kHz) and show it on their internet weather site (www.bbc.co.uk/weather).

The forecast includes a detailed analysis of weather systems in the North Atlantic, gale warnings and sea area forecasts for the following 24 hours for the waters around the UK. The current times are shown in Figure 16.1, but are occasionally changed so you will need to consult your almanac to be sure.

As the majority of weather systems approach the UK and continental Europe from the west, it is a good idea to study the areas to the west of your position to see what the weather is likely to do later on.

Inshore waters forecast

Of enormous relevance to leisure boaters on a coastal passage is the forecast for inshore waters covering the area up to 12 nautical miles

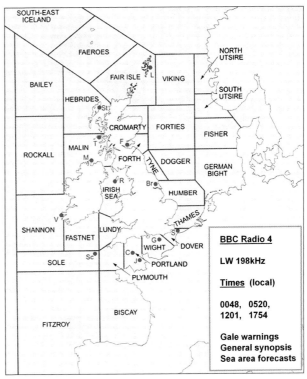

Fig 16.1 *Sea area forecast areas for the UK.*

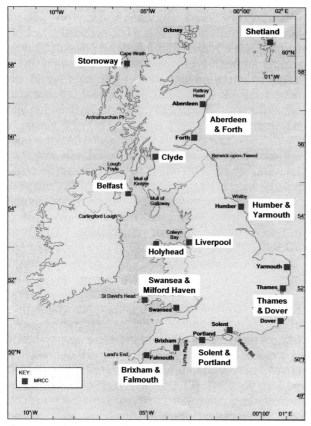

Fig 16.2 *Inshore waters forecast areas covering up to 12 nautical miles offshore.*

offshore. This forecast is updated every 6 hours and repeated every 3 hours by the UK Coastguard in their MSI broadcasts, giving a total of 8 broadcasts within a 24-hour period. The UK has been divided into 12 forecast areas, and information on wind speed, wind direction, weather, visibility and sea state is included. In addition, there is an outlook for the following 24 hours. A map of these areas is shown in Figure 16.2, but consult your almanac for channels and time schedules.

```
WARNINGS: NIL

GENERAL SYNOPSIS
LOW JUST WEST OF BAILEY 1006 MOVING
SLOWLY WEST, DEEPENING 1000 BY
MIDNIGHT TONIGHT. LOW EAST ROCKALL
1008 EXPECTED NORTH FAEROES 1000
BY SAME TIME. THUNDERY LOW MOVING
STEADILY NORTHEAST EXPECTED EAST
THAMES 1001 BY THAT TIME

24-HR FORECASTS

THAMES
EASTERLY 4 BECOMING CYCLONIC THEN
NORTHWESTERLY 5 OR 6. THUNDERY
RAIN. GOOD BECOMING MODERATE OR
POOR
```

Fig 16.3 *Part of a broadcast on a McMurdo ICS Navtex receiver.*

Navtex

A *Navtex* receiver is a great addition to the weather armoury as it quietly prints information gathered during the small hours so that it is ready and waiting for you when you get up. A dedicated antenna is required and, as the service forms part of the Global Maritime Distress and Safety System, it is international and in English. All Navtex sets receive on 518 kHz and some have a second frequency, 490 kHz, for local language broadcasts. The range of these sets is about 300 miles and transmitters at Portpatrick, Cullercoats, Niton (Isle of Wight) and Valentia (Shannon area) cover the whole of the UK and the Republic of Ireland. Stations at Calais and Brest cope with the Brittany coast.

Gale warnings are broadcast as soon as they are received and the Met Office shipping forecast with the extended outlook are given – once again, consult the almanac for times.

Part of a Navtex screen is illustrated in Figure 16.3.

Television and newspapers

Most newspapers print a weather chart and give a forecast, which, although land-biased, can be very useful to give you a feel for the weather trends. Regional television stations serving coastal areas aim to give information more suitable for mariners and always give wind speed and direction.

Local radio

BBC and commercial radio stations that are close to coastal areas offer a good local weather service for boating enthusiasts. Forecasts are usually around breakfast and supper time and include strong wind warnings, extracts from the shipping forecast, and the inshore waters forecast.

Marinas and harbour masters

Marinas generally receive a faxed weather map and display it on a notice board.
French marinas often display two forecasts, one in French and the other in English.

Internet – useful sites

www.metoffice.gov.uk
Shipping and inshore waters forecast, satellite images, etc.

www.wetterzentrale.de
Weather charts from the UK Met Office and European weather centres, and a whole lot more.

www.ndbc.noaa.gov
Useful data collected from special buoys moored in the Atlantic, Biscay and the North Sea is issued by this agency.

www.meteo.fr
Wind charts and a five-day forecast for Europe (including the UK). Wind speed is given in km/hour, so it may not be as strong as you might think at first glance.

www.bbc.co.uk/weather
Synoptic charts, shipping and inshore water forecast, and much more.

www.franksingleton.clara.net
Links to just about every known meteorological site.

What the Forecasts Mean

The wind and the sea state are probably of the most interest, so let's kick off by finding out exactly what is meant when we are told that the wind will be Force 6.

Beaufort scale

Admiral Beaufort published his wind scale, in 1808 so that Royal Navy captains wouldn't keep damaging expensive sails that cost the Admiralty a fortune! It was so successful that it remains, to this day, as the internationally accepted method for classifying wind speeds. An updated version that gives guidance for small sailing and power craft is shown in Figure 16.4.

The wind strengths are average wind speeds, not the maximum that can be expected.

Taking things to the extreme, a Force 4 may give gusts up to 20 knots if it is squally, and if there is a 3-knot tidal stream flowing in the opposite direction, the apparent wind felt will be 23 knots – a Force 6! An unexpected 5-hour leg to windward with this wind-over-tide situation may be impossible for many power craft and an endurance test for even an experienced yacht crew. If you are relatively new to the sport and have chartered a boat for a weekend that turns out windy, try to resist any peer pressure that may push you to set out against your better

BEAUFORT SCALE			
1	Light airs	1- 3 kn	Ripples without foam crests *Power – fast plane. Sail – drifting.*
2	Light breeze	4- 6 kn	Small wavelets. Crests do not break *Power – fast plane. Sail – full sail.*
3	Gentle breeze	7- 10 kn	Large wavelets. Crests begin to break *Power – fast plane. Sail – full sail.*
4	Moderate breeze	11- 16 kn	Small waves. Frequent white horses *Power – slow down in wind against tide conditions.* *Sail –consider reefing main and reducing genoa* *in light yachts.*
5	Fresh breeze	17- 21 kn	Moderate waves. Many white horses *Power – reduce speed going upwind.* *Sail – reef mainsail.*
6	Strong breeze	22- 27 kn	Large waves. White foam crests. Some spray. (sometimes called "The Yachtsman's Gale") *Power – slow down to displacement speed.* *Sail – Further reef main and reduce headsail.*
7	Near gale	28- 33 kn	Sea heaps up, foam from breaking waves blown in streaks. Spray. *Power – displacement speed; head into waves.* *Sail – deeply reefed main, small or storm jib.*
8	Gale	34- 40 kn	**Moderately high waves, crests break into spindrift.** *Power – stay at home or in port!* *Sail – deep reefed main /storm trysail, storm jib.*
9	Severe gale	41- 47 kn	No place for Day Skippers! Try another sport!

Fig 16.4 *The Beaufort wind scale.*

judgement. Tragic accidents have happened in the past when novice skippers were persuaded to venture further than wisdom dictated. Keep your resolve and make alternative plans to explore the sheltered creeks close to base instead.

Wave height

The sea state is usually more important to a small boat than the wind speed itself, and inshore weather forecasts describe the sea using the terms given in Figure 16.5. A moderate sea can produce waves that are about 2 metres high, which means that moving around a yacht and life down below becomes hard-going for many people – and almost impossible in powerboats with wide saloons and few grab handles.

Wind against tide When the wind is blowing in the opposite direction to the tidal stream the sea always gets choppy. As the tidal stream strengthens in its third and fourth hour, the rougher the sea will get. If the wind and the tidal stream are running in the same direction, the sea will probably be at its flattest during the same period. Motor cruisers who can get to their destination in just 2 or 3 hours will find it much more comfortable to take the wind with the

▶ **Fig 16.5** *A moderate sea can feel very rough when the waves are 2 metres high.*

	WAVE HEIGHT		
	metres		metres
CALM	< 0.1m	MODERATE	1.25 - 2.5m
SMOOTH	0.1 - 0.5m	ROUGH	2.5 - 4m
SLIGHT	0.5 - 1.25m	VERY ROUGH	4 - 6m

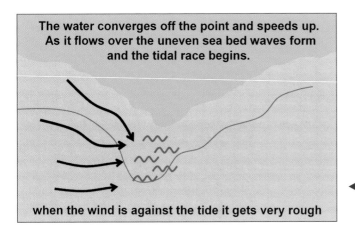

The water converges off the point and speeds up. As it flows over the uneven sea bed waves form and the tidal race begins.

when the wind is against the tide it gets very rough

◀ **Fig 16.6** *A Force 6 blowing against a spring tide can cause rough, confused water.*

tide, even if it means going against both elements. Wind with tide means that the boat can remain at planing speed on a flat sea to reach the destination quickly and comfortably.

Headlands   There are many headlands around the UK and some of them have a tidal race that causes rough water and dangerous waves to form when a strong tidal stream is running (Figure 16.6). The race off Portland Bill in Dorset, the Needles channel and the Pentland Firth off the north coast of Scotland are good examples of water either squeezing around a headland or through a gap. All have a very uneven seabed and all should be avoided when a strong wind is blowing.

Shallow water and rebounding waves   An onshore wind and a shoaling seabed can cause steep waves, which break as surf on the beach. Perranporth, in Cornwall, may be sheer joy to surfers, but would be a nightmare to a boat blown onto the beach. Keep well offshore and give yourself some sea room for safety.

When there is an onshore wind and a swell is running, the incoming waves may bounce back off a harbour wall or cliffs to produce a very confused sea. This can sometimes make a harbour entry difficult where there is a narrow entrance to the port.

Strong Wind Warnings and Gale Warnings

Strong wind warnings are issued when the winds are expected to reach Force 6 and are repeated in the MSI broadcasts throughout the day and night (Figure 16.7).

Gale warnings are broadcast on Marine VHF and Navtex as soon as possible after they are issued and those with Digital Selective Calling (DSC) radios will hear a safety alert before the voice message is broadcast. The warning will be issued for specific sea areas when winds are

STRONG WIND & GALE WARNINGS

A STRONG wind warning is issued if the average wind is expected to be Force 6 or 7

A GALE warning is issued if the average wind is forecast to be F8 or more or gust to more than 43 knots.

There is always an indication as to the timing

IMMINENT	Within 6 hours of issue of warning
SOON	6 - 12 hours after issue
LATER	More than 12 hours

◀ **Fig 16.7** *The definitions used when gale warnings and strong wind warnings are issued.*

VISIBILITY

Good	More than 5 miles
Moderate	2 - 5 miles
Poor	1000m - 2 miles
Fog	Less than 1000m

▶ **Fig 16.8** *Good visibility can be anything from 5 to 30 miles.*

expected to reach Force 8, or to give higher gusts. A 'soon' forecast will generally give the coastal sailor plenty of time to reach shelter.

Visibility

Visibility is given in weather forecasts, and although the descriptions appear rather vague they do have very specific meanings (Figure 16.8).

Fog and reduced visibility at sea need special care and merits a chapter of its own (see Chapter 17).

North Atlantic Weather Systems – Lows and Highs

Synoptic charts are drawn using data sent in by weather stations worldwide. Information on barometric pressure, temperature, humidity and cloud types are all taken into account to produce a chart that shows centres of high and low pressure and any associated disturbances caused by air masses of different temperatures meeting (Figure 16.9).

Very noticeable is the circular pattern of *isobars* – the lines joining points of equal barometric pressure that enable us to calculate the wind speed and direction.

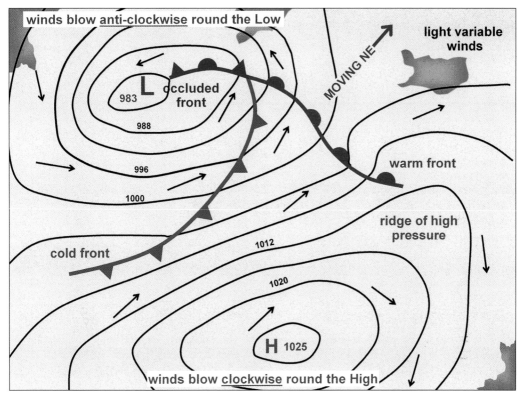

Fig 16.9 *A typical weather chart for the North Atlantic showing a centre of high pressure to the south and low pressure to the north.*

Low Pressure

An area of low pressure is formed when warm air and cool air meet and interact with each other. The warm air rises above the cool air, leaving slack pressure at the surface, and the cool air flows in to replace it (Figure 16.10). The Earth's rotational effect (Coreolis force) kicks in and causes the rising warm air to go into an anti-clockwise and upward spiral in the Northern Hemisphere. South of the Equator it reverses to blow in a clockwise direction around a low.

Air flows from the area of high pressure to the low in an attempt to equalise the pressure, just as it does when a hole is made in a bicycle tyre – the air leaks out.

However, the air does not pass directly from one to the other; instead it more or less follows the line of the isobars except that it pushes out from the high and 'toes into' the low. Follow the flow on the weather chart and you will see that the flow is similar to a figure of eight.

Notice that the wind blowing in from the west between the high and the low converges and the isobars are closer. This means that the wind will be stronger in this area – the closer the isobars the stronger the wind will be.

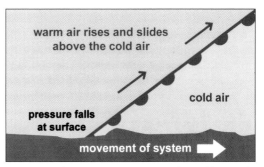

Fig 16.10 *The warm air rises over the cold air and the pressure falls at the surface.*

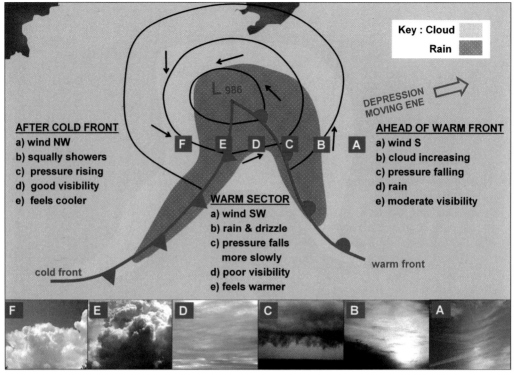

Fig 16.11 *This weather system is moving from left to right. Imagine that you are standing to the right of positon A and the depression is moving towards you.*

Fronts

A 'front' is just the leading edge of an air mass and will be called a warm front if the mass is warm and a cold front if the mass is cold. The chart in Figure 16.9 shows both a warm and a cold front, which is the normal pattern for a depression (a low).

Each front carries its own type of weather, and the cold air – being denser and heavier – moves more quickly than the warm air. The cold front catches up with the warm front close to the centre of low pressure, and as the two fronts 'occlude', the weather from each front combines. Once the fronts begin to occlude the system begins to die, but it is not quite over yet as the weather associated with an occlusion is usually bad.

A depression generally moves from west to east across the UK so the warm front arrives first, together with its own weather. Even if you managed to obtain a forecast, always keep your eye on the sky and barometer. Record the pressure hourly in the ship's log, and if it starts dropping like a stone then seek shelter soon because it *will* blow. Falling pressure is just one of the many indications that a depression is approaching, so let us have a look at the other signs.

The Sequence from A to F

We shall assume that we are at position A on the right-hand side of Figure 16.11, with a clear blue sky and very little wind. Someone on the boat is keeping a good log and is recording everything that happens as the depression passes over.

At Position A

1 We see high *cirrus* cloud that looks hooked by the wind. This means that there is moisture in the upper atmosphere and a possible frontal system may be approaching (Figure 16.12).
2 We are aware that aircraft vapour trails are remaining in the sky and not disappearing just behind the aircraft. There is also a halo around the sun (Figure 16.13). This is caused by a very thin layer of *cirrostratus* cloud veiling the sun. (The prefix *cirro* = high cloud, and *stratus* = layer.)
3 The wind is light, but has changed direction from southwest to south. This means that it has 'backed' – ie, it has swung anticlockwise.
4 The barometer has started to fall.
5 The visibility is reasonably good – more than 5 miles.

At Position B

1 The sky is now completely covered with high cloud and a thickening lower layer – *altostratus*. (The prefix *alto* = medium-height layer cloud.)
   The sky in Figure 16.14 looks as if some nasty weather is on its way.
2 The wind is rising now and the pressure is continuing to fall.
3 It has begun to rain and the visibility has fallen to about 3 miles.

At Position C

1 We are now completely soaked and the cloud has become thicker and lower. It is *nimbostratus* cloud (Figure 16.15). (The prefix *nimbo* = rain-bearing.)
2 We are getting quite close to the warm front and the wind is howling. The pressure has now fallen 6 millibars in the last 3 hours.
3 The visibility has become quite poor and it is quite misty in the rain, but we are feeling a little warmer as we get close to the warm front.

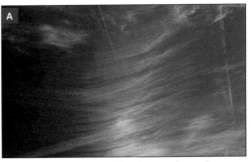

▲ **Fig 16.12** *Cirrus cloud indicates that a front could be approaching.*

▲ **Fig 16.13** *Aircraft vapour trails and thin cirrus cloud.*

▲ **Fig 16.14** *High cirrostratus and the lower altostratus – both are layer clouds.*

▲ **Fig 16.15** *Low nimbostratus cloud.*

At Position D

1 Life is beginning to look up a bit – the heavy rain has stopped and it's now just drizzle or light rain.
2 The cloud has thinned and looks a little lumpier than it did as it is now *stratocumulus* cloud (Figure 16.16). (The prefix *strato* = layer, and *cumulus* = accumulating.)
   Stratocumulus could be described as layer cloud that has a small amount of vertical development.
3 We noticed that the pressure had stopped falling when we did the last log entry – it has steadied now.
4 It is still blowing hard, but the wind has veered round to become southwesterly.
5 The visibility is quite poor – about 1 mile.
6 It is definitely a lot warmer.

At Position E

1 Just when we thought the weather was improving, it has started to pour with rain again (Figure 16.17).
2 The wind is even stronger than it was and getting quite gusty too.
3 It doesn't feel so warm now – quite chilly in fact.
4 Despite the heavy rain, a line of blue sky appears to be creeping towards us from the northwest.

At Position F

1 The rain has stopped and the sky is blue, except for quite a few towering *cumulus* and *cumulonimbus* clouds, which have been giving us some heavy squally showers (Figure 16.18). (The prefix *cumulo* = accumulating or growing, and *nimbus* = rain-bearing.)
2 The wind has veered yet again and is now blowing from the northwest. We think that it has moderated a little.
3 The barometer has risen a lot in the last couple of hours, but is slowing now.
4 The visibility is now very good – we can see coastline about 15 miles away, but in the showers we can hardly see anything. We had hailstones during the last squall.
5 There are not so many clouds to the northwest – the showers will die out and we will have blue skies again.

▲ **Fig 16.16** *Warm-sector cloud – stratocumulus.*

▲ **Fig 16.17** *The cold front with accumulating rain-bearing cloud – cumulonimbus.*

▲ **Fig 16.18** *After the cold front. This well-developed cumulus cloud will give squally showers.*

High Pressure (an Anticyclone)

A cyclone is always associated with extreme weather and an anticyclone is just the opposite with fair or fine weather and light winds at its centre.

Highs that build in pressure slowly but steadily often remain in one place for a time and give long periods of stable weather. They also form ridges between two depressions (Figure 16.19). This should provide a day of sunny weather before the next depression arrives.

During the summer, a high generally has blue skies and calm nights associated with it. In the winter months, though, it can be cold, overcast and gloomy if the air is coming from the north and has passed over a large expanse of sea.

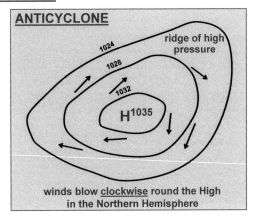

Fig 16.19 *The anticyclone has light and variable winds at its centre.*

Local Winds

The wind systems of the world undergo local modifications due to the presence of topograph-ical and geographical features and the unequal heating and cooling of land and sea. High hills will cause air to blow up the slope when the sun is heating the surface and down again at night when it is not.

The sea breeze

When an area of high pressure is well established in late spring and early summer it is likely that there will be clear skies, light winds and many hours of warm sunshine to heat the land. At this time of year the sea is still relatively cold after the winter as it absorbs heat more slowly

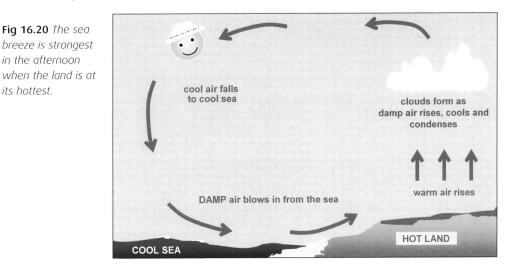

Fig 16.20 *The sea breeze is strongest in the afternoon when the land is at its hottest.*

than the land. This temperature difference can cause a breeze to blow off the sea during the hotter parts of the day in areas close to a large expanse of water.

During the morning the land heats, causing the air above it to be heated and rise. This leaves slack pressure above the land so the cool air from the sea blows in to replace the displaced air. As the land gets hotter during the afternoon, this cycle will continue and speed up – causing the wind to veer. A line of cumulus cloud may form along the coastline as the damp air continues to blow in from the sea (Figure 16.20).

Everything will slow down in the late afternoon and early evening as the heat goes out of the sun. Once sunset comes, there may be no wind at all from the sea and the cumulus cloud will have dispersed over the land.

A sea breeze does not normally exceed a Force 3; it may extend up to 15 miles offshore, and sometimes even further inland when the land is at its hottest. During the late summer the breezes are less pronounced as the differential between land and sea temperature narrows.

Land breeze

In late summer the days are shorter and the temperature of the land falls more quickly than the sea as darkness falls (Figure 16.21). This situation is perfect for a land breeze to blow. This is never as strong as the sea breeze and seldom felt more than 5 miles offshore, although topographical features may cause some variation.

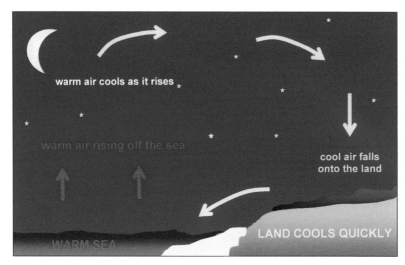

warm air cools as it rises

warm air rising off the sea

cool air falls onto the land

LAND COOLS QUICKLY

WARM SEA

◀ **Fig 16.21** *As the land cools, the warm air radiates off the sea. The air from the land blows towards the sea.*

▼ **Fig 16.22** *This seemingly quiet anchorage could get quite bumpy overnight.*

Downslope winds (katabatic)

In a mountainous region the cool land air can rush down the hill slopes at night and out into what started as a sheltered bay (Figure 16.22). Ask those who have chartered a boat in Greece, Turkey or Thailand and they all have a tale about standing an anchor watch after choosing the wrong anchorage!

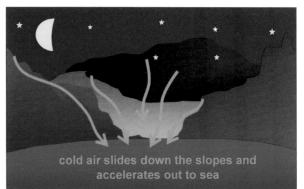

cold air slides down the slopes and accelerates out to sea

This wind, known as a *katabatic* wind, normally blows for just a few hours until sea and land temperatures equalise, but it is wise to keep watch to check that the anchor is holding.

Summary

Meteorology is a fascinating subject and we have looked only at the basics in this chapter. To develop your knowledge further, keep looking at the sky and the barometer when a depression is expected to cross the UK so that you can study the sequence of events. For those who wish to delve more deeply into the subject, my book *Yachtmaster for Sail and Power* (Adlard Coles Nautical) might be of interest. If you just want an easy life, you can always refer to the guidelines used by Gary in Figure 16.23!

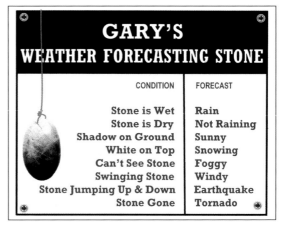

GARY'S WEATHER FORECASTING STONE

CONDITION	FORECAST
Stone is Wet	Rain
Stone is Dry	Not Raining
Shadow on Ground	Sunny
White on Top	Snowing
Can't See Stone	Foggy
Swinging Stone	Windy
Stone Jumping Up & Down	Earthquake
Stone Gone	Tornado

Fig 16.23 *I think we will choose a dry stone with a shadow on the ground, don't you?*

WEATHER: KNOWLEDGE CHECK

1 Which organisation is responsible for broadcasting maritime safety information in the UK?

2 You hear this gale warning on the VHF radio:

'The following gale warning was issued at 1100 BST for the sea areas Portland and Wight. Southwesterly gale Force 8 imminent.'

Between which times could you expect the wind to reach Force 8?

3 When is a strong wind warning issued?

4 Describe the weather conditions that you could expect in the warm sector of a North Atlantic depression.

5 Would you expect the wind speed at the centre of an anticyclone to be light or strong?

6 Would you expect a sea breeze to be strongest at breakfast or teatime? Explain the reason for your answer.

CHAPTER SEVENTEEN

FOG

Fog is forecast when the visibility is expected to be less than 1,000 metres; that is just over half a mile in 'old money', which means that Nelson would not be able to see Buckingham Palace from his column in Trafalgar Square!

Even the most seasoned seafarers feel uneasy in fog; sounds appear to come from many different directions and helmsmen sometimes imagine that they are steering around in circles, despite a steady compass needle. Few of us choose to venture out in the conditions shown in Figure 17.1; most people are sensible and stay put until the fog has cleared. However, with GPS to assist with the navigation, we should be able to find our way to a safe haven should we be caught in it. For those without GPS, we shall be looking at pilotage solutions later in the chapter.

Radar

When shrouded by fog, ships depend on radar to see other vessels. Slab-sided metal hulls reflect radar beams back to the sender extremely well, but unfortunately pass right through glass-reinforced plastic and give a very poor return from wood. The engine is a good reflector, but is usually mounted low in the hull so that it is not visible until a ship is very close. This means that, without a radar reflector, the average glassfibre boat is almost invisible to large ships as the mast and other metal deck fittings give a poor radar return due to their rounded shape.

In 2002, the Safety of Life at Sea Convention (SOLAS) decided that, because of many near misses, all craft, whether commercial or leisure vessels, should fit a radar reflector where practicable.

Fig 17.1 *This is not the day to set sail along a rocky coast.*

Radar Reflectors

Passive reflectors

There are many different types on the market, but some are too small to be effective. I have shown two that work well if one of a reasonable size is used.

Octahedral type This inexpensive 'flat pack' reflector preceded all others, but remains one of the best as long as it is mounted correctly. It may be permanently secured on the arch above the fly-bridge or on a yacht's backstay. It may also be hoisted temporarily on a signal halyard. It is important that it be used in the 'catch rain' position so that it would collect rainwater in one of the hollows if it were watertight (Figure 17.2). If suspended by one of the corners, the metal sheets reflect incorrectly and give a poor radar return.

Care should be taken to see that the aluminium sheets do not get bent when the reflector is stored in a locker.

Cylindrical type The second style of reflector is a high-performance type consisting of a stacked array of aluminium sheets enclosed in a fender-shaped glassfibre cover. More expensive than the octahedral, it is easy to mount on mast or arch and will stow in the cockpit locker if permanent installation is not desired. If they *are* stowed in a locker with the fenders, be careful not to use it by mistake when going alongside – it will make a very expensive crunching noise as the hull touches the dock! The colourful one in Figure 17.3 is mounted on a mast out of harm's way!

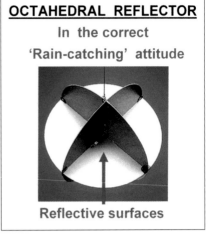

OCTAHEDRAL REFLECTOR
In the correct
'Rain-catching' attitude

Reflective surfaces

Fig 17.2 *An octahedral radar reflector.*

Fig 17.3 *A Firdell Blipper reflector mounted on a mast.*

Active reflectors

A radar target enhancer, such as the 'Sea-me', receives a radar signal, amplifies it, then re-transmits it. This ensures a stronger return signal over the full 360°, with your boat appearing as a larger and more consistent target. Some models also give a visual and audio alarm when the equipment is activated by a radar beam so that you are aware that other vessels are in the area.

This type of reflector is most suitable for those venturing offshore and is more expensive than a passive reflector.

Fig 17.4 *Preparing a pilotage plan.*
Photograph:
www.stephenrichard.co.uk

When the Fog Comes Down

Many skippers keep a 'fog checklist' in the chart table so that they do not forget any of the important tasks that need to be done. The list might read something like this:

1 Hoist the radar reflector and switch on the low navigation lights. (Remember the steaming light if the engine has been started.)

2 Sound a fog signal at least every 2 minutes: one long blast (power), or one long and two short blasts (sail).

3 All crew must be on the deck in lifejackets.

4 Switch the VHF to the port operations frequency to listen for commercial shipping.

5 Set a radar watch if an experienced operator is aboard.

6 Check the boat's position and consider getting out of the big ship channel and into shallow water to anchor.

7 When clear of immediate danger, prepare a pilotage plan for entering harbour.

Finding the Way

Most ports will have commercial ships entering and leaving in both good and poor visibility. Our aim is to keep well clear of them and, if we do not have radar, this means staying in relatively shallow water and creeping into the harbour entrance well away from the shipping channel.

If for some reason you find yourself without your trusty GPS when the fog descends, it is wise to have a cunning plan up your sleeve to save the day.

Following a contour line to a safe haven

Using contour lines to find a safe route into a harbour is a tried and tested method that relies on common sense and simple logic.

The coastline in Figure 17.5 is ideal for our purpose, as it has clearly defined contours with the 5-metre line close to the coast and passing within a stone's throw of the breakwater at Misty Haven. The harbour looks the ideal place in which to wait for improvement in the visibility – but is it safe to approach?

Fig 17.5
*The safe
approach is
from the
west as there
are no off-
lying dangers.*

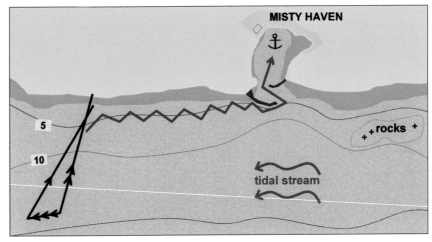

Looking at the chart we see that there is a rocky patch to the east of the harbour, but it is clear for an approach from the south and west.

The navigator considers a straight-line approach, but discards it for two reasons:

1 It may bring the boat close to larger vessels.
2 The tidal stream may sweep the boat past the entrance and, with no GPS, it would be diffi-cult to tell whether the boat is remaining on the intended course over the ground.

The navigator decides that the best plan is to shape a course to make a landfall well to the western side of the entrance and to calculate the height of tide so that he or she knows when the 5-metre contour has been reached. At the correct depth, the helmsman will alter course to starboard and then make the necessary course alterations to stay on the contour. Once the breakwater is sighted, the helmsman will turn to port to enter the haven.

How Fog Forms

There are two types of fog that are likely to affect us on the water. One is sea fog, and the other is a land fog that drifts out over the sea to cause coastal fog patches. Both are formed when air masses of different temperatures interact with each other; moisture is always involved.

Sea fog

This type of fog is most common in the late spring or early summer when the sea tempera-ture is still very low. As the sun edges north of the Equator and the days grow longer, the daytime temperatures can climb when the wind comes from the tropics. This wind, although warm, has passed over many miles of sea and is holding quite

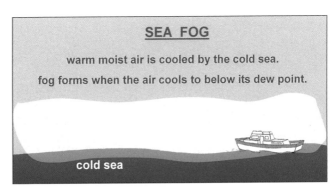

Fig 17.6 *How sea fog is formed.*

a lot of moisture by the time it reaches the UK. A wind and a turbulent cold sea can cool this warm air to below its dew point and fog will be formed (Figure 17.6).

A wind of Force 5 or more should lift this fog off the sea to improve the visibility, but a change to a much colder air-stream should clear it completely. If the warm air-stream continues, then the fog could hang around for a few days.

Land fog (radiation fog)

This fog, which forms on the land, is most commonly found in autumn and in winter.

During an autumn day with clear skies and a light wind, the land can heat up quickly. Once the sun has set, the air above the land cools down quickly with the clear skies, but the land is just like a radiator and will continue to radiate heat for much of the night. If there is no wind at all, then the visibility will remain good but dew will form. The moment a light wind causes turbulence to the warm radiating air it will cool rapidly to below its dew point and fog will form (Figure 17.7). The thickest patches will be found in damp river valleys and over moorland around dawn. Towns may remain clear due to the dry roads, street lamps and heat escaping from buildings.

Once daylight returns and the sun begins to heat the air again, the fog will thin and burn off (Figure 17.8).

Radiation fog lies in river valleys that connect to the sea, and this type of fog often drifts out to sea to a distance of 8 miles or so during the hours of darkness. If radiation fog is expected, then 'coastal fog patches' will be forecast. Once offshore, the visibility should improve dramatically.

▶ **Fig 17.7** *The fog slides out to sea to give coastal fog patches.*

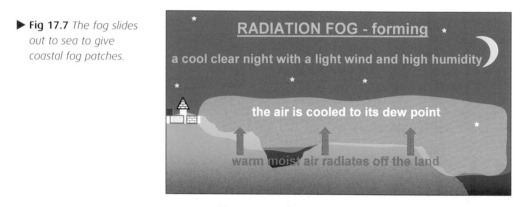

RADIATION FOG - forming

a cool clear night with a light wind and high humidity

the air is cooled to its dew point

warm moist air radiates off the land

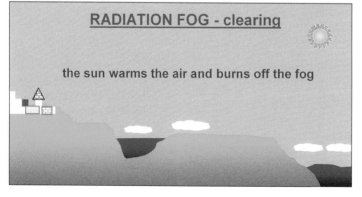

RADIATION FOG - clearing

the sun warms the air and burns off the fog

◀ **Fig 17.8** *The heat of the sun burns the fog off during the morning.*

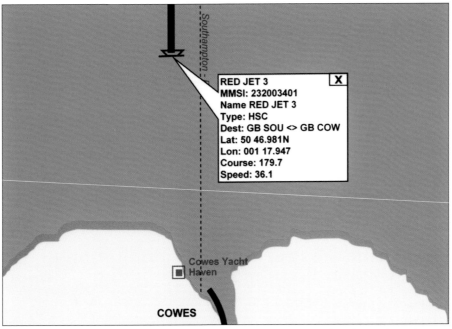

Fig 17.9 *Information about the Southampton–Cowes catamaran displayed on a chart plotter.*

Automatic Identification System (AIS)

Merchant ships over 300 tons carry a box of electronic wizardry called AIS. This is a navigation and surveillance system capable of automatically providing information about a ship to others and to coastal authorities. These commercial craft are fitted with expensive transponders that give the vessel's position, destination, course, speed, VHF MMSI and a lot more besides. An example of a full AIS display is shown in Figure 17.9.

Recently, a leisure version has been marketed that could prove invaluable to small craft in foggy conditions. As it is a receiver only it is relatively inexpensive, but gives all the vital information needed for collision avoidance. However, the small craft would not be visible on the merchantman's display.

FOG: KNOWLEDGE CHECK

1 Did the SOLAS Convention decide that radar reflectors should be fitted to:
   a) commercial craft only? b) leisure craft only? c) all craft?

2 How should an octahedral radar reflector be mounted to give the maximum radar return?

3 List five actions to be taken when entering fog.

4 How often should a fog signal be sounded from a craft under way?

5 Does sea fog form with:
   a) warm air over warm water? b) warm air over cold water? c) cold air over cold water?

6 What clears radiation fog?

CHAPTER EIGHTEEN

PASSAGE PLANNING

In the last chapter of most novels, everything comes together – the plot unravels, the boy wins the girl, or the villain is unmasked. This book is no different; we are going to bring together all our newly acquired knowledge of navigation, pilotage and weather to plan a visit to another port using a boat chartered out of the beautiful River Dart. The proposed date is 18 August, but we have not yet decided whether to take a 9-metre cruising yacht or a 9-metre motor cruiser. We will therefore hedge our bets and prepare a plan for each type.

Choosing the River Dart was a sound decision that has already been part of the planning process, because depending on the weather, the boat could go southwestwards to Salcombe, northwards to Torquay and Brixham, or to the upper reaches of the sheltered River Dart if the weather was bad. Figure 18.1 will give those not familiar with the Devon coast an estimate of the geography and mileage involved. The distances look ideal for our first trip as skipper.

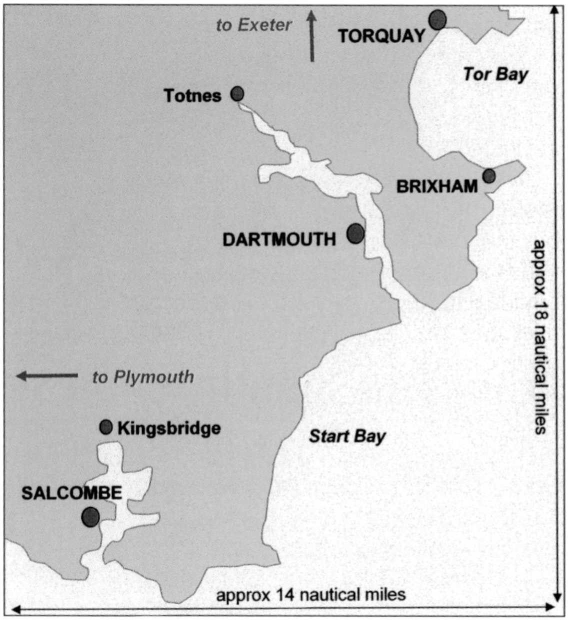

▶ **Fig 18.1** *The coast of South Devon from Torquay to Salcombe.*

Factors to Consider

Before going any further, we have to ask ourselves 'Are both boat and crew suitable for a passage in either direction?'

Boat

Both the boats we are considering are large enough to look after us on a coastal passage in moderate weather. The motor cruiser would be most adversely affected by wind over tide conditions, particularly around the headland to the east of Salcombe, but the yacht should cope with all parts of the passage in moderate winds.

Crew

The crew have joined the boat to have fun. Their enjoyment will be greatly enhanced if they feel safe under the care of a competent, relaxed skipper. Many souls suffer from seasickness, particularly when they are apprehensive, and the very young suffer from boredom if the passage is more than a few miles. A caring skipper will always be willing to adapt a plan to make life more comfortable for everyone on board.

Our crew for 18 August are very inexperienced, and one of them is known to get queasy on the cross-Channel ferry. It will therefore be wise to remain in sheltered water.

Weather

Old salts will begin looking at the weather patterns at least a week before setting out on a passage. The five-day forecast gives a good indication as to how settled the weather will be. A succession of depressions over the area in the days immediately preceding the jaunt may mean that a weather window might be hard to find, so let us look at the weather chart in Figure 18.2.

We seem to be in luck as a high to the west is giving northwest winds and settled weather, but the spacing of the isobars shows that the winds are likely to be too light for a good sail, but ideal for a motor cruiser. Depending on the tidal streams, the weather is suitable for going north or south.

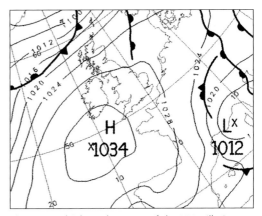

Fig 18.2 A high to the west of the UK will give northwest winds in Devon.

What are the tides doing on 18 August?

Figure 18.3 shows that the tides for Saturday 18 August are:

HW 1001 BST 4.3m
LW 1.1m
HW 2207 BST 4.4m

The range tells us that it is about mid range. Now we need to look at the tidal stream atlas to see in which direction the stream is running during the morning and afternoon.

▶ **Fig 18.3** Dartmouth tides for 18 August.

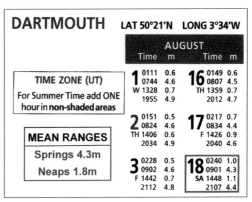

DARTMOUTH LAT 50°21'N LONG 3°34'W

	AUGUST		
TIME ZONE (UT)	Time m		Time m
	1 0111 0.6		**16** 0149 0.6
For Summer Time add ONE	0744 4.6		0807 4.5
hour in non-shaded areas	W 1328 0.7		TH 1359 0.7
	1955 4.9		2012 4.7
	2 0151 0.5		**17** 0217 0.7
MEAN RANGES	0824 4.6		0834 4.4
	TH 1406 0.6		F 1426 0.9
Springs 4.3m	2034 4.9		2040 4.6
	3 0228 0.5		**18** 0240 1.0
Neaps 1.8m	0902 4.6		0901 4.3
	F 1442 0.7		SA 1448 1.1
	2112 4.8		2107 4.4

The tidal streams

If you look at Figure 18.4 you will see that the times of the two high waters have been entered on the HW chartlet together with the 'HW hour' for the morning tide. As we intend to return to Dartmouth before dark, there is no need to write the evening 'HW hour' times as well. As the stream is setting northwards until 1330, southwards until 1937, Torbay seems to be the perfect place to go. The northern part of the bay would remain sheltered should the wind pipe up from the northwest, whereas Brixham would be exposed. We decide to go to Torquay.

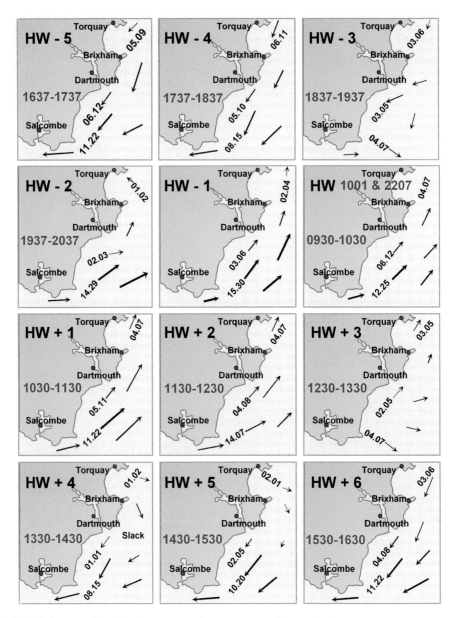

Fig 18.4 *Tidal streams along the Devon coast for 18 August. The two high waters are at 1001 and 2207 BST. That gives a north-going stream during the forenoon and a south-going one for the return to Dartmouth later in the day.*

The Plan

The Admiralty chart for the area shows us that the distance from the Dart entrance is about 10½ miles that will take about two hours in the yacht and under an hour in the motor cruiser. The streams are favourable until lunchtime, so we will carry the stream all the way without having to rise with the lark on a Saturday morning. If we decide to take the motor cruiser and the wind is blowing stronger than forecast, it would give a calmer sea if we left after 1230 when the streams are almost slack. The yacht should depart by 1000 to take advantage of the stronger streams.

The turning points in the passage are entered as waypoints in the GPS – identical points for both types of boat except that the yacht will have to tack between waypoints 3 and 4 because of the wind direction. The GPS entries are checked by comparing bearings and distances on each leg.

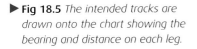

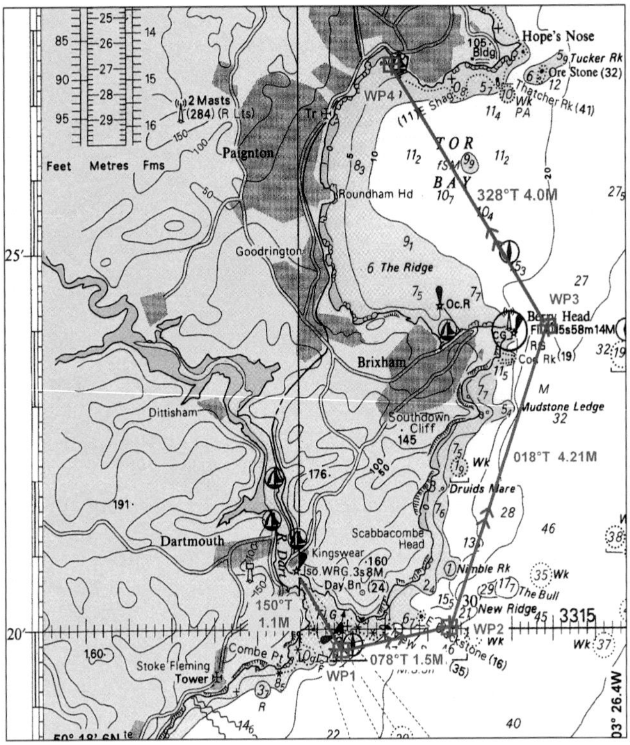

▶ **Fig 18.5** *The intended tracks are drawn onto the chart showing the bearing and distance on each leg.*

Leaving Dartmouth

This is the first time we have cruised from Dartmouth, so we consult our trusty almanac for information about the port (Figure 18.6) and make a few notes on the port plan (Figure 18.7).

DARTMOUTH

Devon 50°20′·66N 03°33′·96W ✱✱✱❄❄❄❄❄❄❄

CHARTS AC *1613, 1634, 5602, 2253*; Imray C5, 2400.1 & 4; Stanfords 2, 12, 22, L15; OS 202

TIDES –0510 Dover; ML 2·8; Duration 0630; Zone 0 (UT)

DARTMOUTH The differences below refer to Dartmouth predictions, not to Plymouth.

Times				Height (metres)			
High Water		Low Water		MHWS	MHWN	MLWN	MLWS
0100	0600	0100	0600	4·9	3·8	2·0	0·6
1300	1800	1300	1800				
Differences GREENWAY QUAY (DITTISHAM)							
+0015	+0020	+0025	+0010	0·0	0·0	0·0	0·0
TOTNES							
+0015	+0015	+0115	+0035	–1·4	–1·5	Dries	Dries

SHELTER Excellent shelter inside the hbr and up-river.

NAVIGATION WPT 50°19′·53N 03°32′·83W, 328°/1·5M in the white sector of Kingswear Dir lt. Bayard's Cove Dir lt leads 293° to abeam Royal Dart YC where the main fairway opens. There is no bar and hbr access is H24, but ent can be difficult in strong SE to SW winds. Speed limit 6kn from Castle Ledge buoy up-river to 1M below Totnes. *Caution:* The Lower and Higher car ferries S and N of Dartmouth have right of way; give way early.

LIGHTS AND MARKS as on the chartlet and/or 9.1.4. E of the ent, on Inner Froward Pt (167m) is a conspic daymark, obelisk (24·5m). Lateral and cardinal lt buoys mark all dangers to seaward of conspic Dartmouth Castle. Within hbr, all jetty/pontoon lts to the W are 2FR (vert); and 2FG (vert) to the E.

R/T, HM: *Dartnav* VHF Ch 11 (summer, daily 0730-dusk). Darthaven, Dart and Noss-on-Dart marinas, Ch 80. Fuel barge Ch 06. Water taxis: *Dartmouth water taxi* Ch 08 or ☎ 07770 628967 (run by Res Nova Inn, next to No 6 buoy). *Yacht taxi (DHNA)* Ch 69 or 11, ☎ 07970 346571, summer 0800-2300. *Greenway ferry* Ch 10 or ☎ 844010 (to Dittisham), daily 364/365. Darthaven marina ☎ 752545, 🖷 752722. www.darthaven.co.uk 250+20 ♥, £2.00 + hbr dues. ME, El, Ⓔ, Gas, Gaz, Ⓞ, ✗, CH, BH (35 ton). Dart marina ☎ 832580, 🖷 835040. yachtharbour@dartmarina.com www.dartmarina.com 100 +10 ♥s, £3.23+hbr dues. C (9 ton), R, Ⓞ. Noss-on-Dart marina ☎ 833351, 🖷 835150. 150 AB, £3.23 + hbr dues. ME, El, ✗, C (18 ton), CH, Gas, Gaz, Ⓞ, good repair facilities.

YACHT CLUBS (visitors welcome): **Royal Dart YC** ☎ 752272, M, short stay pontoon, FW, Bar, R ☎ 752880. **Dartmouth YC** ☎ 832305, L, FW, Bar, R. **Royal Regatta,** last week Aug.

SERVICES Fuel Barge next to No 6 buoy, Ch 06, D, P; ☎ 07801 798861 summer 0800-1800; winter, 'phone to check. **Creekside BY** (Old Mill Creek) ☎ 832649, Slip, dry dock, M, ME, ✗, El, C (14 ton), CH, AB (customer only), FW. **Dartside Quay** (Galmpton Creek): CH, D, FW, L, M, C (6 ton), ME, ✗, SM, BY, Slip, ⬚Ⓓ, BH (65, 16 ton), El, Ⓔ.

Fig 18.6 *Dartmouth port information.*

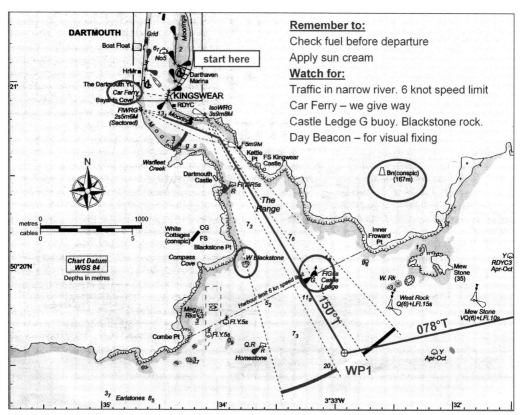

Fig 18.7 *Dartmouth is accessible at all states of the tide and is sheltered from northwest winds.*

Dangers en route

There are numerous rocks outside the Dart entrance, but looking at Figure 18.5, all the ones en route are marked with cardinal buoys.

Nimble Rock (off Scabbacombe Head) has 3 metres of water over it at LW, which gives us a good clearance. Watch out for swimmers and canoeists in the controlled areas that are marked with yellow special buoys (SPM) in Tor Bay.

Torquay

We decide to go into the marina so that we can have a look at the town, so we make further notes about the harbour using Figure 18.8:

1 Access 24 hours.
2 Good lookout needed at the marina entrance due to a blind bend.
3 Marina listens on Channel 80 VHF.
4 Visitors berth at the ends of A, B and C pontoons.

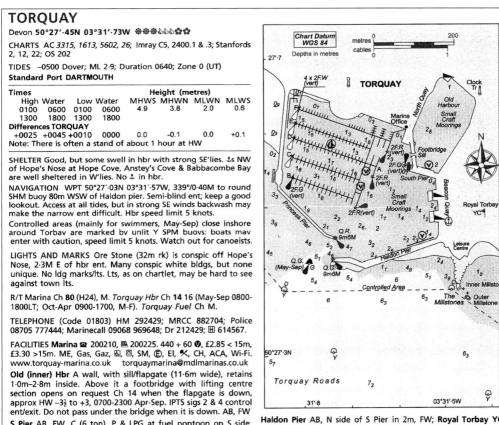

TORQUAY

Devon **50°27'·45N 03°31'·73W** ❄❄❄�☆☆

CHARTS AC *3315, 1613, 5602, 26*; Imray C5, 2400.1 & .3; Stanfords 2, 12, 22; OS 202

TIDES −0500 Dover; ML 2·9; Duration 0640; Zone 0 (UT)
Standard Port DARTMOUTH

Times				Height (metres)			
High Water		Low Water		MHWS	MHWN	MLWN	MLWS
0100	0600	0100	0600	4.9	3.8	2.0	0.6
1300	1800	1300	1800				
Differences TORQUAY							
+0025	+0045	+0010	0000	0.0	-0.1	0.0	+0.1

Note: There is often a stand of about 1 hour at HW

SHELTER Good, but some swell in hbr with strong SE'lies. ⚓s NW of Hope's Nose at Hope Cove, Anstey's Cove & Babbacombe Bay are well sheltered in W'lies. No ⚓ in hbr.

NAVIGATION WPT 50°27'·03N 03°31'·57W, 339°/0·40M to round SHM buoy 80m WSW of Haldon pier. Semi-blind ent; keep a good lookout. Access at all tides, but in strong SE winds backwash may make the narrow ent difficult. Hbr speed limit 5 knots.

Controlled areas (mainly for swimmers, May-Sep) close inshore around Torbay are marked by unlit Y SPM buoys: boats may enter with caution, speed limit 5 knots. Watch out for canoeists.

LIGHTS AND MARKS Ore Stone (32m rk) is conspic off Hope's Nose, 2·3M E of hbr ent. Many conspic white bldgs, but none unique. No ldg marks/lts. Lts, as on chartlet, may be hard to see against town lts.

R/T Marina Ch **80** (H24), M. *Torquay Hbr* Ch **14** 16 (May-Sep 0800-1800LT; Oct-Apr 0900-1700, M-F). *Torquay Fuel* Ch M.

TELEPHONE (Code 01803) HM 292429; MRCC 882704; Police 08705 777444; Marinecall 09068 969648; Dr 212429; ⊞ 614567.

FACILITIES **Marina** ☎ 200210, 🖷 200225. 440 + 60 ⓥ, £2.85 < 15m, £3.30 >15m. ME, Gas, Gaz, 🔌, 🔋, SM, ⒺE, EI, ✖, CH, ACA, Wi-Fi. www.torquay-marina.co.uk   torquaymarina@mdlmarinas.co.uk
Old (inner) Hbr A wall, with sill/flapgate (11·6m wide), retains 1·0m–2·8m inside. Above it a footbridge with lifting centre section opens on request Ch 14 when the flapgate is down, approx HW −3½ to +3, 0700-2300 Apr-Sep. IPTS sigs 2 & 4 control ent/exit. Do not pass under the bridge when it is down. AB, FW
S Pier AB, FW, C (6 ton), P & LPG at fuel pontoon on S side: Torquay Fuel ☎ 294509 & VHF Ch M (Apr-Sept, 0830-1900 Mon-Sat, 1000-1900 Sun).

Haldon Pier AB, N side of S Pier in 2m, FW; **Royal Torbay YC** ☎ 292006, R, Bar.

Town 🚉, D, 🔋, Bar, R, @, ✉, Ⓑ, ⇌, ✈ (Exeter or Plymouth).

Fig 18.8 *An extract from* Reeds Nautical Almanac *giving Torquay port information.*

Using a Chart Plotter to Plan a Passage

You may remember that, when we were planning the trip to Torquay, we drew the intended tracks and waypoints onto a paper chart, measured the latitude and longitude of the waypoints, and then entered the waypoint co-ordinates into the GPS (Figure 18.5). Finally, we needed to check that the bearings and distances from waypoint to waypoint in the GPS were the same as those on the chart.

This task could have been done more easily using an electronic chart plotter as the waypoints can be entered visually

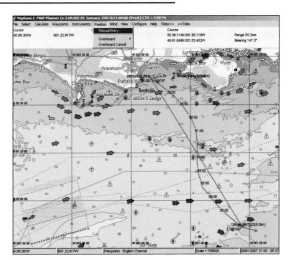

Fig 18.9 *A Neptune passage planning program displayed on a PC.*

instead of using measured co-ordinates from the chart. Lines are drawn electronically, and it is easy to see whether a line passes through safe water or over a rocky patch – altogether much easier and arguably safer when planning a trip.

Passage planning software packages that can be run on a laptop computer or pocket PC are also available. Figure 18.9 illustrates a cross-channel passage on one from the reliable Neptune range of programs in which C-Map charts are used. Notice that the straight line represents the ground track from Poole and the red arrows show the tidal stream.

PASSAGE PLANNING: KNOWLEDGE CHECK

1 List four factors that should be considered when planning a short coastal passage.

2 Using Figure 18.3, will the tidal stream be running southward or northward at 1645 off Dartmouth?

3 Using Figure 18.6, will the LW time at Totnes be earlier or later than LW Dartmouth?

4 List three features that could be used to check your position with a hand-bearing compass from the centre of Tor Bay? Use Figure 18.5.

5 Which wind direction may make Torquay marina entrance difficult to negotiate?

6 Is fuel available at Torquay marina?

ANSWERS TO KNOWLEDGE CHECK QUESTIONS

1: ABOUT BOATS – SAIL AND POWER

1 The leeward side.
2 Luff.
3 Badly.
4 Pilots, police boats.
5 Port tab up.

2: KNOWING THE ROPES

1 Mooring lines.
2 Polypropylene.
3 A mooring line that prevents the boat moving astern.
4 Clockwise.
5 Make sure that is led through a fairlead. Use plastic tubing to cover the rope at chafe points or wrap the rope in material.
6 Sideways movement is minimised so that the transom remains at right-angles to the quay.

3: ANCHORS AND ANCHORING

1 A windlass under load drains the battery so the engine should be run to keep the batteries healthy.
2 Depth – nature of the seabed – shelter – swinging room – out of channel – out of strong stream – close to landing – able to leave safely in darkness.
3 Into tide.
4 At least 30 metres – preferably 40 metres if sufficient cable.
5 An all-round white light.

4: KEEPING SAFE

1 2 x Red parachute plus 2 x Red handheld plus 2 x Orange smoke.

2 When the cooker is not in use.

3 This is how much weight the jacket can support; 150 Newtons should support the average adult.

4 The windward side.

5 So that they do not blow downwind too quickly once deployed.

6 The bow of the boat is turned through the wind without releasing the foresail sheet. This leaves the boat in the 'heave-to position' which will stop the boat making any appreciable way forward.

5: COMMUNICATIONS

1 Low power.

2 Any three from:
Broadcasting music and football scores.
Indecent or profane language.
Sending a hoax distress.
Sending a distress message without the Master's permission.
Passing on information heard over the radio.
Using the radio unsupervised if not the holder of an operator's licence.
Transmitting without identification.
Using the hand-held radio when ashore.
General chitchat.

3 Channels 6, 8, 72, and 77.

4 A unique 9-digit number which identifies a craft using Digital Selective Calling.

5 When there is grave and imminent danger to life, a vessel, an aircraft or other vehicle where immediate assistance is required.

6 Channel 67.

6: AVOIDING A COLLISION

1 A black ball hoisted in the rigging in the fore part of the vessel.
2 One prolonged blast (5 seconds) at intervals not exceeding 2 minutes.
3 One short blast means that he is a power-driven vessel and that he is altering course to starboard.
4 The overtaking vessel.
5 **b)** Ensign upside down.
6 No. The tri-lantern is for sailing only; it should not be used in conjunction with any other light.

7: THE ENGINE

1 Suck, squeeze, bang, blow.
2 The pre-filter, sometimes called the water trap, filters water and large particles of dirt from the fuel.
3 The alternator will not turn so the batteries will not be charged. The water pump will also not turn so the engine will overheat.
4 Black smoke.
5 When the filters are changed and if air is sucked in from a nearly empty fuel tank.
6 To stop the boat flooding (low strainer) and to prevent an air lock (high strainer).

8: ABOUT CHARTS

1 **a)** 1,852 metres.
   b) 185 metres.
2 Longitude.
3 Because of the projection method, distortion occurs with an increase in distance from the Equator.
4 Metres.
5 **a)** Dangerous wreck.
   b) Rock, which covers and uncovers.
   c) Major light.
   d) Public slipway.
   e) Overfalls or tide rips.
6 Online from UKHO website (www.ukho.gov.uk) or from some yachting magazines.

9: COMPASSES

1 You are heading southeast.

2 The compass would be reading 225°.

3 **a)** 130°M. **b)** 004°M. **c)** 170°M.

4 **a)** 321°T. **b)** 352°T. **c)** 275°T.

5 Deviation on 045°M = 1°E.

6 A heading of 045°T + 5°W = 050°M.
Compass reads 055°C so there is 5° deviation.
The compass reads BEST (greater), so the deviation must be 5°W.

10: CHARTWORK – FIRST STEPS

See chart extract opposite.

1 It is best to use a 2B pencil because it is soft and does not damage the chart.

2 1.5 nautical miles.

3 033°T.

4 327°T 3.7 nautical miles.

5 **a)** 216°T = 221°M.

6 **b)** 3.0 nautical miles.

11: TIDES AND TIDAL STREAMS

1 Springs.

2 Clearance heights are measured above Highest Astronomical Tide.

3 1.8m.

4 Corrections should be added to the UT time.

5 110°T 1.2m.

6 False.

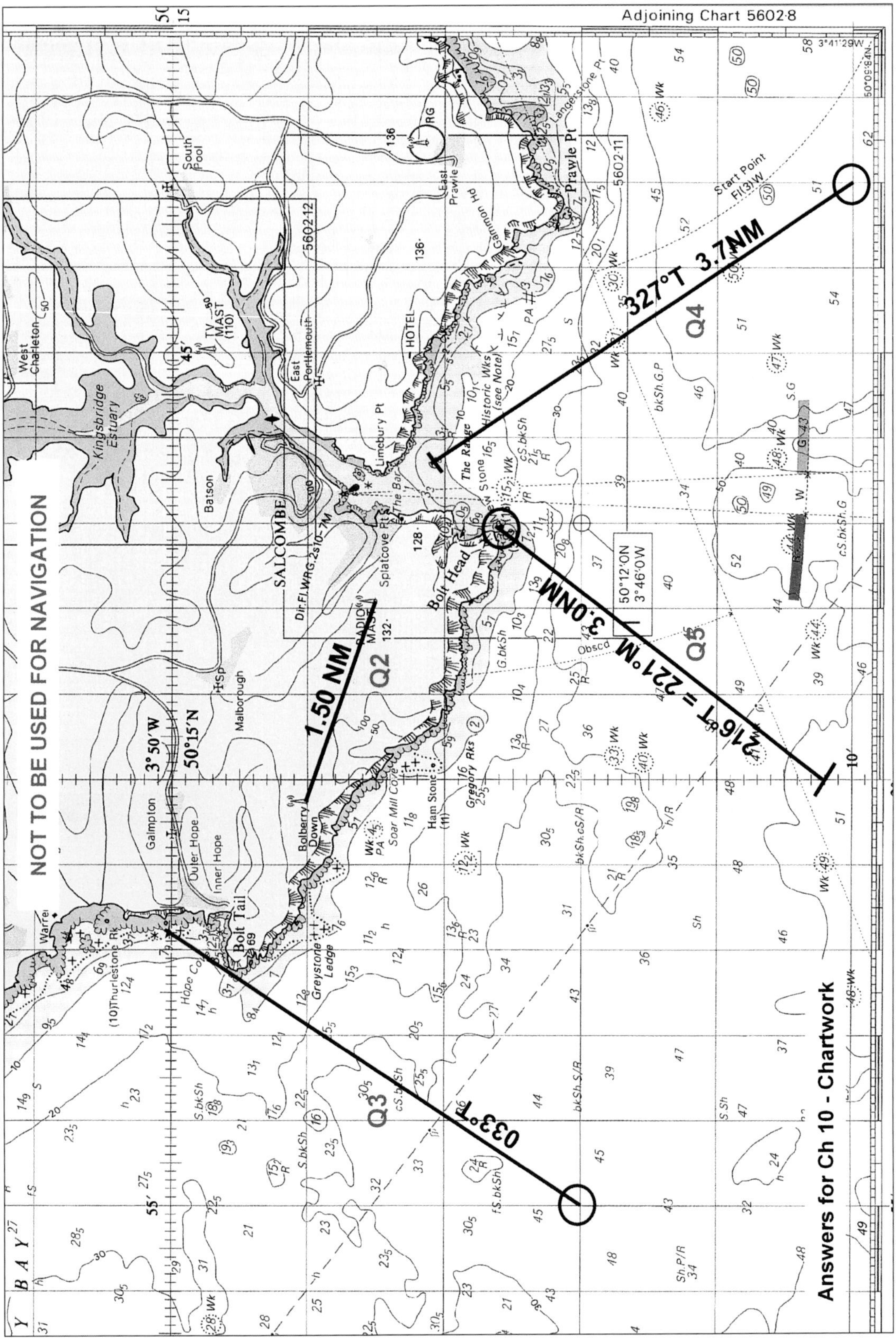
Answers for Ch 10 - Chartwork
NOT TO BE USED FOR NAVIGATION
Adjoining Chart 5602·8
Q2
1.50 NM
Q3
033°T
Q4
327°T 3.7NM
Q5
216°T = 221°M
3.0NM
SALCOMBE
Bolt Head
Bolt Tail
Prawle Pt
Start Point
Kingsbridge Estuary
50°12'·0N
3°46'·0W
3°50'W
50°15'N

12: FINDING OUR POSITION

See chart extract opposite.

1 50° 19'.20N 4° 15'.65W.

2 50° 21'.25N 4° 19'.10W.

3 **a)** 50° 17'.55N 4° 06'.10W.
   b) the boat covers 3 miles in 10 minutes. The SOG is therefore 18 knots.

4 **a)** 50° 15'.75N 4° 12'.50W.
   b) She passes to the east of the wreck.

5 **a)** See plot on chart.
   b) No. The boat will track down the line with two arrows.
   c) The COG will be 316°T.

6 **a)** See plot on chart.
   b) 50° 16'.40N 4° 17'.35W.

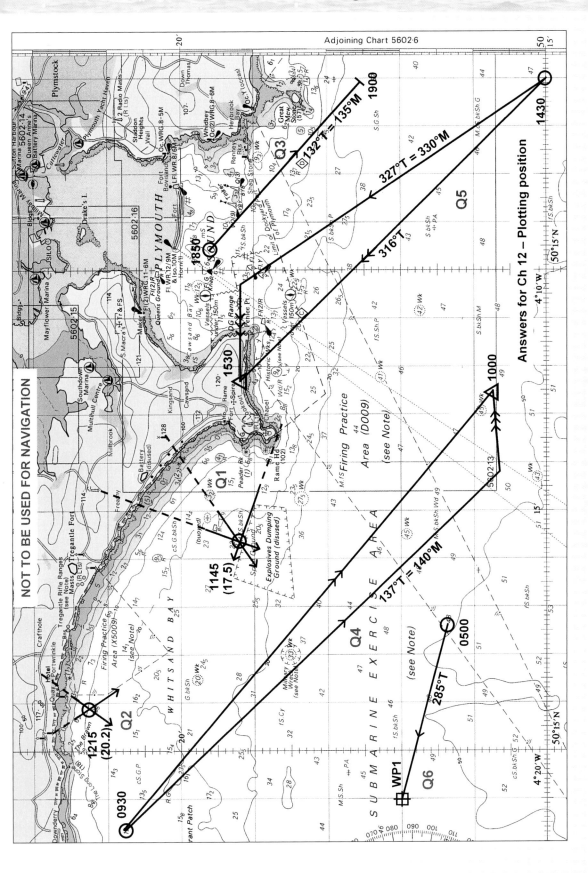

13: COURSE TO STEER

See chart extract opposite.

1 a) 348°T + 3°W Variation = 351°M.
  b) More than one hour.

2 a) 289°T = 3°W Variation = 292°M.
  b) Speed over ground = 4 knots.

3 a) 300°T + 3°W variation = 303°M.
  b) 5.0 miles in 30 minutes = 10 knots.
  c) 304°M less 10° leeway = 294°M. Aim into the wind.

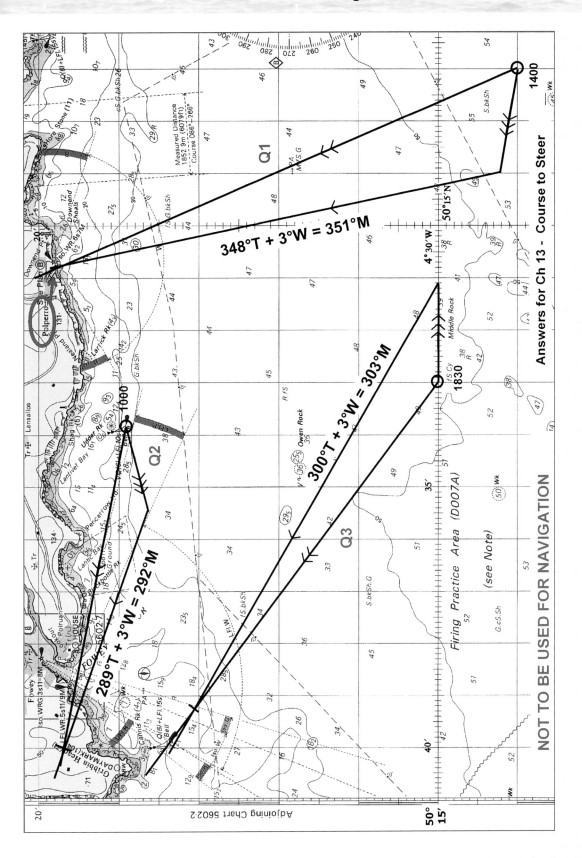

Answers for Ch 13 - Course to Steer

NOT TO BE USED FOR NAVIGATION

14: BUOYS, BEACONS AND LIGHTS

1 Yellow. Used for racing marks, water-ski areas and gunnery ranges, etc and not considered to be of navigational significance.
2 The period of light and darkness are equal.
3 Two black cones with the points together, bases of the triangles at the top and bottom.
4 The northern side.
5 Starboard.

15: PILOTAGE

1 To starboard.
2 Proceed only when instructed. Small craft may be exempt.
3 Course over the ground.
4 Admiralty chart 1267, 148, 31. Imray C6,2400.7/8, Stanfords 2, 23.
5 Channel 12.
6 Udder Rock, Cannis Rock, Punch Cross Rocks and Boddinnick Ferry.

16: WEATHER

1 HM Coastguard.
2 Within six hours from the time of issue. Between 1100 and 1700.
3 When the wind is expected to reach Force 6.
4 Windy, overcast, intermittent rain and drizzle, poor visibility and barometric pressure falling more slowly.
5 Light.
6 Teatime. This is because the land is at its hottest and air is rising away from the surface quickly. Air blows from the high pressure area over the sea to fill the low pressure area over the land.

17: FOG

1 **c)** All craft.
2 The octahedral reflector should be hoisted in the 'catch rain' position.
3 Any five from:
   a) Hoist radar reflector.
   b) Turn on navigation lights.
   c) Sound a fog signal.
   d) Crew on deck in lifejackets.
   e) Consider making towards shallow water.
   f) Plot the boat's position.
   g) Listen on port operations frequency.
   h) Consider anchoring.
   i) Prepare pilotage plan for entering harbour.
4 At intervals not exceeding 2 minutes.
5 **b)** Sea fog forms when warm air blows over a cold surface.
6 The heat of the sun will burn off radiation fog.

18: PASSAGE PLANNING

1 Any four from:
   a) The boat – suitability for the passage.
   b) The crew – experience and strengths/weaknesses.
   c) Weather and shelter.
   d) Tidal stream – direction and rate, around headlands.
   e) Dangers en route, areas to be avoided.
   f) Access times to port of departure and destination.
   g) VHF information for marinas and harbourmasters.
   h) Availability of fuel, water, etc.
2 The stream will be south-going.
3 Later.
4 Any three from:
   Berry Head lighthouse.
   Church in Paignton.
   Brixham breakwater.
   Radio masts west of Paignton.
   Ore Stone (32 metres).
   Thatcher Rock (41 metres).
   Hope's Nose (headland).
5 Strong southeast winds.
6 No, it is available at South Pier.

GLOSSARY OF NAUTICAL TERMS

AIS	Automatic Identification System.
Abeam	At right-angles to the fore-and-aft line of the boat.
Ahead	The direction directly in front of the boat.
Aloft	Above deck level; up the mast.
Anchor buoy	Small buoy attached to a tripping line on the crown of the anchor.
Anchor light	A white all-round light hoisted up the mast or positioned at the masthead.
Anchor winch	Winch used to assist with the raising and lowering of the anchor and its cable.
Astern	Direction directly behind the boat.
Back (1)	The wind backs when its direction shifts in a counter-clockwise direction.
Back (2)	To 'back the headsail' is to turn the boat so that the headsail is on the 'wrong' side.
Back spring	A securing rope that prevents the craft from moving aft.
Backstay	A wire between the top of the mast and the stern of the hull.
Bar	An area near the mouth of a river where the water flow causes silting, resulting in a shallow patch.
Bathing platform	A structure on the stern of a boat for easy access to the water. Frequently provided with an 'after swim' shower.
Batten	A stiff slat, of either wood or composite material, used to control the curve of a sail.
Batten pocket	A pocket on the sail where the batten is inserted.
Beam	The width of the boat.
Beam reach	A point of sailing with the apparent wind on the beam.
Bear away	To alter course away from the wind.
Bearing	The direction, normally measured in degrees, from the observer to the object described.
Beat	To sail on alternate tacks towards a position that is upwind of the boat.
Beaufort scale	Admiral Beaufort's scale of wind strengths used in maritime forecasts.
Bilge	The area of a boat underneath the cabin sole (floor) where water can collect.
Bilge keel	Twin keels that enable the hull to remain upright on the seabed at LW.
Bilge pump	A hand or electrical pump designed to empty the bilge.
Binnacle	A structure near the helmsman's position housing the compass and other instrumentation.
Black ball	A single black ball hoisted by day near the bow of the vessel to indicate that it is at anchor. Required by the International Rules for Preventing Collisions at Sea.
Boathook	A hook on a pole used to pick up mooring buoys, etc. Using it to hold onto another boat is unpopular!
Bollard	A strong metal pillar on a dock or quay around which a rope is placed for securing the craft alongside.
Boom	Metal or wooden spar to which the foot of the mainsail is attached. Hurts if it hits you!

Boom vang   A device for pulling the boom down in order to flatten the mainsail.

Bottlescrew   A screw fitting on guardrails and fixed rigging (shrouds and stays); used to tension the wire.

Bow roller   A metal roller at the bow of a boat over which the anchor chain runs.

Bow thrusters   An electrically driven propeller fitted low on the bow of a craft to aid manoeuvre at slow speeds in confined spaces.

Braided rope   A low-stretch rope protected with a woven cover.

Breast ropes   Mooring lines run at right-angles to the fore-and-aft line of the vessel.

Broach   When a heavy following sea causes the boat to slew round towards the wind. In a sailing boat, this can result in a large angle of heel.

Broadreach   A point of sailing between running with the wind astern and sailing with the wind on the beam.

Broken water   An isolated area of the sea with small breaking waves. Often caused by a rough seabed and a strong tidal flow.

Bruce   A type of claw anchor.

Bulkhead   A partition built across the width of the hull.

Burgee   A small triangular flag flown from the masthead or crosstrees to indicate membership of a yacht club or organisation.

COG   The course over the ground. The resultant of heading, tidal movement and leeway.

Cable   A distance of one-tenth of a nautical mile. Approx 185 metres.

Calm   A state when the sea is smooth with little or no wind.

Cardinal marks   Navigational buoys marking the geographical position of a danger: North, East, South and West.

Cast off   An instruction to release or let go of a rope or line.

Catamaran   A twin-hull yacht.

Centre of buoyancy Geometric centre of that part of the hull that is below the waterline.

Centre of gravity A theoretical position where the weight of the vessel appears to be centred.

Chain plate   A metal strip on the hull to which the rigging wires (shrouds) are attached.

Chart datum   The level from which depth soundings are measured. It approximates to the level of the lowest astronomical tide.

Charted depth   The height of water between the seabed and chart datum. This measurement is printed on charts with 'soundings'.

Charted height   The height of a structure such as a lighthouse above MHWS.

Chine   The corner-like intersection where the bottom of the boat is joined to the hull.

Clearance height   The height of a bridge or cable above HAT (Highest Astronomical Tide).

Clearing bearings The limits of a sector drawn on a chart that will enable the skipper to keep clear of dangers when entering a harbour or anchorage.

Cleat   A fitting, normally on deck, for securing lines and ropes.

Clew   The lower aft corner of a sail.

Close-hauled   Sailing as close to the wind as efficiency permits, with sheets hauled tight.

Cocked hat   The triangle formed on a chart when three (or more) position lines are drawn. Gives some indication of the size of the measurement error.

Companionway   Steps from the deck to the cabin below.

Courtesy ensign   A small ensign of the country being visited, normally hoisted on the starboard crosstrees as a courtesy to the host country.

CQR	A plough-style anchor.
Cringle	A small metal ring fitted to the sail.
Current	Movement of water caused by geographical features, eg 'the Gulf Stream'.
Cutter	Similar to a masthead sloop, but has a second foresail.
DTG	The distance to a waypoint or destination.
Danbuoy	A floating pole with flag used to mark the position of a man overboard.
Danforth	A two-part anchor.
Davit	A hoist for lifting a tender at the stern of a motor cruiser.
Deck log	Book in which all events and navigational data are recorded.
Delta	A one-part anchor.
Depth contours	Lines on a chart joining positions with the same charted depth.
Deviation	A correction to magnetic North to counteract errors caused by magnetic objects in a particular boat. It varies with the boat's heading.
Displacement	The weight of the craft. Equal to the weight of water displaced.
Drag (anchor)	A condition when the anchor slides over the seabed.
Drift	The distance the boat is carried by the tidal stream in a fixed time.
Drying height	The height of land that is uncovered at chart datum, but is covered at MHWS.
DSC	Digital Selective Calling – an electronic system for initiating radio contact between radio stations.
Ebb	The tidal stream that occurs when the tidal height is falling.
Echo sounder	An instrument that measures the depth of water by using sound waves.
Ensign	A flag flown at the stern of a boat which indicates the nationality of the craft.
EP	Estimated position. A calculated position, taking into account the heading through the water, leeway and the tidal stream.
EPIRB	Emergency Position Indicating Radio Beacon.
Fairlead	A fitting on the deck edge to reduce chafe on mooring lines.
Fairway	A passage of deeper water permitting entry to a port or harbour.
Fender	Strong, cylindrical inflatable plastic shape used to protect the hull when alongside a dock or another boat.
Fix	The geographical position of a boat obtained from compass or electronic bearings.
Flood	The tidal stream that occurs when the tidal height is rising.
Fluxgate compass	An electronic compass that can interface with navigation equipment.
Fly-bridge	An abbreviation for 'flying-bridge', an upper deck on a motor cruiser fitted with a second open-air steering position.
Fog	Visibility of less than 1,000 metres.
Foot	The lower edge of a sail.
Fore spring	A securing line that prevents the craft from moving forward.
Foredeck	The main deck at the fore end of the boat.
Foresail	A sail set on the forestay or inner forestay.
Fractional rig	When the forestay of a yacht is attached to the mast slightly below the masthead.

Freeboard	The distance between the waterline and the deck level.
Furl	To roll a sail – normally applies to a headsail when it is rolled around the forestay.
Genoa	A large headsail that overlaps the mainsail.
Go about (to)	To tack. To move the bow through the eye of the wind and set the sail on the other side.
Gooseneck	A jointed fitting that secures the boom to the mast.
GPS	Global Positioning System.
Great circle	A line on the surface of the Earth with the same circumference as the Equator. The shortest route between two points on the Earth's surface.
Ground (to)	To touch the seabed. To run aground.
Gybe	To turn the boat so that the stern passes through the wind permitting the sails to be set on the other side.
Halyard	The wire or rope used to hoist a sail.
HAT	Highest Astronomical Tide – the highest sea level, above chart datum, reached under normal meteorological conditions. HAT is used for clearance heights under bridges and cables.
Hawser laid	A rope, normally of three strands, twisted together in a clockwise direction.
Hatch	An opening in the deck with a sliding or hinged cover.
Haze	When the visibility is between 1,000 and 2,000 metres.
Head-to-wind	With the bow pointing directly into the wind.
Heading	The direction in which the boat is pointing.
Heads	The marine toilet. In days past, nearly always situated near the ship's head.
Headsail	Sail set forward of the mast.
Headway	Moving through the water in the direction the bow is pointing.
Heave-to	To stop a yacht at sea without lowering the sails. In a motor cruiser, to stop the engine at sea.
Height of tide	The vertical distance between the level of chart datum and the actual height of water.
Hi-line	Line passed from a search and rescue helicopter to a boat during a rescue.
Hoist	To raise an object such as a sail or flag using a halyard.
IALA	International Association of Lighthouse Authorities.
IALA A	System of buoyage used in areas other than the USA and Pacific rim countries.
IALA B	System of buoyage used in the USA and Pacific rim countries.
IMO	International Maritime Organisation.
IRPCS	International Rules for Preventing Collision at Sea.
Isobar	Line joining points of equal barometric pressure on a weather map.
Isophase	Light characteristic with equal periods of light and dark.
Jib	A triangular headsail set on the forestay.
Kedge anchor	Small anchor, often kept in a locker, used when anchoring for a short time or as a second anchor in strong wind conditions.
Ketch	Two-masted yacht where the after mast is forward of the rudder post.

Kicking strap	Device for pulling the boom down to flatten the bottom of the mainsail.
LAT	Lowest Asronomical Tide.
Lateral mark	Buoys marking the port and starboard side of a navigable channel.
Lead line	Length of cord, with lead weight at the end, used to measure the depth of water.
Leading lights	Lights erected by a harbour authority so that, by keeping the lights in line, a craft can remain in safe water while approaching the harbour at night.
Lee	The direction downwind.
Leech	The after edge of a sail.
Leeward	The opposite side of the boat from which the wind is blowing.
Leeway	Angular difference between the boat's heading and its course through the water caused by the wind pushing on the side of the boat.
Lifting keel	Keel that can be raised into the hull, permitting the boat to enter very shallow water.
LOA	Length overall – the maximum length of the craft.
Local time	Clock time at a specified place.
Log (1)	Instrument for measuring the distance run through the water.
Log (2)	Book in which an official record of the boat's movements is kept.
Luff	The front edge of the sail.
Luff (to)	To alter course towards the direction of the wind.
Magnetic North Pole	Geographical position in northern Canada to which the compass needle points.
Making way	A craft is 'making way' when it is moving through the water.
Mast-deck stepped	Mast that sits on the cabin roof.
Mast-keel stepped	Mast that passes through the cabin roof and sits on the top of the keel.
Masthead rig	The forestay is attached to the top of the mast.
Mercator projection	Technique used by cartographers to project the image of spherical Earth onto a flat sheet of paper.
MHWN	Mean high water neaps.
MHWS	Mean high water springs.
Mizzen mast	The aftermost mast on a yawl or ketch.
MLWN	Mean low water neaps.
MLWS	Mean low water springs.
MMSI	The nine-digit number given to DSC radios to identify the boat.
Monkey's fist	Large knot on the end of a throwing line.
Mooring buoy	An anchored buoy used for securing a boat.
MSI	Maritime Safety Information. Broadcasts made every three hours by HM Coastguard giving the weather forecast and navigational warnings.
Nautical mile	A unit of distance based on 1 minute of latitude (approx 1,820 metres).
Navtex	An electronic instrument for receiving weather forecasts and navigational data while at sea.
Neap tide	A tide when the tidal range is small and streams are at their weakest.
No Go Zone	The sector, close to the wind, within which a yacht cannot sail.

Nominal range   The nominal range of a light is dependent on the intensity of the light in meteorological visibility of 10 miles. Note that this takes no account of the curvature of the Earth. This range is shown on charts.

North-up mode   A radar picture, when North is at the top of the screen.

Not under command   A vessel that through some exceptional circumstance is unable to manoeuvre as required by the Rules for Preventing Collisions at Sea.

NUC   Not Under Command.

Occulting (Occ)   A light where the periods of light are longer than the periods of dark, ie it is on for longer than it is off.

On the bow   A sector within 45° either side of the bow.

On the quarter   A sector within 45° either side of the stern.

Open   When the leading marks are not in line they are described as 'open'.

Outboard engine   A portable engine clamped to the transom of a craft.

Overfalls   Turbulent sea caused by a sudden change in water depth. Effect increases in a strong tidal stream.

Overtaking light   The 135° white light at the stern.

Overtaking sector   An angle from 221.5° aft of the port beam, through the stern, to 221.5° aft of the starboard beam.

Painter   The line used to secure a dinghy.

Pay out   To ease out a line or rope slowly.

Period (of a light)   The time that a navigational light takes to complete one cycle.

Pick-up buoy   A small buoy attached to a large mooring by a pennant which can be hauled onto a boat when securing.

Pilotage   Using visual marks to navigate into creeks and harbours.

Plaited rope   Has eight strands; four plaited clockwise, four anticlockwise. Frequently used as an anchor warp.

Plot   To transfer a position to a chart.

Port   The left-hand side of a boat when looking forward.

Port beam   The direction on the left-hand side of the hull at right-angles to the fore-and-aft line.

Port bow   The sector from the fore and aft line to the port beam.

Port quarter   The sector from the port beam to the astern line.

Port tack   A point of sailing with the mainsail filled on the starboard side of the boat. (Wind to port.)

Position line   A line drawn on the chart giving one component of a fix.

Power trim   Allows the drive leg on the more powerful outboard engines to be trimmed away from the hull to help the propeller operate more efficiently.

Preventer   A line rigged to secure the boom to prevent an accidental gybe.

Prime meridian   An imaginary line drawn on the Earth's surface from the North Pole to the South Pole passing through Greenwich, London. Used internationally as the origin of longitude measurements.

Pulpit   Metal frame round the bow at deck level to protect the working crew.

Pushpit   Metal frame round the stern at deck level to protect the crew.

Radar reflector   When hoisted up the mast, this enhances the radar echo seen by shipping.

Range of tide	The difference between water height at HW and water height at LW.
Reach	A point of sailing between close-hauled and running free.
Reefing (to reef)	To reduce the area of a sail.
Reefing pennant	A rope used to reduce the area of a sail.
Registered tonnage	A measure of the volume of the craft – not the weight. Originally used for taxation purposes.
Relative wind	The wind you feel. The resultant of true wind and boat movement.
Repeater	A duplicate instrument display used when information is required in more than one position on the boat, ie on the fly-bridge and close to the inside steering position.
Rhumb line	A line that crosses each meridian of latitude at a constant angle on a Mercator chart. NOT the shortest route.
RIB	Semi Rigid Inflatable Boat with a rigid glassfibre base and inflatable tubes above the waterline.
Riding turn	Occurs when the turns on a winch become crossed and then jam.
Roach	Outward curve on the mainsail leech supported by battens.
Rope clutch	A jamming device that grips a rope, making a cleat unnecessary.
Rubbing strake	Wooden moulding on outside of the hull to reduce chafe when alongside.
Running	Sailing with the wind from astern.
Running by the lee	When the wind is blowing from the same side of the boat as the mainsail. There will be the possibility of a gybe.
RYA	Royal Yachting Association. The governing body of the sport of sailing in the UK.
SOG	The speed of the vessel over the ground.
Sail ties	Lengths of light line or tape used to secure a sail to the boom after lowering.
Schooner	A yacht in which the after mast is taller than the mainmast.
Sea anchor	A device used to hold the head of the boat into the wind when neither sailing nor anchored.
Sea clutter	A control on a radar display that reduces unwanted beam reflections caused by a wave close to the ship.
Self-tailing winch	A winch fitted with a rope-gripping device above the drum.
Set	The direction towards which the tidal stream flows.
Sheet	A control rope attached to the clew of a sail (or to the boom in the case of the mainsheet).
Shorten sail	To reef the sails or change the sails to a smaller size.
Shroud	A wire providing athwartship support to the mast.
Shroud laid	A rope, normally of four strands, twisted together in a clockwise direction.
Sill	A wall or dam across the entrance to a harbour or marina.
Slip line	Shore lines that are passed from the boat, round a fitting and returned to the boat to permit easy release without standing on the shore.
Sloop	A one-masted sailing boat designed for one headsail.
SOLAS	Safety of Life at Sea Convention.
Special marks	Buoys that have no navigational marks, eg marks used for racing. Coloured yellow.
Sports bridge cruiser	A fast motor cruiser with no fly-bridge.
Spreaders	An athwartship strut on the mast to spread the shrouds to support the mast.

Spring tide	A tide where the tidal range is large and streams are at their strongest.
Springs	Ropes rigged to prevent a boat from moving forward or aft when secured alongside.
Stanchions	Metal poles that support the guardrail lines.
Starboard	The right-hand side of the boat when looking forward.
Starboard beam	The direction on the right-hand side of the hull at right-angles to the fore-and-aft line.
Starboard bow	The sector from the fore and aft line to the starboard beam.
Starboard quarter	The sector from the starboard beam to the astern line.
Starboard tack	A point of sailing with the mainsail filled on the port-side of the boat. (Wind from starboard.)
Steaming light	An alternative name for a masthead light. Used when a vessel is driven by power.
Stern	The after end of the craft.
Stern drive	Often called inboard/outboard, the main engine unit is installed inside the craft close to the transom, but the propeller is mounted on a drive leg outside the hull, The craft is steered by turning the entire drive leg without the need for a rudder.
Stern thrusters	An electrically driven propeller fitted low on the hull near the stern of the craft to aid manoeuvre at slow speeds in confined spaces.
Storm	A wind of, or exceeding, Beaufort Force 10 (48 to 55 knots average).
Storm jib	A small headsail set in strong winds.
Swashway	A channel of deeper water, normally into a harbour or river.
Swing a compass	To prepare a list of corrections to a magnetic compass.
Swing keel	A keel on a pivot that can be raised or lowered.
TTG	The time to go to a waypoint or destination.
Tack (1)	To change the course through the wind and set the sails on the other side.
Tack (2)	The lower forward corner of a sail.
Telltails	Small pieces of wool or cloth on the luff of a sail to indicate the path of the wind over the sail.
Tender (1)	A description of a lightweight and lively boat.
Tender (2)	A dinghy for transport from boat to shore.
Tidal diamonds	Magenta diamonds on charts that refer to a table of known tidal streams for various states of the tide.
Tidal range	The vertical distance between the level of LW and HW.
Tide	The vertical rise and fall of the water level.
Topping lift	A lie from the masthead to the end of the boom, used to support the boom when the sail is lowered.
Traffic separation scheme	An area of one-way traffic lanes where special rules apply.
Transducer	The unit of an instrumentation system that converts depth, speed, etc into electrical pulses.
Transit	Two objects are 'in transit' when they are seen one behind the other.
Transom	The flat part of the hull across the stern.
Traveller	A metal car on a track that allows the mainsheet lower end to move across the boat from one side to the other.

Tri-coloured light	A red, green and white light at the masthead, which may *replace* the lower red, green and overtaking lights *when under sail*.
Trim tabs	Metal plates mounted below the waterline on the stern of a performance motor cruiser, used to trim the level of the boat.
Trip line	A light line between the crown of an anchor and the anchor buoy.
True North	The geographical North Pole.
Trysail	A small heavy sail used to replace the mainsail in very strong winds.
Under way	A ship is under way if it is not attached to the seabed.
Up and down	The state of the anchor cable, when being weighed, just before it breaks out of the seabed.
UT	The Greenwich time zone. Same as GMT and UTC.
Variation	The angle between Magnetic North and True North.
Veer	A wind is said to veer when it alters its direction in a clockwise direction. (The opposite to 'backing'.)
VHF	Very high frequency radio. The range of signals is limited to 'line of sight'.
Warp	A rope used as a shoreline.
Water track	A plotted line showing the movement of the boat through the water.
Waypoint	A geographical position which is stored in the GPS and later used as a turning point or destination.
Weigh (the anchor)	To raise the anchor.
WGS84	A geographical location used by chart makers as the basis for deriving the position of all points on the chart.
Wildcat	A type of windlass for both chain and rope.
Winches	A mechanical device used to enhance the hauling power of running rigging.
Windlass	Power-driven winch used to raise and lower the anchor and its cable.
Windward side	The side of the hull from which the wind is blowing.
Withies	Small sticks or saplings used in rivers to mark the boundary between deep and shallow water.
Yawing	Swinging from side to side of the desired course.
Yawl	A two-masted yacht with the after mast aft of the rudder post.

RECOMMENDED EQUIPMENT FOR INSHORE CRUISING BOATS

(Boats remaining within 10 miles of the coast and within approximately 4 hours passage time of a safe refuge.)

MEANS OF PROPULSION – SAILING CRAFT
Deep-reefed mainsail or storm trysail.
Under 6m in length with no auxiliary engine
1 x pair of oars or paddles.
With auxiliary engine
Battery whose sole purpose is to start the engine and is isolated from any battery used for domestic systems or a method of starting the auxiliary engine by hand.

MEANS OF PROPULSION – POWER DRIVEN CRAFT
1 x pair of oars or paddles.

ANCHORS
2 x anchors with length of warp and chain or chain only, appropriate to the cruising area and diameter appropriate to the size of the boat.
1 x fairlead at the stem capable of being closed over the anchor chain and warp.
1 x strong point on the foredeck, either a cleat, Samson post or anchor winch securely fitted to the structure of the hull.

BAILING AND BILGE PUMPING
2 x buckets (1.2 to 3 gallons/7 to 13.5 litres)
1 x hand bilge pump.
1 x set softwood plugs kept adjacent to all through-hull fittings.
All through-hull fitting able to be closed.

DETECTION EQUIPMENT
1 x radar reflecting device, properly mounted with as large a radar cross section as can reasonably be carried.
1 x set fixed navigation lights.
1 x foghorn.
1 x powerful torch or searchlight.
1 x anchor ball and light.
1 x motoring cone (sailing craft only).

FLARES
4 x hand-held red distress flares.
2 x red parachute distress flares.
2 x hand-held orange smoke signals.
4 x hand held white anti-collision flares.

FIRE FIGHTING EQUIPMENT
1 x fire blanket for craft with cooking equipment.
1 x 5A/34B multi purpose fire extinguisher (for craft fitted with a galley *or* carrying fuel for an engine).
2 x 5A/34B multi purpose fire extinguisher (for craft fitted with both a galley *and* carrying engine fuel).
1 x 13A/113B multi-purpose fire extinguisher (or smaller fire extinguishers giving the equivalent rating.

PERSONAL SAFETY EQUIPMENT FOR EACH MEMBER OF THE CREW
Warm clothing and waterproof foul weather clothing.
Sea boots and hat.
Lifejacket (BS EN 396) 150 Newtons
Safety harness for each crew member for craft with open cockpit (for 50 per cent of the crew if wheelhouse is closed).
Jackstays and cockpit clip-on points.

LIFERAFT
1 × liferaft designed specifically for saving life, of sufficient capacity to carry everyone onboard.
1 × emergency grab bag.

MAN OVERBOARD RECOVERY EQUIPMENT
1 × horseshoe lifebelt fitted with drogue and self-igniting light.
1 × 30m buoyant heaving line with quoit.
1 × boarding ladder capable of rapid and secure attachment.

RADIO
1 × marine band VHF fitted with digital selective calling (DSC).
1 × Navtex receiver
1 × waterproof hand-held VHF radio.

NAVIGATIONAL EQUIPMENT
1 × recent charts, tide tables and navigational publications of the intended cruising area and adjacent areas into which the craft may have to go due to adverse weather.
1 × ship's logbook.
1 × steering compass with light.
1 × hand-bearing compass.
1 × set of navigational drawing instruments.
1 × barometer.
1 × lead line and echo sounder.
1 × GPS
1 × watch or clock.
1 × distance measuring equipment (distance log).
1 × binoculars (7 x 50 magnification is ideal).

FIRST AID KIT
1 × first aid kit.

GENERAL EQUIPMENT
1 × current first aid manual.
6 × mooring warps.
6 × fenders.
2 × waterproof torches.
1 × inflatable or rigid tender.
1 × tool kit for engine, electrical and general use.
1 × sail repair kit (sail only).
1 × bosun's kit containing spares for engine, electrical shackles, twine, hoses etc.
Spare can of engine oil.
1 × emergency tiller on wheel steered vessels.
1 × bosun's chair (vessels with mast only).

INDEX